Ancient Rome
From Romulus to Augustus

Ancient Rome

From Romulus to Augustus

GEORGINA MASSON

A STUDIO BOOK

THE VIKING PRESS . NEW YORK

Frontispiece A patrician, carrying busts of his ancestors (based on death-masks). This marble statue of the first century B C/A D embodies the strong Roman sense of the dignity and continuity of the family.

Published in 1974 by The Viking Press, Inc.
625 Madison Avenue, New York, N.Y. 10022

SBN 670-12265-3
Library of Congress catalog card number: 73-7434

Printed and bound in Great Britain by
Jarrold and Sons Ltd, Norwich, England

Contents

Legends and beginnings

Rome was founded on 21 April in the year 753 BC on the Palatine hill. This tradition of date and place, hallowed by legend, has been handed down through the ages and 21 April is still celebrated in Rome today as the birthday of the city. Although ancient historians were not dogmatic about the matter – there were many legends and many versions of them, subjected to a process of rationalization in the later days of the Republic – and modern archaeologists differ in their opinions, nevertheless the majority of the latter believe that their findings agree with the tradition.

The legends state that this momentous event occurred during the Parilia – the spring festival of the pastoral deity Pales – and describe the rustic ceremonial with which it was surrounded. A pit was dug on the hill and into this were cast propitiatory offerings of grain from the previous harvest. When the pit had been refilled an altar was made on the spot. The consecration concluded, the confines of the city-to-be were traced by a plough drawn by a heifer and a bull, the furrow symbolizing the moat, the earth thrown up from it the site of the walls. The ploughman was Romulus, whom the gods themselves had chosen by favouring him with a good omen. From the summit of the Palatine, Romulus had seen a flight of twelve vultures, whereas his twin Remus had seen only six from the Aventine, where he wanted to found the city. According to the legends Remus was jealous, in mockery he jumped over the beginnings of his brother's city wall, and in a rage Romulus killed him, shouting, 'So perish all who ever cross my walls.'

Again according to the legends, Romulus and Remus were the sons of Rhea Silvia, daughter of the King of Alba Longa, a descendant of Aeneas (himself a son of Venus) who had married King Latinus' daughter when he arrived in Italy after his escape from Troy. Rhea Silvia had been forced to become a Vestal Virgin by a usurping uncle, but was loved by Mars and bore him twin sons. Various interpretations are given of their mother's fate, but it is generally agreed that Romulus and Remus were exposed at birth and laid in a basket which was consigned to the Tiber floods. The basket floated and, when the floods subsided, was deposited at the foot of the Palatine. The twins were saved and suckled by a she-wolf. Ultimately they were found under a fig tree by the shepherd Faustulus and brought up by him and his wife Acca Larentia, who lived in a hut on the south-west corner of the hill.

When Romulus and Remus grew up, they killed the usurping King of Alba Longa, placed the rightful one on the throne and received from him instructions to found the colony of Alba Longa which was to become the city of Rome. The legends relate how, in order to swell the population of his new colony, Romulus accepted within its walls homeless, stateless wanderers from all Latium. The problem then arose as to how wives could be found for the colonists.

2 *Opposite* The she-wolf suckling Romulus and Remus, the most familiar symbol of ancient Rome, harking back to the city's legendary origins.

3, 4 According to tradition, Rome was founded in 753 BC on the Palatine hill, *above*. The outlines of the future city were then traced by Romulus with a plough, no doubt like the one shown in this Etruscan bronze, *right*.

This was solved by holding a festival, later commemorated as the Consualia, and inviting the inhabitants of all the nearest towns, some of which were inhabited by Sabines. The upshot is well known: at a prearranged signal each Roman seized a girl and bore her off. The young men's intentions were strictly honourable, however, and the couples were married according to the *confar-reatio* – a rite devised by Romulus which was indissoluble and gave the husband absolute power over his wife. The Sabines naturally declared war on the Romans, and the fighting continued until one day the Sabine wives of the Romans flung themselves between the combatants. The peace was made, including the stipulation that no wife of a Roman should be called upon to perform servile tasks.

From now on Romans and Sabines worked together to build up the new city. Romulus invited the Sabine chief, Titus Tatius, to share the throne with him. Titus Tatius seems to have played a minor part, however, as the legends make little mention of him; on the other hand, they refer to Romulus as the founder of the oldest Roman institutions such as the Senate, the assembly of the people and the earliest Roman form of marriage. After thus having provided for the welfare of his people and winning several wars, Romulus disappeared. This event is said to have occurred in the midst of a violent thunder-storm in full view of all the people of Rome, assembled on the Campus Martius. As a result of what appeared to be divine intervention, Romulus was proclaimed a god, curiously changing his name to that of an old Sabine deity, Quirinus, whose altar stood on the Quirinal hill.

With the rape of the Sabine women and the ensuing war and peace, the legends emerge from the realms of myth and ritual into a story which may sym-bolize some real historical fact. Archaeological discoveries show that other settlements, coeval with that on the Palatine, existed on the neighbouring hills. At some time these settlements were united and became a community. Possibly owing to the size, favourable site and defensive character of the hill itself, the Palatine settlement proved the dominant one, while a Sabine settlement on the Quirinal may only have joined the community after a struggle – hence the legends. It seems, however, that this 'city' of Rome came into being as a result of the fusion of these primitive hill settlements, though whether their number had already reached the historic figure of seven is uncertain. Strange as it may seem, and in spite of the fact that one of Rome's most ancient festivals was called the Septimontium, neither ancient historians nor modern archaeologists have ever been able to decide exactly which were the original seven hills of Rome. Indeed there is no certainty that they were all hills in the physical and geographi-cal sense, for one of the earliest lists included the Suburra, which was always low-lying land. The word 'hill' is itself somewhat misleading as the hills are in fact spurs of the higher land of the surrounding Campagna that protrude into the Tiber valley.

To those of us who are accustomed to think of Rome in terms of Augustus' famous phrase as having been built of brick before his day and of marble after-wards, it is not easy to envisage what primitive Rome must have looked like. The Romans of Cicero's time, however, had an object-lesson before them: standing on the south-west corner of the Palatine beside the patrician houses of what was then the fashionable quarter of the city, was a thatched hut. The Romans called it 'House of Romulus' and were proud of it, though not all of

5 The rape of the Sabine women, represented on a Roman coin of 88 B C.

6 Hut foundations discovered during excavations on the Palatine hill.

them necessarily believed that, even allowing for necessary restoration, it was the shepherd's hut in which Romulus had grown up six centuries earlier. Whether the hut was the product of a conscious antiquarian spirit or a genuine folk-memory of the distant past is not known, but the astonishing fact remains that a village of just such huts had stood on this spot in the eighth century B C. Excavation during the twentieth century has revealed groups of holes cut into the rock which held the posts that formed their framework – the method of construction was very similar to that still employed for herdsmen's huts in remote parts of Italy today.

There was nothing dramatic or obviously strategic about this site which was destined to become one of the most famous spots on earth. Much play has been made of the fact that Rome grew up at the place nearest the Tiber mouth where the river could be bridged by primitive means, but such an undertaking would have been beyond the capacity of the founders. Nor do suggestions of a ford existing at this point seem to have any factual foundation. The swift current would also have rendered upstream navigation impossible – against it a modern rowboat can just make headway. It seems more likely that Rome derived her origins from the salt used in her primitive cooking-pots. Since time immemorial salt, extracted in the pans at the river's mouth, had reached central Italy by way of a trail that followed the left bank of the Tiber, and this Via Salaria may have been the first road that led to Rome, or rather to the site where the city was one day to arise. It seems that from very early times the valley to the north of the Palatine was also a primitive communications centre – a meeting-place of trails which connected Campania and central Italy with the Tiber mouth. The valley was well watered, which may have been one of the reasons why several trails con-

verged there, and wells were dug to serve the users of this highway. Already at some time between the end of the ninth and the beginning of the sixth century B C the inhabitants of the Palatine had adopted the custom – which was to be continued by the Romans for two thousand years – of burying their dead on both sides of the highway.

At some stage the Palatine settlement overflowed into this valley, huts were built in it and for a while it seems that the huts and cemetery existed side by side. What gave the inhabitants the confidence to forsake the security of the Palatine heights and set up their homes beside an open highway? The answer, as supplied by the legends, is of course the peace made between the Romans and the Sabines. Then the valley ceased to be a no-man's-land and became instead a dwelling and meeting-place for Romans, Sabines and wayfarers alike. At the north-western end of the valley there still stand the remains of an altar hewn from the live rock; it was dedicated to Vulcan and is called the Vulcanal, and according to tradition this was the actual spot where Romulus and Titus Tatius made peace. Other sites in the valley are still associated with those momentous early times: the Comitium, the gathering-place of the assembly of the Roman people, instituted by Romulus, and possibly the near-by shrine of Janus (now vanished), whose doors were opened only in time of war. Apparently the high-way continued to be lined by tombs and huts, but it would also have formed a natural place in which the inhabitants and wayfarers met and exchanged their wares. Part of it was in fact to become the most famous meeting-place in the whole world – the Roman Forum.

Some idea of the life lived in this village may be pieced together from fragments recently excavated on the site. These include the remains of spools and spindle

7 Reconstruction of a herds-man's hut of the eighth century B C.

whorls – thick rings of stone or metal used in primitive spinning to increase the momentum of the spindle. Evidently Roman women were already accomplished spinsters – a craft for which they were still esteemed in Imperial times and one which must have kept them well occupied in the eighth century BC when all clothes were made of wool. On this site were also found sherds of cooking-pots and even traces of what was cooked in them – broad beans and grains of wheat and barley. Cooking was evidently already done not only on open fires, but on special earthenware cooking-stands for holding the glowing embers – like those still used in the Orient today.

These fragments build up a very domestic picture and it is not surprising to find that the archaeologists who have examined them believe that the cult of Vesta, the goddess of the hearth, probably originated in this village. Certainly her temple arose very close at hand. At first this would simply have been a round thatched hut with a central hearth and a vent-hole for the smoke at the apex of the conical roof – huts of this type still existed in eighteenth-century Italy and were drawn by J. R. Cozens. Small models of such huts were used as funerary urns, and some of these have been found on the site of the Forum village. The fire which burned continually within the temple, only being re-kindled annually at New Year (1 March), symbolized the perpetuity of the Roman state. The virgin priestesses who attended it could originally have been just the young girls of the village to whom was entrusted the task of keeping a communal fire alight. The Vestals were also the guardians of the *sacra pignora* of Rome, the city's own household gods and pledges of her welfare. With the exception of the Palladium, an image of Pallas supposed to have been brought by Aeneas from Troy, nothing is known of the nature of these sacred fetishes which were seen only by the Vestals and the Pontifex Maximus, nor has excavation revealed the slightest trace of their hiding-place. Traditionally the origins of the worship of Vesta were ascribed to the reign of Romulus or his Sabine successor Numa Pompilius; the building of her first temple is usually attributed to the latter, who was the great organizer of Roman religion.

To King Numa, who was believed to have reigned from 717 to 673 BC, is assigned the building of the original Regia, the ruins of whose Republican successor still stand beside the old highway. This road came to be called the Via Sacra, or Sacred Way, because of the religious buildings which grew up beside it and its use as the principal route followed by religious processions. Later generations believed that the Regia had been Numa's royal residence, but its small size and subsequent usage seem to indicate that it was really the administrative centre of his high-priestly activities. From the first the Regia was a religious building. It contained two shrines, one dedicated to Ops Consiva, goddess of crops and plenty; in the other were preserved the spears and shield of Mars, who in Rome was originally a god of the fields. Through the centuries the Regia was officially the residence of the High Priest, although like Numa the Pontifex Maximus never lived there. It was also the repository of the religious records of the city. Numa was believed to have been the founder of the priestly colleges which, with subsequent additions, endured until the final suppression of paganism in the fourth century AD.

Among these colleges the one that was ultimately to enjoy the greatest and most lasting importance was that of the *pontifices*, whose head, the Pontifex Maximus, became the High Priest of the Roman state. Strangely, the origins

8 Funerary urn in the form of an early Roman hut.

9 *Opposite* Reconstruction of a grave from the Forum cemetery, dated after the mid-eighth century BC.

of this famous title are still a mystery, though in historical times the Romans themselves mistakenly associated it with the word for bridge – *pons*.

The Roman religious system was unusual in that it possessed no sacred writings except invocations and prayers and that its priesthood was not a caste set apart. Though originally the exclusive preserve of the patricians, later nearly all offices were open to men of good family and standing. The one enduring exception was that of the *flamines maiores* (chief priests), all of whom had to be patricians born of parents married by the ancient rite of *confarreatio* and married in a like manner to wives to whom the same rule applied.

After the death of Numa Pompilius, Rome is said to have been ruled during some fifty years by a Latin king, Tullus Hostilius, then a Sabine one, Ancus Marcius. To the period of the former's reign is attributed the war with Alba Longa which resulted in the destruction of the parent city and the transference of its population to Rome. Alba had been the leader of a federation of Latin cities since well before the foundation of Rome. The federation's common place of worship was Jupiter's sanctuary on the Alban Mount (now Monte Cavo, the highest peak of the Alban hills); this continued there though the leadership of the federation had now definitely passed to Rome.

The origins of two Roman monuments were attributed to the period of Tullus Hostilius' reign: one, the dread state prison called the Tullianum (now believed to have been a cistern built later and fed by a spring or *tullius*), the other, the Curia Hostilia, the first meeting-place of the Senate, which was said to have been named after the King. Certainly, according to Livy, the numbers of this council of *patres* or heads of families were increased about this time by the admission of six of the Alban tribal chiefs. If the Curia Hostilia was indeed built by Tullus Hostilius it was a remarkably solid construction for the period, as apparently it stood up to the vicissitudes of more than six centuries. The Curia was first rebuilt by Sulla in 80 BC, then reorientated and rebuilt by Julius Caesar, and completed by Augustus. Finally it was rebuilt for the last time, by Diocletian, to survive into our own day, still standing beside the Comitium.

Although Rome's fourth king, Ancus Marcius, was on his mother's side the grandson of the great Numa, the legends are less communicative about his reign. He is, however, credited with the foundation of a colony at Ostia, by the mouth of the Tiber and, more important still, the building of the first Roman bridge – the famous Sublician – which spanned the Tiber just opposite the south-west corner of the Palatine. Another action of Tullus Hostilius was to have even more far-reaching consequences. For reasons unknown, he is believed to have taken the Etruscan 'Lucumo' (really the Etruscan title for a chief) into his household and made him the guardian of his children. The Latinized form of the man's name was Lucius Tarquinius Priscus and his responsible position in the royal household finally led to his becoming Ancus Marcius' successor. Thus in 616 BC Lucius Tarquinius Priscus became the first Etruscan King of Rome, and according to tradition he ruled the city until 579 BC. His accession was a complete break with what seemed to have become an established practice of Latin and Sabine monarchs reigning alternately and thus preserving the balance of power between the two former factions in the state. Though all the kings are more or less shadowy figures, the mere fact that it was believed that at this stage in Rome's development an Etruscan had become her

ruler, places the whole situation of the city in a different context. It no longer appears as an isolated entity exclusively concerned with its own parochial affairs, but as part of the complex political situations then reigning in the Italian peninsula, a circumstance which was to exercise a profound influence upon its own character and development.

The 37 years of Tarquinius Priscus' reign cover the turn of the seventh and sixth centuries B C, which coincides with the halfway period of the expansion of Etruscan power in Italy. At this time Etruscan influence was spreading rapidly beyond the confines of Etruria proper – which lay between the Tyrrhenian seaboard, the Arno and the Tiber – and extending over an area that was finally to stretch from the Po valley in the north to Campania in the south. It did not ever really penetrate the central mountain massif of Italy, which continued to be the stronghold of the primitive Italic tribes, and in the south it was to be checked by the outposts of a superior civilization, that of the Greek colonies of the Italian seaboard and Sicily. The most northerly of these colonies was Cumae, Etruscan Capua's bitter rival. The third great power then present in the western Mediterranean was Carthage, but at this time its influence was from the Roman point of view peripheral, being limited to settlements in Sardinia and western Sicily.

Thus at the end of the seventh century B C the Etruscans were the dominant power in central Italy and primitive Rome was increasingly exposed to the influence of a people whose civilization was greatly in advance of its own and who were then rapidly extending their sphere of influence. The effect of this confrontation upon Rome's development can hardly be exaggerated. At some time about 600 B C a process began which was rapidly to transform Rome from an agglomeration of rustic villages into a city recognizable as such in the Etruscan or even Greek conception of the word. That this was not achieved by a gradual process of indigenous evolution but occurred almost in one bound, as it were, indicated the impact upon Rome of a fully fledged civilization, which proceeded to dominate it. Whether this domination was personally imposed by the Etruscan king, Tarquinius Priscus, or whether the legend of his existence was afterwards invented to explain Rome's transformation, are two sides of the question which will no doubt long continue to provide fuel for learned argument. The fact remains, however, that the period attributed to his reign coincides approximately with that of the beginnings of Rome's transformation under Etruscan influence.

Little trace of this period of the conversion of Rome of the villages into the beginnings of Rome the city has survived, but one alone is enough to indicate how radical it must have been. Somewhere about 600 B C – the actual date is debated by archaeologists – the huts and tombs in the Forum valley were demolished and over the site an open space was laid out and paved with pebbles. Gradually the thatched wattle huts standing by this primitive forum were replaced by buildings whose foundations and some of whose walls were of cut and dressed stone. This process of urbanization would hardly have been possible if the formerly marshy valley had not been drained; and, significantly, tradition attributes the making of the Cloaca Maxima to one of the Tarquin kings. The existing vaulted underground channel of the Cloaca Maxima is of a considerably later date; the original drainage system was simply a series of ditches which carried the stagnant waters down to the Tiber by way of the

Velabrum and Forum Boarium, where the Cloaca Maxima still flows underground today.

If the orderly physical development of the city of Rome was begun by Tarquinius Priscus, to his successor Servius Tullius is attributed the introduction of similar processes governing the life of her citizens. According to Etruscan tradition – later endorsed by the scholarly Emperor Claudius – Servius Tullius was actually an Etruscan named Mastarna, who was born to a slave of Tarquinius Priscus' household. His birth had been followed by one of those prodigious happenings to which so much significance was attached in Rome. As a result the King took a friendly interest in the boy and eventually married him to his daughter. Thus in story-book fashion Servius Tullius' way to the succession was prepared.

Servius Tullius' succession did not, however, come about by election in the usual legal fashion. According to Livy (writing some five centuries later) the custom of electing kings began after Romulus, who had been selected by the gods to rule, was carried away alive to join them. This remarkable event naturally posed a problem with regard to the succession but, after some friendly debate, the Senate and the assembly of the people agreed that in future kings should be nominated by the people and ratified by the Senate. The Roman monarchy thus officially became an elective one, and Ancus Marcius seems to have been the first king who was a blood relation of a previous sovereign. At his death, however, no tie of blood was evidently considered, and Tarquinius Priscus was elected. Ancus Marcius' sons may have been minors at the time, for later they evidently regarded Tarquinius Priscus as a usurper and conspired to have him murdered. The plot miscarried, the assassins were caught and Tarquinius Priscus' widow concealed his death until her son-in-law, Servius Tullius, had gained control of Rome. Or at least this was the story told to justify Servius Tullius' strong-arm method of seizing power. Whatever his origins and whatever the means he employed to get the throne, Servius Tullius was an outstanding king and one indeed who left his mark upon Rome and its institutions. When he came to the throne in 579 BC the Roman people were divided

10 A battle of Etruscan heroes, in a wall-painting of about 300 BC – a scene from the life of Mastarna (Servius Tullius).

into three tribes; these were subdivided into 10 *curiae* and together the 30 *curiae* formed the assembly of the people, or *comitia curiata*. Our knowledge of this primitive organization of Rome is largely derived from the accounts of historians, such as Livy, who wrote about them centuries later and probably rationalized the story in the light of later events. But it seems that originally the *comitia curiata* possessed considerable powers, including the very important one of the right to bestow the *imperium* upon the kings after their election. The Roman conception of this absolute power of *imperium* is difficult to interpret in terms understandable to us, but it runs like a thread right through Roman history and some last traces of its influence may even be perceived in the Roman Catholic Church, one existing institution which has spanned the centuries from pagan times until today. The *imperium* combined the normal powers of sovereignty – the right to rule, to administer justice, to command in war and to summon the people to assemblies – with the religious functions inherent in maintaining correct relations with the gods. The most important of these was Jupiter, who, as he had been the presiding deity of the Latin confederation, of which Rome was originally an offshoot, was also the founding god and protector of the city. The *imperium* had first been conferred upon Romulus as the chosen of the gods; he was thus the first *imperator*, and as such appears almost to have been regarded as an earthly personification of Jupiter himself. The Romans envisaged him attired like the god in purple embroidered robes, riding in a chariot drawn by four white horses. Just how the right of bestowing the *imperium* on subsequent sovereigns devolved upon the *comitia curiata* is not clear, but after Servius Tullius' reforms the *comitia*'s powers were radically restricted and in time seem to have become largely religious and ceremonial.

Servius Tullius began his reforms in a thoroughly orderly manner by having a census taken of the inhabitants of Rome and of their property, which at this period meant landed property. He then proceeded to divide the Roman people into five classes, graded according to the property they owned, the richest in the top class, the poorest in the bottom one. The members of the four higher, propertied classes were then subdivided into *centuriae* or centuries. These centuries had both a political and a military connotation. In the ballot each century had one vote; for purposes of mobilization the centuries represented groups of men already classed according to military trades. Thus the centuries of the richest top class of landowners and those who could afford to buy and equip a horse, provided the cavalry. The less well-off classes were distributed among the other variously equipped forces according to their means: the third and most important class, forming the mass of armoured pikemen of the phalanx; the fourth, who could not afford such heavy equipment, being employed as scouts and skirmishers. Even at this early period men with special skills, such as blacksmiths and carpenters, were drafted into centuries resembling the modern Corps of Engineers. At this same time there already also existed an embryo Signal Corps, consisting of buglers and trumpeters. Only the pauper citizens of the fifth class were altogether exempt from military service.

The Roman people as represented in the new Servian classification was known as the *comitia centuriata* and for all effective purposes this new body replaced the old *comitia curiata*. The practical effect of this reform was to give power and also responsibility to those who had the greatest financial stake in the state. For naturally, then as now, there were fewer wealthy men than poor

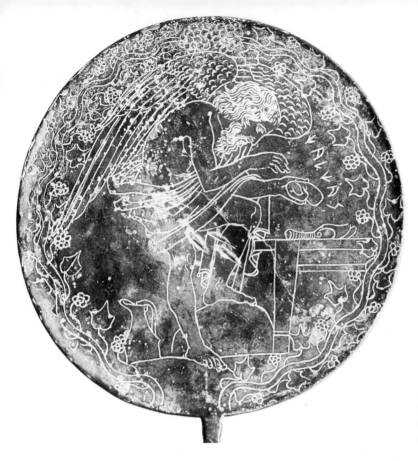

11 A Roman soothsayer ex-
amining a liver; engraved back
of a fifth-century BC bronze
mirror.

ones, but the single vote of the centuries of the richer classes, which represented
a much smaller number of people, counted in the ballot just the same as the
single vote of a much more numerous poor century. In fact the poor were really
given very little say, as voting started with the centuries of the higher classes and
once the majority was reached, proceeded no further down the scale. By these
Servian reforms the old *comitia curiata* was shorn of all its voting powers, though
as a tribute to its ancient origins, it retained the right of endorsing the finding of
its successor by means of a religious ceremony.

   This, to us very strange, Roman system of voting also had a religious significance; the auspices were taken before voting began and, in later times at any
rate, it was surrounded by very considerable ceremonial. This was because the
Romans believed that the vote thus given by the assembly of the people expressed the will of the gods and that of the first century to vote – the *centuria
praerogativa* – constituted an omen. This concept of investing civic or even
military activities with religious significance was the rule rather than the exception in Rome and an appreciation of this fact is essential to an understanding of
Roman life.

   Even so matter-of-fact an occasion as the taking of the census was a religious
ceremony. On these occasions the entire *comitia centuriata* was drawn up on the
Campus Martius in military formation and the three sacrificial animals used
only in the great state sacrifice of the *suovetaurilia* (a pig, a sheep and a bull) were
led in solemn procession around the assembled men and then sacrificed. The
object of this rite was the purification of the entire (male) population of Rome.

17

Servius Tullius' reforms were also extended to the physical aspects of the city. He divided Rome into four regions and was believed (though this is contested by archaeologists) to have surrounded it with a wall. It seems probable that this last really consisted of an agger and other earthworks constructed at particularly vulnerable places, rather than the stone wall whose surviving fragments are still called the Servian Wall, though they are now believed to date from the early Republic. Servius Tullius' four regions were, however, destined to endure and to become the nucleus of the 14 into which the city was divided in Imperial times. His four original regions were the Suburana, which included the Suburra and the Coelian; the Esquilina, consisting of the western part of the Esquiline; the Collina, composed of the Viminal and Quirinal; and the Palatina, which comprised the Velia as well as the Palatine.

The flat land lying in the bend of the Tiber, which we now look upon as the heart of old Rome, was not included in the four regions. Due no doubt to difficulties of defence and its being subject to frequent flooding by the Tiber, this area was not inhabited but was used instead for military training and exercises, from which it came to be called the Campus Martius or Field of Mars. Nevertheless, the Rome of the four regions covered a surprisingly large area – approximately a third of that enclosed by the Aurelian Wall in late Imperial times – for a city still in its infancy. In all probability this may be explained by the fact that at this time each region comprised tracts of land used for cultivation and grazing; in time of war these open spaces would also have served as a refuge for farmers and their flocks and herds from the surrounding countryside.

Evidence of the importance of pastoral life in Servius Tullius' Rome, and indeed in the city for long after his time – is provided by the name of Forum Boarium, given to the strip of land lying between the Palatine and the Tiber, where the Sublician bridge already spanned the river. The Forum Boarium was the cattle market and, according to some authorities, it may have come into being before the Forum proper and even have antedated the foundation of Rome itself. In any event its importance during the early period of the development of the city is attested by the fact that two temples, dedicated to the Mater Matuta (the Dawn Mother) and to Fortune, are believed to have been built there as early as Servius Tullius' reign. Remains of their terracotta decorations – great acroteria, resembling in form the curling sprouts of ferns or bracken – have recently been found in the area. These are dated to the sixth century BC and would probably have been placed above the gable or pediment of these early wooden temples, standing up on each side of the ridge-pole in the centre of the roof, much as the rafters appeared in Villanovan huts.

All in all, Etruscan though he might be, Servius Tullius stands out as a man who deserved well of Rome. His vision seems to have enabled him to conceive of her as a corporate whole and to plan for the future, while with his practical sense of organization he laid the foundations of that administrative machine which was to become one of Rome's outstanding features.

It might have been expected that at the end of his long reign such a king would have closed his days in peace. Evidently Servius Tullius hoped to do so and believed that he had made provision for the succession by marrying his two daughters to the sons of Tarquinius Priscus. Here, however, if the legends are to be believed, a domestic tragedy intervened. His younger daughter Tullia was ambitious, like her brother-in-law, Lucius Tarquinius. They conspired together and she is believed to have been responsible for the death of their respective spouses, after which she married Lucius Tarquinius. This well-matched couple now planned a *coup d'état* against Servius Tullius. With a band of his supporters, Lucius Tarquinius burst into a meeting of the Senate, succeeded in overawing the Senators and getting them to proclaim him king. Informed of what was happening, Servius Tullius hurried to the Curia, but arrived too late and was forced to flee. On his way home he was murdered in the street. Horror is piled upon horror in the legend, which goes on to relate how, as Tullia was driving back to her house on the Esquiline from the Curia, the driver of her chariot halted when he saw the body of Servius Tullius lying in the street, but Tullia herself seized the reins and drove over the dead body of her father. To the Romans this was a deed more terrible than murder itself and for centuries the street where it was believed to have occurred was called the Sceleratus Vicus – the name still appeared on maps of Rome made two thousand years later.

Such were the deeds, so the Romans believed, that ushered in the reign of Lucius Tarquinius, or Tarquinius Superbus – Tarquin the Proud – as he soon came to be called. According to their own calculations, however, this much-hated king ruled over the Romans for twenty-five years and to do so he cannot have lacked either ability or courage. Although he was born and brought up in Rome, Tarquinius Superbus seems to have been more Etruscan than either his father or his father-in-law, who appear to have identified themselves more closely with the city of their adoption. But political circumstances may explain his attitude. The year 534 B C, in which Tarquinius Superbus seized the throne, coincided with the apogee of Etruscan power in Italy. This was the result of the Etruscan and Carthaginian defeat of the Greeks at Alalia in Corsica, which ended Greek penetration in the western Mediterranean. Ten years later, however, the Greeks halted the Etruscan advance in southern Italy

12 Terracotta acroteria from the Temple of Mater Matuta, built in the sixth century B C.

by their heroic defence of Cumae. Thus at the end of the sixth century BC the future of Italy seemed to tremble in the balance – was she to become an Etruscan or a Greek domain? Naturally, Tarquinius Superbus threw the whole weight of his power on to the Etruscan side, hoping thus to tip the balance, but in doing so he was not tender to Roman susceptibilities. The Romans afterwards claimed that Tarquinius ruled as a tyrant, ignoring the existence of the Senate and all other Roman institutions. Nor, apparently, was he much more amiable to the cities of the Latin Confederation. Between them, Ardea, Aricia, Fidenae, Gabii, Labicum, Laurentum, Lanuvium, Nomentum, Tibur and Tusculum controlled the land stretching from the Sabine and Alban hills to the Tyrrhenian coast. Tarquinius had no intention of allowing any of these buffer states to stray from his allegiance and even less of permitting them to enter into friendly relations with the Greek cities in Campania, but the King neglected to use the velvet glove in achieving his ends.

Like other tyrants before and since, Tarquinius Superbus had a taste for grandeur, especially in architecture. In fact he seems to have been the prototype of that succession of domineering figures, recurrent throughout Roman history, who, though hated during their lifetimes, nevertheless left the city architecturally the richer. Tarquinius is credited with having introduced chariot-racing into Rome and with having first laid out the Circus Maximus, though according to some sources Tarquinius Priscus drained the site. This primitive circus would have been built of wood and probably resembled the one which can still be seen in the paintings of the Tomb of the Chariots at Tarquinia – the city from which the House of Tarquin originally came. These paintings, dating from about 500 BC, indicate that this sport, which was to become a Roman passion, originated in Etruria.

13 Wall-painting from the Tomb of the Chariots at Tarquinia, showing a chariot race.

Tarquinius Superbus decided to build a temple on the Capitol in Rome which was to be the largest in central Italy, and to dedicate it to Jupiter, Juno and Minerva. The custom of dedicating a temple to a triad of deities was a

common practice in Etruria, but as Jupiter was the protector of Rome the Capitoline temple was usually known as the temple of Jupiter Optimus Maximus. It is said that it was Tarquinius Priscus who first vowed to build the temple if he was successful in a war against the Sabines and that Tarquinius Superbus thus fulfilled his father's wishes. However, there could also have been some political calculation behind his act, as Jupiter was not only the great god of Rome and the Latin Confederation but, as Tini, a member of the Etruscan pantheon as well. Thus, in the troubled times that central Italy was then experiencing, the dedication of what was to be the most magnificent temple in the whole area, to a triad presided over by Jupiter, would emphasize the religious links of the Romans, Latins and Etruscans.

The building of the temple probably began about 520 B C. It stood on the south-western crest of the Capitol, thus dominating the entire city. The foundations were well laid, for much of the podium still stands, its massive stone blocks having weathered the centuries and survived fire and siege, sack and ruin for close on 2,500 years. The temple was orientated to face south-east overlooking the Forum and the Palatine. For the period its size was truly remarkable; it formed a rectangle measuring 185 by 200 feet. A wide flight of steps, some ten feet high, led to the portico in which 18 Tuscan columns were ranged three rows deep, while colonnades continued down each side of the building to a solid wall at the back.

Many aspects of the old Capitoline temple would have been different from the general impression of Roman temples received when viewing their ruins today. The podium and columns were of stone – not marble – the *cellae* and back wall were built of unbaked brick, the roof of wooden beams and terracotta tiles. If the basic materials of the construction were of the most sober and simple kind, the decoration, on the other hand, was brilliantly coloured. Painted terracotta reliefs and antefixes decorated the roof, while the three angles of the pediment were surmounted by acroteria of the same materials. We know from Livy that the group on the apex of the Capitoline temple, representing Jupiter in a quadriga drawn by four milk-white horses, was also of painted terracotta and that Vulca and other Etruscan sculptors came from Veii to execute this and other decorations. Vulca is also believed to have made the cult statue of Jupiter which stood in the *cella*. The face and body of this image were painted red and it was robed in a purple tunic embroidered with flowers and a gold-embroidered purple toga. These robes were among the Etruscan symbols of royalty which were also assumed by the kings of Rome and later used by the consuls and emperors in their triumphs, when they drove up the Sacred Way in a quadriga drawn by four white horses. On these occasions the triumphator's face and body were also painted red like the cult statue of Jupiter and other Etruscan gods. In fact the triumph, like many other Roman religious ceremonies, derived from Etruria.

Tarquinius Superbus was, however, destined never to drive up to the Temple of Jupiter Optimus Maximus in triumph, nor even to see his temple completed. The story of his fall is related in a legend as blood-stirring as any that the Romans told of their kings.

In Livy's version, Tarquinius Superbus was besieging Ardea (not far from Anzio), when the train of events began which were to end in personal tragedy but also to bring about Rome's liberation from tyranny. One day when two

14 A detail of the surviving podium of the Temple of Jupiter Optimus Maximus in Rome, built in 509 B C.

of the King's sons, of which one was named Sextus Tarquinius, were drinking with their cousin L. Tarquinius Collatinus, they jokingly laid bets with one another as to how their wives were behaving in their absence. In order to put the matter to the test, they decided to return home. In Rome the Tarquins found their wives enjoying themselves at parties. Having lost their bets, the two princes insisted on riding the nine miles out to their cousin's home at Collatia near Tivoli. Although it was late, they found Collatinus' beautiful young wife Lucretia, industriously spinning with her maids. Thus Collatinus won his bet.

The story goes on to tell how Sextus Tarquinius returned to Collatia some days later and asked to stay the night in his cousin's house. During the night he entered Lucretia's bedroom and told her that if she did not yield to him he would kill not only her but also one of the slaves and leave his body in her room. No one would then be able to contradict his tale that he had found Lucretia and the slave together and, as her husband's kinsman, exacted vengeance. Next day Sextus Tarquinius rode off, confident that his act would never be discovered. Lucretia, however, summoned her father, Spurius Lucretius, her husband and the men of her family. Her husband was on his way to Collatia with Lucius Brutus, the captain of the King's guard, when the message reached him and he hurried home.

To this family council Lucretia told the story of the terrible choice forced upon her by Sextus Tarquinius between death and apparent dishonour. All those present swore to take revenge, whereupon Lucretia stabbed herself and died at their feet. Brutus then drew out the dagger stained with Lucretia's blood and holding it up swore an even more terrible oath, not only to take revenge upon Sextus Tarquinius, but upon the entire House of Tarquin, including the King himself. Lucretia's body was carried to Rome and laid in the Forum, where Brutus pronounced her funeral oration and recounted the whole story. The people of Rome vowed to take revenge and to expel the King and all the Tarquins from the city. When Tarquinius Superbus hurried back to quell the revolt he found the city gates barred and the situation so threatening that he had to flee to Etruscan soil, to Caere (Cervetre), for refuge.

Whether or not the tale of Lucretia is true, it is possible that some such incident was the spark which fired the train leading to the overthrow of the Tarquins, but there seems little reasonable doubt that the train itself had been carefully laid beforehand. The speed with which an alternative form of government appeared in Rome, with Brutus and Collatinus as its leaders, confirms this, while the fact that Tarquinius Superbus was forced to flee to Etruria, indicates that the conspiracy was widespread, involving not only Rome but the entire Latin Confederation. As all the principal figures in the drama – Brutus, Collatinus and Lucretia's father, Spurius Lucretius – were closely connected with the King, it is evident that the conspiracy was led by the young nobles who, either out of a genuine desire for revenge or as a matter of cold-blooded calculation, or for both reasons, used her death to fire the passions of the mob. Even afterwards the title of king was dreaded and hated in Rome. Until the very end, tyrant though he might be, no emperor ever dared to call himself king although the dynasty of Constantine ruled by hereditary right. Thus, although the tales told of the kings of Rome may be legendary, their influence endured for nearly a thousand years.

2

Rome the city state (509–27 B C)

'The whole period of monarchical government, from the founding of Rome to its liberation, was 244 years. After the liberation two consuls were elected by popular vote, under the presidency of the Prefect of the City; the voting was by centuries, according to the classification of Servius Tullius. The two consuls were Lucius Junius Brutus and Lucius Tarquinius Collatinus.' Thus, writing nearly five centuries later, Livy described the foundation of the Republic, of which he himself had witnessed the extinction in all but name.

This traditional date, 509 B C according to our reckoning, is regarded as approximate by modern historians, who place the rise of the Republic, governed by two annually elected consuls or praetors, as they were originally called, at some time around 500 B C or even later. They exercise similar caution in their acceptance of the epic tales of Rome's struggles to prevent the restoration of the monarchy, although they admit it is unlikely that she was able to free herself from Etruscan hegemony without a fight. Whether or not we believe these heroic legends of the early days of the Republic, it cannot be denied that they illustrate the qualities which enabled the inhabitants of this small town beside the Tiber eventually to conquer most of the known world.

If indeed it was only hindsight that made the Romans of a later age attribute these heroic actions to the founders of the Republic, the virtues they personified were the traditional ones which Romans of all ages most admired. They were also recognized by others, even her enemies, as Rome's particular virtues. The Greek historian Polybius, who was brought to Rome as a hostage in 167 B C, attributed the Roman conquests – including that of his own country – to the austerity, discipline and honesty of the Roman, whose word was his bond.

15 This bronze head of the late fourth or early third century B C is known as 'Brutus'.

The early Romans owed these steadfast qualities to two things: a devotion to Rome and all she stood for that went beyond the modern concept of patriotism, and the dour endurance typical of yeoman farmers. Although they called themselves citizens, the early Romans were in fact farmers who possessed the toughness and common-sense characteristics of men of the soil, qualities which also made them excellent soldiers. The Senators who were the leaders of the new Republic were also countrymen – these *patres* were the heads of the great landowning families which in certain respects seem to have resembled Scottish clans. In fact the importance of land ownership, as giving a man a stake in the country, runs right through Roman history; still under the Empire, to own land in Italy and to have an income (ostensibly) entirely derived from land, were prerequisites for becoming a Senator.

Such were the men who had pitted their wits against the no doubt more brilliant and intellectual Etruscan kings, and ousted them.

The first test of Republican hardihood was not long in coming. At the head of an army recruited from Tarquinia and Veii, Tarquinius Superbus advanced

upon Rome. Brutus was killed in the first battle, which was not really decisive though the Romans claimed that the Etruscans withdrew after it, and the surviving consul, Publius Valerius (successor to Collatinus, who was banished along with all members of the Tarquin family), claimed a victory. Valerius' failure to ensure the election of another consul to replace the dead Brutus soon aroused suspicions that he wished to become king. However, he disarmed these by introducing various democratic measures, including that of granting all Roman citizens the right to appeal against the verdict of a magistrate to the assembly of the people; thus he earned for himself the name of Poplicola or 'friend of the people'.

Any prospect of a Roman victory must have seemed remote, for the Tarquins had gained the support of Lars Porsenna, the powerful King of Clusium. However, after Lars Porsenna's direct attack on Rome had failed owing to the heroism of the 'immortal three' and other epic events, the existing political situation in Italy played into the Romans' hands in their struggle to prevent Etruscan efforts to restore the monarchy. After withdrawing from Rome, Lars Porsenna turned his attention to the other Latin cities and sent his son Arruns to attack Aricia. The Etruscan conquest of Latium would have represented a threat to the Greek colony at Cumae; hence its ruler came to the assistance of Aricia and, in the words of Livy, 'the men of Cumae saved the day'. Nevertheless the Etruscans finally succeeded in rousing the Latin cities against Rome. The situation was so serious that Aulus Postumius was made dictator and on 15 July 497 B C (499 and 496 B C are also given as the date of the battle) he defeated the army of the Latin Confederation at Lake Regillus. This brought the Tarquin threat to an end, as Tarquinius Superbus died shortly afterwards. The victory, however, must have been won by a narrow margin for, according to the peace terms, Rome had to acknowledge that she was no longer *primus inter pares* as she had been in the days of the kings, and accept the other Latin cities as her equals.

According to Livy, in the heat of the battle of Lake Regillus, Aulus Postumius had vowed to build a temple to Castor, but an ancient Roman legend tells an even stranger tale. On the day of the battle, two riders appeared in the Forum and, after watering their horses at the spring of Juturna, they told the people of the victory at Lake Regillus and then disappeared. Realizing that these messengers had been none other than the heavenly twins, Castor and Pollux, the Romans themselves vowed to build a temple to them on the spot. This was finally completed and dedicated by Aulus Postumius' son 15 years later. Fifteen years may seem a long time for the construction of a temple, but the mere fact that it was possible to build it at all illustrates the continuation of normal life in Rome during the stirring events which followed upon the founding of the Republic. Nor could there be a picture more typical of daily life in any Italian town, now or in the fifth century B C, than that of the population gathered round the fountain in the piazza on a summer evening to hear the news. For in 497 B C the spring of Juturna, rising as it does between the Palatine and the Forum, would have been *the* fountain of the city. The Temple of Castor and Pollux was in fact not the first to be built in Rome after the fall of the Tarquins. That of Saturn, at the other end of the Forum, had already been dedicated in 497 (or 493) B C, and a public holiday in honour of this god who was believed to have taught the people farming, was inaugurated. The

Saturnalia, which was celebrated annually on 17 December (later the holiday was extended to seven days) was in effect the pagan Christmas. There was feasting and presents were given, though probably in these early days they would have been limited to such simple things as candles for adults and clay dolls for children. The Saturnalia was one of the few ancient festivals that never fell into disuse, its continued popularity no doubt due to the fact that it was one of the rare occasions upon which all Romans unbent and enjoyed themselves playing the fool.

Freedom has its price, an unpalatable truth that was soon brought home to the Romans. As brave men they were prepared to lay down their lives for their freedom, but not for the fact that if they returned home from the battle it might be to face bankruptcy. As we have seen, the rank and file of the Roman army were small farmers, and wars have always brought ruined harvests and financial loss in their train. In Rome bankruptcy could mean that a man became the slave of his creditors. While the Senate debated this first great internal crisis of the Republic, the plebeians took matters into their own hands.

Drawn up in military order they marched out of the city and entrenched themselves on a hill some miles away, still known as Monte Sacro – the Sacred Mount. Menenius Agrippa was dispatched by the Senate to parley with the plebs. He was a wise and honourable man, and by recounting a fable about a body which wasted away because its members could not agree, he managed to convince his hearers to negotiate a settlement. As a result the plebs obtained the right of electing their own magistrates, who possessed the power of forbidding any action being taken in the state which they considered was contrary to the plebeian interest. Thus in 494 BC the first two tribunes of the plebs were elected and armed with their formidable power of veto, their persons were declared inviolate – to lay hands upon a tribune was sacrilege; but their powers

16, 17 *Above left* The fountain of Juturna in the Roman Forum, where, according to legend, the Dioscuri, Castor and Pollux, watered their horses after the battle at Lake Regillus. *Above* One of the Dioscuri, with his horse.

did not extend further than a mile outside the city, which they were never able to leave during their year of office. At the same time the office of aedile was created, one aedile being assigned to each tribune as his assistant.

Thus for the first time the plebs had a share in the government of Rome. It came at an opportune moment for them, as the city was now faced with a serious economic crisis which would naturally hit the poor more heavily than the rich. This crisis was probably an indirect result of the proclamation of the Republic: Etruscan hostility would have excluded Rome from trade with central Italy and the fighting had an adverse effect on agriculture, the main source of wealth in any country in ancient times. In any event, Rome suffered from famine and pestilence in the miserable years which followed, and gradually, over a period of some thirty years, the struggle between the patricians and the plebs resolved itself into a battle for power between successive consuls and tribunes. Finally, to one of these last occurred the ingenious idea that, as the tribunes' powers had been defined at the time of the creation of the office, those of the consuls should be, too. The Senate was naturally appalled; knowledge of the law was an aristocratic preserve in Rome as in other early civilizations and to define the powers of the consul was inevitably to indicate their limits. The struggle continued for several years, sometimes almost in an atmosphere of farce. At one moment the Capitol was seized by allegedly dissident elements; the tribunes swore that these were in reality patricians who were trying to alarm the people.

The only edifying episode of this dismal period is the tale of old L. Quintius Cincinnatus, who was declared dictator in order to save Rome from Sabine attack. The impoverished patrician was stripped to his shirt and engaged in clearing a ditch in one of the few fields left to him, when a Senatorial delegation arrived to inform him of his appointment. His wife helped Cincinnatus into his toga, and thus decently clad he received the delegation and departed forthwith to take up his command. Cincinnatus made short work of the Sabines and then, presumably, returned to his ditch. His story was never forgotten and more than two thousand years later some flat land on the right bank of the Tiber was still marked on maps of Rome as Prati de' Quinti – the field of the Quintian family.

Because of the political struggle it had been impossible for five years to pass any new legislation in Rome. Attempts to mollify the tribunes by increasing their number to ten had no effect; for another three years they continued to block all legislation. At last the tribunes changed their tactics and proposed that not only the consular powers but the whole legal framework of the state should be reviewed. Written codes of law already existed in southern Italy, Sicily and Greece. It was therefore decided that these codes should be examined by a committee of three, who actually went to Athens to study the working of Solon's code on the spot. A commission of ten men – the *decemviri* – was now set up to examine the committee's report. Appius Claudius was appointed president of the commission and all normal offices of state were abrogated for a year, which was the time limit set upon the *decemviri's* deliberations. The upshot at first appeared to be highly satisfactory. After some discussion and amendments, the new legal code drawn up by the *decemviri* was approved by the vote of the assembly of the people, and the laws were inscribed on 12 stone tablets which were set up in the Forum. These Laws of the Twelve Tablets became the basis of all subsequent Roman law and future generations of Roman schoolchildren had to learn them by heart.

The basic principles of some of these laws would seem to us to be self-evident – for instance that 'No person shall be beyond the law' and that 'The law last made should be the one in force' – but this is because Roman law has influenced that of Europe and much of the world ever since. Lord Hewart's dictum of 1923, 'Justice should not only be done, but manifestly and un-doubtedly be seen to be done', is in effect derived from the same concept as one of the Laws of the Twelve Tablets which stated that there should be 'No judicial decision after sundown', i.e. that judgment must be made in public.

The success which they had achieved in compiling such an admirable legal code seems, however, to have gone even to the hard Roman heads of the *decemviri*, for having tasted almost absolute power, they were now unwilling to relinquish it when their year's term of office ended.

Once again the plebs withdrew to the Sacred Mount. The *decemviri* were forced to give way and to agree to the restoration of the tribunate and the citizens' right of appeal. The plebs then marched to the Temple of Ceres on the Aventine and there they duly elected their tribunes, one of whom was Lucius Verginius. The tribunes were thus the first state officials to be returned to office after the rule of the *decemviri* had ended. At the first meeting of the assembly of the people which followed, it was noted that a consular election should be held at once and the right of appeal should be restored. Two men who had resisted the *decemviri*'s usurpation from the start were duly elected consuls. Some doubt as to the legality of their election now arose, because it had come about as the result of the vote of the council of the plebs and not of the whole people as represented in the *comitia centuriata*. A law was therefore passed which stated that a decision of the assembly of the people was binding for the whole state. At the time this was intended only to confirm the legality of the consuls' election, but it created a precedent which was eventually to result in the council of the plebs becoming the legislative body of the Republic; the laws concerned were called the Valerio-Horatian laws, after the consuls who promulgated them.

Five years of calm followed, but again it was broken by a tribune's startling proposals. He suggested that the law forbidding marriages between patricians and plebeians should be rescinded and that in future one of the two consuls should be a plebeian. Though no doubt gritting their teeth, the patricians played the game in true Roman style. After discussion among themselves they agreed to change the marriage law, it seemed a fairly safe concession as the *pater familias* even of a plebeian family had absolute power over his children, let alone the head of a great patrician house. This fact was not lost upon the tribunes, who now placed their veto on the military levy in order to force through the infinitely more important consular reform which struck at the root of patrician power.

Once again the Roman capacity for compromise triumphed. The patricians came forward with a proposal for the creation of a new magisterial office which would be open to patricians and plebeians alike. There were to be six of these new magistrates who were to be called 'consular tribunes' and vested with many of the consular powers, though subject to certain limitations. They would not, for instance, be eligible for the Senate at the termination of their office, or to classify citizens for taxation, military service and the call-up. The plebs accepted this compromise which opened military leadership to them and had obvious practical advantages in providing for six potential commanders in time of war. In the event, however, it proved to be a temporary expedient that gave the patricians breathing-space in which to accustom themselves to the revolutionary idea of sharing the consulate with the plebs which came about forty-three years later. The administrative duties of classification for taxation, military service and the call-up were finally allocated to a new patrician magistracy, that of Censor, for which two men were elected ostensibly for a period of five years, though it became customary for them to resign after holding office for 18 months, when the census had been completed. It also became the custom to elect only elder statesmen of great personal reputation to this office as they enjoyed the extraordinary power, almost entirely at their own discretion, of censuring citizens for their private conduct, and placing on them the 'brand of infamy'.

Having settled its political problems, Rome was again confronted with the even more serious ones of famine and pestilence, which were recurrent during the years 438 and 426 B C. Probably this was due to a rapid increase in population and insufficient land upon which to grow food, for in 425 Rome declared war on Veii. This first attempt at expansion was unsuccessful; after capturing the near-by small town of Fidenae, the Romans were forced to make a truce of 18 years with Veii. They were 18 years of famine, pestilence and internal unrest in Rome, and no sooner was the truce ended than they decided to try again.

The tribunes entertained well-founded doubts about the difficulties of the whole venture, but for once the Senate and the majority of the plebs were in agreement. Possibly prospects of pay while on active service had already been held out to the citizen-soldiers by way of encouragement, for they certainly received it before the campaign came to an end. In any event the war party carried all before them and in the spring of 405 the legions marched out of Rome, taking the first step on the road which was eventually to lead Rome to world conquest. For this war with Veii proved to be something quite different from the usual seasonal forays into the Roman Campagna to subdue hostile Latins or repel raiding tribesmen from the hills. During the bitter years which followed, Roman endurance was tested to the full and these citizen-soldiers learned the techniques of siege warfare and evolved tactics which would provide the foundations of the military machine that was to surpass all others in the ancient world.

These war years tried the home front almost as sorely as the soldiers entrenched before Veii. Apart from the inevitable squabbles about military leadership and tactics in any war of unexpectedly long duration, startling natural phenomena convinced the Romans that they had incurred the gods' displeasure. There was a terrible winter during which the Tiber froze and the land was covered with snow. This was followed by a ferocious summer when plague again broke out in Rome. The Sibylline books were consulted and propitiatory rites conducted, but the Romans now became aware of an even more alarming phenomenon. Without any natural cause the waters of the Alban lake rose to an unprecedented height. Superstitious terror was increased by the news that an old man in Veii had prophesied that Veii would never fall until the excess water in the Alban lake was drained off. The old man was kidnapped by a

Roman sentry and brought before the Senate, but he stood his ground. The Delphic Oracle was now consulted and upheld the prophecy, adding that the water must be used to irrigate Rome's fields if Rome was to conquer Veii.

A tunnel some 2,500 metres long, cut through the rocky wall of the crater containing the Alban lake, still exists and regulates its level to this day. And the surplus water still flows through the fields and vineyards of the Roman Campagna. If indeed this remarkable feat of engineering was completed on the traditional date of 397 BC it is not surprising that the Romans having achieved it, returned with renewed confidence to attack Veii and to gain a great victory under the dictator, Marcus Furius Camillus.

Camillus' triumph after the ten years' war with Veii was the greatest Rome had ever seen. Indeed it was so splendid that it aroused foreboding among the people. As they watched the victor's chariot with its four milk-white horses thundering up the Via Sacra, the Romans began to doubt whether so much splendour might not invite jealousy of the gods. For the present, at any rate, it was not the gods who displayed their jealousy, but mere men. Rome was rent with quarrels about the disposal of the booty of Veii, especially over the distribution of the conquered Etruscan land. As usual the Senate was unwilling to allow the large estates to be broken up, thus arousing discontent among the plebs, many of whom now wanted to emigrate to Veii and set up a new state there; they said with reason that the site was more healthful and the city finer. The Senate, who were acutely aware that a Roman Veii could become an even more dangerous rival than its Etruscan predecessor, opposed the move. In the end they won by adopting a judicious mixture of patriotic appeals and extensive distribution of Veiientine land among the plebs.

18, 19 Etruscan warriors: *opposite*, a figure that may represent Mars; *left*, two soldiers carrying a dead comrade. All are armed and wear the distinctive Etruscan helmet with ear-like projections.

20, 21 Gallic helmet and crude sculpted head of a Gallic war-rior, both of the third century BC.

An embassy now arrived from Clusium to warn Rome and ask her aid against the Gauls. To the Romans this name probably meant little or nothing, but the ambassador's accounts of these savages' descent upon the city and their arrogant demands for land, struck at that innate Roman sense of justice and the propriety of the observance of due legal form. Thus, although they had no cause to love the city of which Lars Porsenna had once been king, the Romans agreed to send an embassy to warn the Gauls that, if need be, they would come to Clusium's aid. Three sons of Marcus Fabius Ambustus were chosen as ambassadors; no one could boast a nobler name, but their subsequent be-haviour suggests that the Fabii were too young and hot-headed for the task in hand.

At this first confrontation with the Gauls, the Romans were appalled by the Gauls' retort to their protests at the injustice of demanding Clusium's land with threats. The reply that 'all things belong to the brave who carry justice on the point of their swords', was not a concept calculated to appeal to Romans who prided themselves upon observing the rules even in war. Not surprisingly, hot words were soon followed by hostilities. Now, however, the Fabii be-haved with as little respect for law as the Gauls themselves, for they joined in the fight against these people to whom they had been sent as ambassadors, and Quintius Fabius killed a Gallic chief.

The Gauls in their rage were determined to settle accounts with Rome itself. Nevertheless they proceeded diplomatically, sending an embassy to the city to ask for the surrender of the Fabii. The Senate were not prepared to hand three Roman patricians over to the Gauls, so they temporized and submitted the matter to the vote of the people. The plebs' reaction was as emphatic as

it was disastrous: they elected all three Fabii as consular tribunes for the coming year, while the Gallic ambassadors were still in the city.

22 A mounted soldier fighting a Gaul; from a third-century BC Etruscan funerary stele.

Sheer ignorance of what force the despised barbarians represented, combined with euphoria over the defeat of Veii, seem to have lain at the root of the madness which seized Rome. The phrase 'Quem Jupiter vult perdere dementat prius' ('Whom God would destroy he first sends mad') was written two thousand years later, but it might have been coined to describe the situation in the city in the year 390 BC. All forebodings of the jealousy of the gods were forgotten, and, in Livy's words, 'Calamity of unprecedented magnitude was drawing near, but no adequate steps were taken to meet it.'

The Gauls galloped down the Tiber valley on their huge horses, and were within eleven miles of Rome before they encountered any resistance at all. Finally, at a point near where the Allia joins the Tiber, they came upon the hastily raised Roman levies, drawn up in a ragged line. Before the onslaught of the Gallic cavalry the Romans broke and ran; many of them were drowned trying to cross the Tiber, but a large part of the army escaped to Veii.

The few stragglers from the battle who had not escaped to Veii arrived in Rome to tell gruesome tales of the débâcle. No one knew whether or not the whole of the rest of the Roman army had perished on the Allia. In these terrible straits, desperate action was taken. The walls were judged to be indefensible, and all men of military age were reserved for the defence of the Capitol. They were joined there by those able-bodied Senators who could also fight and at the same time represent the emergency government of Rome. Women and children were permitted to take refuge on the Capitol, but the rest of the population was told to evacuate the city, and many women left with their families.

The Priest of Quirinus and the Vestal Virgins were ordered to leave with the sacred emblems and to make for some safe place. They were also ordered to continue to observe their rites as long as one of them remained alive.

The dismal exodus streamed across the Sublician bridge. The more fortunate piled into carts and wagons, thousands hurried up the steep slope of the Janiculum on foot.

In the city, the aged Senators who had refused to take refuge in the Capitol and thus burden the garrison with useless mouths, resolved to withdraw to their homes and there await their fate at the hands of the Gauls. They did indeed prepare to meet their end 'after the high Roman fashion'. After taking a solemn oath to offer themselves as a sacrifice for their country and the Roman people, arrayed in all their ceremonial robes, these elder statesmen seated themselves upon their ivory curule chairs in the *atria* of their deserted homes, there to await the coming of the Gauls.

As night fell upon the empty city, there was silence in the summer heat, except for distant echoes of war-songs coming from the Gallic camp. Dawn came and no Gaul had yet set foot in Rome. Then, cautiously at first, suspecting some trick, the Gauls started to explore what seemed to be a city of the dead. Where they had expected ferocious resistance they found instead empty streets, deserted houses and closed, silent temples. Near the Forum they came upon the great patrician houses and espied the first human beings they had seen in Rome. But were they human? The old men sat in motionless dignity, the Gauls gathered round to stare, then one of them touched the grey beard of Marcus Papirius and the outraged patrician struck him with his ivory rod. The spell was broken; Papirius and all the rest were killed.

The Gauls now started to sack and burn, their violence increasing as the days went by. The wooden houses blazed, temple roofs came crashing down and the city which had taken 250 years to build was reduced to a smouldering heap of ruins.

The garrison on the Capitol looked down, not daring to intervene, for on their survival depended that of Rome – if indeed it was destined to survive. As in the days of its first struggles against Lars Porsenna, so now again Roman history was enriched by tales of individual heroism. One of the Fabii, a member of the same family as the hot-headed ambassadors who had provoked the disaster, carried out his House's ritual obligation to make an annual sacrifice on the Quirinal. He walked alone through the Gallic hosts to do it and, his duty completed, returned unscathed.

In Veii the fugitives' spirits had begun to revive. They determined to try and get a message through to Camillus who had retired to Ardea, asking him to take command. Even in these desperate conditions the Roman regard for legal and religious form held good. If Camillus was to become dictator, he must be invested with the *imperium* by a magistrate. A young soldier volunteered to act as messenger to the beleaguered government. He made his way from Veii by floating down the Tiber on a lifebuoy and climbed up the Capitol by an approach so precipitous that the Gauls had left it unguarded. Then, duly armed with written authority for Camillus' appointment, he returned to Veii.

The Gauls evidently discovered some trace of the soldier's ascent, for, following the same route, they now attacked the Capitol by night. The cries of the sacred geese, who gave the alarm and thus saved the Capitol, have earned for them a place in Roman history as famous and familiar as that of the she-wolf.

The struggle for Rome became a test of endurance. Gauls and Romans alike were starving, but in the summer heat, to which they were unaccustomed, the Gauls were attacked by a mysterious sickness and died in great numbers: they were the first of many northern armies to discover that pestilence could be Rome's most redoubtable ally. No doubt some rumours of Camillus' activities had by now reached the ears of Brennus, the Gallic chief, for he proceeded to make it known to the defenders of the Capitol that he would be prepared to accept a comparatively modest sum as Rome's ransom. One thousand pounds of gold was the agreed price, but Brennus had one more humiliation in store for Rome. When the gold was being weighed out, the Romans discovered that the Gauls were using weights which were heavier than the accepted standard and they protested. Brennus' answer was to throw his sword into the balance on top of the weights and when the astonished Romans asked what he meant, he replied, 'Woe to the vanquished.'

The fortunes of war now favoured the Romans. Camillus and the hastily reorganized forces from Veii pursued the retreating Gauls and in the end defeated them. Camillus did not resign the dictatorship until the ritual purification of Rome's desecrated temples had been accomplished.

When this had been done the dictator celebrated the Capitoline games as a thank-offering to Jupiter for his protection of the Capitol and ultimate liberation of Rome. Camillus' meticulous observance of these religious rites and ceremonies among the dust and ashes of the ruined city was in fact inspired by policy as much as piety. He was seeking to underline the fact that the destiny of its people was indissolubly linked with the soil of Rome itself, because they owed their unity to the forms of worship of their tutelary gods, the bonds of common custom and the traditions which were the product of the *genius loci*.

This was not a popular view at the time. With all the problems that beset them in the ruined city, the plebs were agitating even more strongly for the entire population to emigrate to Veii. Their arguments now had infinitely greater force, but Camillus and the Senate felt instinctively that Rome up-rooted would no longer be Rome and that the force of tradition which was its mainstay would be lost. Nevertheless, so strong was the support for the migration that the question was debated in the Senate. Even after Camillus had made an impassioned appeal to the people, the decision was still in doubt. Then, by chance, some soldiers returning from guard duty passed through the Comitium and there were given the order to halt. The centurion's command rang out clearly and was heard by the Senators in the Curia, as was his added instruction to the troops, 'We might as well stay here.' Coming at so tense a moment, this chance utterance was accepted by the Senate and the people as an omen that they should not abandon the city. By so narrow a chance did Rome survive.

The decision to remain once made, all worked to rebuild the city and it seems that every effort was made to replace as many as possible of the old inflammable wooden buildings with solid ones of stone and brick. The state-owned quarries were opened to the public for their use; the state also supplied bricks and tiles. But inevitably in the feverish haste of the reconstruction – it is said that Rome was rebuilt in a year – the poorer classes could not

23 The sacred Capitoline geese, in front of the Temple of Juno Moneta; detail of a second-century AD marble relief.

24 The Tarpeian Rock, scene of many Roman executions.

afford the time and labour necessary for such solid construction. Little is heard of new religious buildings in Rome after the sack, except the Temple of Juno Lucina, built in 375 BC on the Esquiline, where the cult of this revered mother goddess continued to flourish right into the fifth century AD.

One major public work was, however, initiated about this time, the so-called Servian Wall. This was built of massive blocks of stone and probably incorporated some of Servius Tullius' primitive defences. Fragments of the Republican Wall, as it is now usually called, can still be seen in various parts of Rome. One of the most conspicuous remains is beside the Stazione Termini. The wall was 11 kilometres in length and the area it enclosed included the Capitol, the Quirinal, the Viminal, a large part of the Esquiline, the Coelian, the Aventine and the Palatine. The fact that the line of the perimeter was evidently not dictated by the military advantages of the terrain, has led archaeo-logists to believe that the 426 hectares of land thus enclosed, corresponded with the built-up area of the city about 378. Thus in the first half of the fourth century BC Rome was already by far the largest city in Italy – Capua, the second largest, occupied a mere 180 hectares.

Such rapid expansion following so soon upon a catastrophe resulted in severe financial stress, which was felt by most of the population of Rome – the tribunes were probably not exaggerating when they said that half the plebs were bankrupt. It was an explosive situation and inevitably someone tried to make political capital out of it. By repeated references to himself as the saviour of the Capitol and constant attempts to try and curry favour with the plebs, Marcus Manlius incurred grave suspicion of trying to seize power. In 382 he was tried by the assembly of the people on the charge of aspiring to the monarchy and was condemned, suffering a traitor's death by being flung from the Tar-peian rock.

Manlius' execution provided no solution for the problems which had brought it about, but in the end a way was found. This was the achievement of two men, the patrician M. Fabius Ambustus and his plebeian son-in-law, G. Licinius Stolo. Both were convinced that the problems of the plebs could only be solved by their having a share in the consulate, by the reduction of debts and by the redistribution of land. Their project was revolutionary, but the most amazing thing about it was not that it took 10 years to get it accepted, but that during all that time the contending parties played the game according to the law, no act of violence was committed, and in the end a peaceful settle-ment was reached. Thus, in the year 368 (or 367), the Licino-Sextian laws were passed, which laid down that one consul should always be a plebeian, that no one was entitled to hold more than 500 jugera (about 310 acres) of Roman state land, and gave legal sanction for the cancellation of certain debts.

The seal was set upon the patricians' acceptance of these laws when the great Camillus, who had served his country five times as dictator, came forward with an appeal to them to do so. Camillus died two years later and was ever afterwards remembered as one of the greatest figures of the Republic, one of the originators of her military system and the personification of the traditional Roman virtues of piety and self-discipline. One of the last acts of his life was to build the Temple of Concord, to commemorate the passing of the Licino-Sextian laws; some fragments of Tiberius' reconstruction of the original building still stand at the foot of the Capitol not far from the Curia.

3

Rome, capital of Italy

Rome enjoyed peace and prosperity for 14 years after the passage of the Licino-Sextian laws. New treaties were negotiated with the Latin and Etruscan cities, extending the Roman sphere of influence so that it reached from southern Etruria to the borders of Campania. Even more significant as an indication of Rome's increasing status was a treaty negotiated with distant Carthage, one of the greatest powers in the Mediterranean. During this peaceful period a temple was built on the *arx* of the Capitol and dedicated to Juno Moneta, which gave its name to the first Roman mint later built beside it and to us our word money. Such tranquillity could not last for long in the period of political flux through which the Italian peninsula was then passing, and being hard pressed by the Samnites, some of the Campanian cities now invoked Rome's aid. Its citizens hesitated, as well they might, with the long-drawn-out agony of the war with Veii still fresh in the minds of the older generation, but finally they took the plunge. Two years of war were enough to send the Samnites back into the mountains, and Rome was now mistress of much of Campania.

Alarmed at the rapidly expanding power of Rome, which had formerly simply been a member of their confederation, the other cities of the Latin League presented an ultimatum. This would have made them an integral part of the Roman state, with equal rights of representation in the consulate and Senate. It seemed a reasonable suggestion; they were, after all, of the same stock. But this time Rome did not temporize. Expansion was one thing, integration quite another. During the weary years of recovery after Veii and the Gallic sack, the Romans had come to realize the truth of Camillus' words, that it was their common tradition and their institutions painfully evolved over the years which made them what they were. This was their particular heritage and they were not going to place it at risk, especially as they were beginning to reap the first fruits of their long struggle for independence and self-sufficiency.

The war that followed was perhaps the bitterest that Rome had ever fought or was ever to fight. The defeat of a coalition of more than fourteen Latin cities and their Campanian allies took three years to accomplish, whereas the reduction of Veii alone 58 years earlier had taken an exhausted Rome ten years. It was indeed a changed Rome that in 338 dictated peace on its own terms to the cities that had once been its equals. Moreover, the shrewd calcula-tion which underlay the generosity of those terms showed that Rome's political judgment was keeping pace with its military strength. Rome was generous in that the cities preserved their own identity and freedom within certain limits. Their status was that of allies whose foreign relations were now directed by Rome. They were also obliged to provide military levies, not exceeding a stated number, for the Roman army. In Rome itself the Latins enjoyed preferential rights not accorded to other non-Romans. They were Latin citizens, however, not Roman ones. Land confiscation, ostensibly for the benefit of the Roman plebs, was extensive only in the case of the cities that had put up a strong resistance. Some Roman colonies were set up, notably at the important seaport of Antium (Anzio), whose fleet had been destroyed during the war.

No doubt Roman losses had been heavy, but there was a new feeling of unity in the city, the plebs now had an active part to play in all decisions in the state. These decisions came to affect an ever-widening area.

Evidence that life in Rome was changing and giving rise to a new sense of civic pride is afforded by various developments which occurred about this time. In 339 the first permanent buildings were set up in the Circus Maximus. These were the *carceres* or enclosures, from which the chariots started for the races. A year later the *rostra*, the bronze beaks used for ramming from the prows of the warships of defeated Antium, were affixed to the orators' platform in the Comitium. Until this date the spoils of victory are usually mentioned in Roman history as votive offerings to temples. Possibly the *rostra* were too large or for some other reason considered inappropriate for this purpose – in any event, they seem to have been the first prizes of war used for civic embellishment in Rome.

25 Prows of ships with *rostra*, on a coin of *c.* 47 BC.

These were the outward and visible signs of the city's evolution, but already they had been preceded by the beginnings of a civic administration. Among the first functionaries to carry on this work were the *quaestores*, the consuls' assistants in their day-to-day legal work, particularly criminal cases. The *quaestores*, of whom there were originally only two, also had charge of the state treasury which was housed in vaults beneath the Temple of Saturn. One of the most familiar official figures in Rome was the Praetor Urbanus, who was to be seen on court days trying civil cases in full public view in the Forum. From early morning until late afternoon he sat in a small open pavilion on his ivory curule chair, this last the prerogative of magistrates exercising the *imperium*. The curule chair was actually a camp stool, and its name is believed to have been derived from the fact that a magistrate originally carried it in his *currus* or war chariot. It was this practice which gave rise to the association of the curule chair with magistrates of the highest rank whose jurisdiction was not limited to a particular place.

The officials who were most closely associated with the day-to-day administration of Rome were the aediles. Originally a plebeian office, the number of aediles had been increased from two to four in 367 by the addition of two curule aediles. These four men were, between them, responsible for policing the city, for its food supplies, for the maintenance of public buildings and for the organization of the games. This last was to become an exceedingly onerous function as the aediles were expected to contribute to the expenses out of their own pockets, but lavish spending won them popularity with the citizen-voters and election to this junior magistracy was often the first step on the ladder of a political career.

The Ides of September 366 BC was a memorable day in the history of Roman festivities, for it was on this date that the first series of annual games – the Ludi Romani or Ludi Magni – was instituted. As we have seen, the circus had existed since the days of the Tarquins, and ever since then games had been held at different times to celebrate outstanding events. But from now on the four days of the Ludi Romani were declared a regular public holiday, and in time this was extended until it lasted from 4 to 19 September. During the centuries to come, many other public games were instituted that rivalled the Ludi Romani and lasted nearly as long. In early times, however, nothing could match the pomp of the Ludi Romani, which almost equalled that of a triumph.

The games' festivities opened with an offering made to Jupiter Optimus Maximus; this was followed by a banquet held on the Capitol and attended by all state dignitaries. The feasting over, a procession set out from the Capitol for the Circus Maximus. It was headed by a consul, attired in purple triumphal robes and wearing a crown of oak leaves on his head; behind him came the citizens of Rome, marching in their civil cadres. The competitors in the games followed, surrounded by mimes and dancers; then came the band of trumpeters, flautists and tambourine players. These ushered in a procession of litters upon which the most precious objects of the sacred treasuries were laid out – bowls and vases of gold and silver and pots of precious unguents. Finally, the gods appeared, also borne aloft. In early times these were lay figures attired in the robes and carrying the traditional attributes of each deity; later the actual cult statues were carried in the procession.

The concept of embellishment as a matter of civic propriety – what Italians call *il decoro della città* – originated in Rome towards the end of the fourth century BC. Then, public consciousness appears to have awakened to the fact that, spartan virtues notwithstanding, the word *decorus* applied equally to the beautiful and to moral fitness. Thus, some thirty years after the *rostra* had been installed in the Comitium, a colossal statue of Hercules was raised in the Capitoline area – this was one of the first of that multitude which was later to people the streets of Rome. Changes had also been occurring in the Forum. Balconies, called *maeniana* after Gaius Maenius who first built them, now overhung the entrances of the *tabernae* or shops that lined the Forum, where the ruins of the Basilica Aemelia and Basilica Giulia still stand. The character of the shops themselves was also changing – *argentarie*, bankers and money-changers, were replacing the butchers, and since 310, they had advertised their trade in decorative fashion by hanging gilded shields outside their place of business. The houses behind this commercial façade, however, belonged to great patrician families like the Scipios: in fact the *domus* of the Scipios stood on the south-east of the Forum where the Basilica Giulia was later built. This, to us, curious juxtaposition of shops and patrician abodes was so much a Roman custom that it was still true of palaces built two thousand years later.

The first years of the third century witnessed further notable developments in this process of adding to the dignity of Rome. Gaius and Quintius Ogulnius, who were curule aediles in 296, used the funds confiscated from usurers to instal 'brazen thresholds' on the Capitol and to enrich 'the three tables in the shrine of Jupiter' – presumably the altars of the triad of deities in the Capitoline temple – with silver plate, and placed a statue of Jupiter in a four-horse chariot on the roof. This may have been a replacement, possibly of bronze, for Vulca's original terracotta group which would by then have been more than three hundred years old. The usurers must have been highly successful ones, for the money confiscated from them also paid for a sculptural group of the she-wolf suckling Romulus and Remus, set up beside the fig tree, Ruminalis, marking the traditional spot where the twins were discovered by the shepherd. Nor was this all; money from the same source enabled the plebeian aediles to present golden bowls to the Temple of Ceres, to hold games and to pave the road between the Porta Capena and the Temple of Mars.

What renders these developments even more remarkable is that in the years between 327 and 304 the Romans were fighting desperately in their second war against the Samnites. Like Rome, the confederation of Samnite cities was then an expanding power, whose territory reached from Lucania in the south to the River Liris in the north. The establishment of a Roman colony at Fregellae in the Liris valley was the immediate *casus belli*, but a collision between two such warlike peoples was no doubt inevitable. That they were equally matched in the military sense is evident from the fact that Rome struggled for 14 years in vain, and in 321 suffered a humiliating defeat at the Caudine Forks. No wonder even Roman nerves began to twitch, if not actually to fail, and that there were rumours of faithless Latin allies and conspiracies, all of which proved to be groundless. Roman common sense reasserted itself, however, and found its personification in one of the new Censors, Appius Claudius, who was elected in 312. Members of the Claudian house were rarely popular and Appius was no exception, nor were his activities calculated to alter this; but his censorship proved to be the turning-point in the Samnite War.

Rather in the manner of a modern business efficiency expert, Appius cut through the dead wood of the antiquated property assessments, based only on land ownership, by which citizens were divided into classes for taxation and military service. He thus made available greatly increased resources of men and money for the prosecution of the war. On the civilian side, Appius' innovations also gave greater opportunities to able men. Livy tells the story of Cn. Flavius, the son of a freed slave, who, to the scandal of the diehards, became a curule aedile. Flavius proved his worth, however, by publishing (possibly at Appius' instigation) the first legal handbook, the *Legis Actiones*. This made available to all the formulae employed in the praetor's court, which had hitherto reposed in the secret archives of the *pontifices*. Flavius also posted notices in the Forum giving a calendar of court days, thus rendering justice more readily accessible to the people.

Naturally such innovations did not endear Appius to either the diehard patricians or the *nouveaux-riches* (and now heavily taxed) plebeians, but this did not prevent the formidable Censor from completing the public works which make his name familiar to us even today. He was the builder of the first great Roman road, the Via Appia, that linked Rome with Casilinum (Capua), the Roman base of operations against the Samnites. Like so many Roman roads in the centuries to come, the Via Appia also led to victory. If Appius Claudius must share some of the credit for his road-building with that stern mother of invention, military necessity, the same does not apply to his other great innovation – the first aqueduct. This was not a spectacular feat of engineering like those of later times (only for the last 80 metres of its course was it supported by a wall or arcade), but rather the adaptation of old agricultural methods of irrigation to a new use. The creation of the Aqua Appia does however reveal, perhaps more clearly than anything else, that combination of practical knowledge and vision which made Appius Claudius what he was.

Even in wartime, life in Rome did not lack moments of light relief. In fact the year 311 witnessed what is probably the first recorded strike in trade union history. The flute-players of the city struck and departed to Tibur (Tivoli) because they were not allowed to celebrate their annual festival in the Temple of Jupiter. They thus precipitated a serious situation, as no sacrifice to the gods could be made without its ritual accompaniment of flute music. The whole machinery of Roman state religion was thrown out of gear at a time when divine protection was particularly necessary to the city, and Roman gods were known to be not only jealous but punctual in their requirements. The government of the day, however, displayed a good deal more guile than many modern ones in dealing with the situation. Evidently, even then, artists did not lead the lives of sober citizens, for the Senate persuaded the inhabitants of Tibur to entertain the flautists so royally (presumably they also footed the bill) that they were soon all dead drunk. By night the errant musicians were piled into carts, driven back into Rome and deposited in the Forum.

These colleges or unions of men practising the same trade were of very ancient origin in Rome; the foundation of that of the recalcitrant flute-players as well as goldsmiths, woodworkers, dyers, shoemakers, leather-workers and copper- and pan-smiths, were even attributed to Numa Pompilius. This legendary origin probably indicates that these were the earliest trades to be practised on any scale in the city. That Appius Claudius had discovered a fruitful source of revenue in taxing plebeian fortunes suggests that commerce was already well established in Rome, while the existence of recognized trade signs for moneylenders and bankers indicates not only their numbers but

26 Samnite warriors, from a fourth-century BC wall-painting; during the second half of this century Rome was engaged in war against the confederation of Samnite cities.

27 Ruins of temples in the Largo Argentina; 'Temple C' is in the foreground.

suggests the extent of money and goods reaching Rome from other parts of Italy and possibly from overseas.

The end of the Second Samnite War in 304 would have provided further impetus for this trade expansion. Peace and prosperity also encouraged the growth of the city's own production of luxury goods, such as bronzes, silverware and jewels. Livy's first specific mention of such things in Republican Rome is a reference to a golden bowl sent to Delphi as a thanks-offering after the defeat of Veii, though this could, of course, have been Etruscan loot. But even before then Roman gold-workers, and even dentists, had evidently been active, as one of the Laws of the Twelve Tablets stated that the only gold which could be buried with a man was that in his teeth. The gold and silver vessels presented to the temples and the statues erected by the aediles in 296 also indicate that there was money in the city – even if it was in the hands of usurers.

The legionaries returned from the wars would have found quite a number of changes in Rome. Possibly the most startling actually occurred during the brief interval between the Second and Third (298–291) Samnite Wars. In 300 the plebs had gained a victory of their own, bloodless but hardly won, against the determined resistance of Appius Claudius. This was the passage of the *lex ogulnia* which increased the numbers of the pontifices and augurs to eight and nine respectively and stipulated that four of the first and five of the second should

28 Relief of the ship of Aesculapius, with his snake symbol.

always be plebeians. As practically no action could be taken in the state without priestly consultation, this was far from being a purely prestige victory. The wars themselves had probably been directly responsible for the three fine new temples that had been built on the Palatine between 298 and 294. The several dedications to Bellona (goddess of war), Victory and Jupiter Stator (the stayer of flight) seem to indicate that they were votive ones, promised in the heat of battle by army commanders. We know nothing about the aspect of these temples, but in all probability they resembled the tetrastyle 'Temple C', their near contemporary, whose ruins can still be seen in the Largo Argentina, but the dedication of which is unknown. This is the oldest surviving stone-built temple in Rome and it still displays certain characteristics common to the old wooden ones. The decorative elements were of terracotta, the wide intercolumniation recalls that of the primitive temples, while lines of columns flank the *cella* and meet lateral extensions of the back wall, as in the Capitoline Temple of Jupiter.

A remarkable religious event occurred in Rome shortly before the end of the Samnite Wars. This was the first ceremonial induction of a foreign god into the city. It was brought about by a plague and the resulting consultation of the Sibylline books, which prescribed the introduction of Aesculapius, the Greek god of medicine, as the only remedy. An embassy was sent to Epidaurus and in

due course returned with a representation of the god and his serpent. According to the legend, a great serpent was seen to leave the ship bearing the god, as it was proceeding up the Tiber, and swim to the Tiber island. This was regarded as an indication of the spot where the god wished to take up residence. A temple was built and later the whole island was walled with travertine to represent a ship, with an obelisk placed in the centre to simulate the mast. Remains of the wall and a relief of the serpent are still to be seen.

The opening years of the third century B C were also the closing ones of an epoch in Roman life. Rome was then still in many ways the stern but simple patriarchal city to which the Romans of later ages looked back with nostalgia, extolling the life of their forefathers as one unsullied by foreign influences, in which the old Roman beliefs and virtues – 'the old ways', as they were called – held sway. The family was the centre of this life, as indeed it was the pillar of the Roman state. The *paterfamilias*' word was literally law for members of his household, though the responsibility for running the home rested with his wife – the *domina*, as she was called by the entire household. As the third century advanced she would, however, probably have achieved a modicum of independence as the free form of marriage became general. In this the wife retained her property and remained under the jurisdiction of her father until she was 25; afterwards her *tutor* maintained a formal guardianship. Long before this the lower classes had contracted marriage by simple cohabitation for a year or by a form of bride purchase made in the presence of five witnesses. Patricians, however, held to the ancient, indissoluble and ceremonious rite of *confarreatio*, in which the bride and groom partook of *panis farreus* – bread made of a primitive type of wheat called *far* (*Triticum spelta*).

29, 30 Domestic life in Roman Italy: the marble relief, *opposite*, shows a family at dinner; the wall-painting, *left*, a woman with her slave.

By the beginning of the third century BC the old tradition of the children receiving their education entirely from their parents was practically a thing of the past. The custom survived, however, of boys accompanying their fathers to the Forum and quite early being placed in a kind of apprenticeship to one of their father's friends in order to learn about the conduct of public affairs. Girls continued to lead a secluded life until their marriage, usually about the age of thirteen. This way of life was, of course, limited to well-to-do people of the type of family which lived in a *domus*, or more or less stately home. That of the mass of the population was undoubtedly very different.

Nevertheless all classes met in the Forum and even the great were expected to recognize anyone who greeted them. The intimacy of life in the Forum is something which the modern world has lost, even in its closest equivalent, the piazza of an Italian country town, and owing to the differences in climate and mentality there was never any real parallel in northern life. Perhaps for the English to picture what life in the Forum was like is to imagine a place in which members of both Houses of Parliament could meet and discuss the events of the day with barristers, stockbrokers and members of the armed forces, in a setting in which the Law Courts and the Stock Exchange were combined with Covent Garden and Smithfield, filled with milling crowds intent upon shopping and gossiping. But even in the midst of this furore a magistrate would be expected to put a name to anyone who saluted him. It is only at the end of the Republic that we hear of the *nomenclator* – the slave with the card-index mind – who could whisper the appropriate name hastily into his master's ear.

It can scarcely be marvelled at that in this world personal contacts were all, and personal amiability – *blanditia*, as it was called – was of the greatest importance.

31 The Temple of Vesta with the curule chair, voting urn and the initials A C – *absolvo condemno* (I acquit, I convict) – representing the voting tablets used by juries. From a coin dated *c.* 57 B C.

The Roman lived in a crowd. It was the sign of a popular and powerful man, and attracted votes which were of the essence in a state where the highest offices were all elective.

In the third century B C the appearance of the Forum was very different from that of the Imperial era, of which we see the ruins today. The square appeared as a practically unbroken space, paved with pebbles, in the manner of paths often still to be seen in Italian Renaissance gardens. The *tabernae* that lined its northern and southern sides would also be familiar to anyone acquainted with Ostia Antica or the medieval and Renaissance quarters of Italian towns. For this kind of shop, with a balcony sheltering the entrance and the large opening below, combining shop window, counter and entrance all in one, continued to be built for centuries. The balconies were said to have been first built for watching gladiatorial displays. However, this seems unlikely as the first displays of this kind in the Forum are believed to have taken place in 264 at the funeral of Junius Brutus; possibly the balconies were first used for watching less gruesome spectacles.

There would have been plenty of space for such events to be held in the Forum at the beginning of the third century B C. Then, apart from the altar and paved area of the Lacus Curtius – marking the site of a spring or marsh, but also the legendary chasm into which Mettius Curtius jumped on horseback and disappeared – only the praetor's canopied seat and a couple of commemorative monuments are believed to have stood in the Forum. One of these last is said to have been a column which was also used to determine the hour of sunset, when the sun sank behind it. The eastern confines of the Forum were bounded by the Regia and the Temple of Vesta, its western end by the Vulcanal and the Temple of Saturn. Apart from the Via Sacra, which traversed the Forum valley from the Velia to the Capitol, and was called the Clivus Capitolinus where it climbed the hill, three other streets now led out of the Forum. These were the Vicus Jugarius and the Vicus Tuscus, connecting it with the

Velabrum and the Tiber bank, and the Argiletum, the street of the shoemakers and later the barbers and booksellers, that led northwards to the Forum Piscarum and the popular Suburra district.

On the left side of the Argiletum, as it led out of the Forum, lay the Comitium, which was the political centre of Republican Rome, as the Forum was the legal, social and commercial one. In the Comitium the old original *comitia curiata* had gathered to vote, as its successor the *comitia centuriata* now did in the Campus Martius. The citizen voters, however, still thronged to the Comitium to listen to the orators speaking from the *rostra* and to await the results of any momentous senatorial debate in the Curia, which faced on to the square.

During the third century the Comitium was to witness many momentous scenes, with anxious crowds waiting for the thundering hooves of couriers' horses, bringing dispatches from the battlefield to the Senate. There were days of rejoicing, but more of catastrophe, when Rome's very existence seemed to hang by a thread. But in the end Rome and Roman institutions triumphed, and the wars which laid the foundations of her world power were directed from this small patch of Roman soil.

The *lex hortensia* of 287, which recognized the *concilium plebis*, council of the plebs, as the sovereign power of the state, completed the liberalizing process of the basis of government that had begun with the second secession of the plebs and the Valerio-Horatian laws of 449.

Authorities, ancient and modern, do not agree as to the processes by which this was eventually achieved – probably it was by gradual stages – but they recognize that the *lex hortensia* was the definitive measure which placed this great power in the hands of the people. In typically Roman fashion, however, this did not mean that the state was governed by *vox populi* alone. Far from it; the third century was in many ways the golden age of Senatorial power, which was based on influence and custom. This was, of course, aided and abetted by the client system that provided the great families with a legion of supporters. Power might legally reside in the hands of the people, but when elections came round these influences combined to persuade many of them still to vote for patrician candidates, and it was the *cursus honorum* – the official career which consisted of holding a succession of magisterial offices – that led to membership of the Senate. The men who achieved it, however, whether they were patricians or, as they increasingly came to be, plebeians, had great experience of government behind them.

The Senate's powers were in fact enormous. For one thing it held the purse-strings of the state. For another it administered the *ager publicus* or state lands, as well as those gained by conquest; these included cultivated and uncultivated land, forests and mines, all of which could be leased to individuals. One outcome of this was that the Senate also controlled the setting up of colonies. Among the Senate's other prerogatives was the appointment of ambassadors and, later, provincial governors. The Senate's functions were, of course, advisory: it was summoned to discuss a given question by a magistrate, usually a consul, though he was not bound to follow its advice. This was expressed by a majority vote which, in later times at any rate, was recorded in the *senatus-consultum* or minutes of the meeting. Nevertheless, consuls and most magistrates held office for only a year, members of the Senate were there for life, and few magistrates, with their careers to think of, would have cared to ignore the

32 King Pyrrhus of Epirus, the invader of Roman territory whose victories were his undoing; a marble bust from Herculaneum.

Senate's opinion. Thus, at this period, a consul would be most likely to accept the Senate's view and act accordingly.

This, then, was the body of men who were now to be called upon to pit their wits against those of two of the most able men of the age and later against one of the great military geniuses of all time. For, just as expansion into Campania had brought Rome into collision with the Samnites, so now victory over them had resulted in Roman confrontation with the Greek cities of Apulia, Lucania and Bruttium (modern Calabria). The cities were rich and civilized – a great deal more highly civilized than Rome – but, partly because they had been founded as colonies by emigrants from different parts of Greece, they were not even united in a confederation as the Samnites had been.

Tarentum (Taranto), with the finest harbour in southern Italy and surrounded by rich corn-lands, was one of the richest of these cities on the Italian mainland. It was also close to Greece where King Pyrrhus of Epirus carried on the Macedonian military tradition. The Tarentines invited Pyrrhus to be their leader, and got a bit more than they had bargained for, as he arrived with his own professional army and twenty war elephants. Their presence, nevertheless, must have been comforting to the Tarentines, who were not militarily inclined, for the Roman people – not the cautious Senate – had, under the leadership of the tribune G. Aelius Paetus, taken Tarentum's rival Thurii under their protection. Although the people's assent had in the past been necessary for the declaration of war, this move on the part of the popular assembly was something new: something, perhaps, inspired by the *lex hortensia* – for to protect Thurii was to threaten Tarentum and now also to wage war against Pyrrhus. The outcome was the battle of Heraclea, the first of the Pyrrhic victories, which brought King Pyrrhus to Anagnia (Anagni), within easy striking distance of Rome.

Whatever his hopes may have been, not one of the Latin cities or even the Greek ones of Campania rallied to the King during his spectacular advance. Accordingly Pyrrhus dispatched his minister Cineas to Rome as his ambassador to negotiate a treaty. The ambassador evidently knew a good deal about the Romans, for Plutarch records that on the day of his arrival in the city he was able to address all the Senators and knights by name. How he recognized them Plutarch does not say, nor does he explain how Cineas came to be so ignorant of Roman feminine psychology – his rich gifts for the wives of influential men were refused with disdain. Nevertheless, under the spell of Cineas' eloquence, the Senate might have accepted the conciliatory terms offered by Pyrrhus. These amounted to Roman recognition of the *status quo* existing before Pyrrhus' victory and included the return of Roman prisoners. The more wide-awake Senators, however, immediately seized upon the fact that the terms gave no guarantee that Pyrrhus would leave Italy; he could simply bide his time and attack again. A stormy debate in the Senate followed, culminating in a moment of pure drama, when Appius Claudius the Censor, now old and blind, was led to his place by his sons. Whatever reservations Senators might have entertained about Appius in the past, he carried them with him now. He said: 'Pyrrhus must leave Italy and then we will treat with him.' Thus the maxim that Rome must never negotiate with enemies bearing arms and never make peace with an enemy on Italian soil became one of the basic principles of Roman policy.

46

Cineas had to return to his master empty-handed.

Pyrrhus did not risk another direct advance upon Rome. Evidently he was trying to turn the enemy flank when he encountered the Roman army at Asculum (Ascoli Piceno). He was forced to fight on difficult ground and he won, but at such a cost that his comment – 'another victory of this kind will finish me' – has passed into history.

The Carthaginians feared that, as Pyrrhus had become the champion of the Greek cities in Italy, he might now wish to extend his assistance to those in Sicily as well, and Sicily formed part of the Punic sphere of influence. Support of Rome, the Carthaginians hoped, would keep Pyrrhus pinned down in Italy. The Greeks of Syracuse, however, now appealed to Pyrrhus for aid and he went to their assistance. The Carthaginians were not so tough as the Romans and in three years Pyrrhus conquered all Sicily except the Carthaginian stronghold of Lilybaeum. In the spring of 275 the King returned to Italy, for Rome had not wasted time either, and much of Lucania was now in Roman hands. Pyrrhus made a swift march to Beneventum and there engaged the Roman army, commanded by Manius Curius Dentatus. The result of the battle of Beneventum was not even a Pyrrhic victory; the King was soundly beaten. Manius Curius stampeded the war elephants by using fire and they turned and charged Pyrrhus' own army.

Manius Curius Dentatus' triumph was the first in Rome to include elephants. There was a note of incongruity about this for, far from being a stately aristocrat, Manius Curius was a plebeian of homely habits. He is said once to have received the Samnite ambassadors in the kitchen of his Sabine farm while eating a meal of turnips. Apparently the Samnites thought that they could expedite their cause by offering a Roman a bribe but Manius' reply was, 'I don't want gold, what I want is to govern the men who have it.'

Nevertheless, a taste for luxury was beginning to creep into Rome. In the same year as Manius Curius celebrated his triumph, the plebeian G. Fabricius Luscinus was Censor, and he had the patrician Publius Cornelius Rufinus expelled from the Senate for disobeying the sumptuary laws and owning more than 10 pounds weight of silver plate. That the law was applied in all its rigour seems to indicate that Publius Cornelius' case was exceptional. But it was a straw that showed which way the wind was blowing and above all that it was a wind of change. The war against Pyrrhus had brought the Romans into contact with the much higher civilization of the cities of Magna Graecia and, by 272, resulted in Rome's becoming the mistress of Italy from the Ionian Sea to the Po valley. Inevitably this meant that wealth was flowing into the city. Evidence of this is provided by the construction of a new 40-mile-long aqueduct, the Anio Vetus, which was begun in 272 but completed in 269. About the same time the first regular Roman silver coinage came into use; the bullion probably came from the Carthaginian mines in Spain. Such were the developments that the war against Pyrrhus brought to Rome – they extended its power and made it aware of the world beyond the confines of the Italian peninsula, so that the next step may not at first have seemed to be so momentous as it eventually proved to be. In 264, by vote of the assembly of the people, Rome committed itself to go to the assistance of the Mamertines of Messana (Messina): this meant crossing the straits and waging war in Sicily against Carthage.

33 Coining implements, represented on a silver *denarius* of *c.* 45 BC.

4

Rome versus Carthage

The morality of the decision to wage war was not quite up to the standards of Fabricius and Manius Curius Dentatus. Rome had lately signed a treaty of alliance with Carthage; though this had admittedly really been only a defensive alliance against Pyrrhus, who had now left the scene. But Sicily was rich, particularly in wheat. In the summer of 264, a Roman army liberated Messina and in the following year Rome concluded a treaty with Hiero, the ruler of the great Greek city of Syracuse. Two years later, after a five months' siege and the rout of a Carthaginian army, Agrigentum was captured by the Romans, who sacked it and sold the population as slaves. This was a warning to Carthage's other Sicilian allies who might be tempted to resist Rome.

Rome might conquer the mountainous heart of Sicily, but could not hold the prosperous ports and coastal plains without a fleet. No doubt this was explained to the Romans by their ally Hiero, for with Greek aid they set to work to build a fleet. Their ships were not like those of the Greeks; the Romans still put their trust in the superiority of their infantry and their ships were therefore designed to carry troops who could board and seize an adversary, not to ram and sink one as in Greek naval tactics. In their first naval battle the Romans were successful. In 260, off Mylae (Milazzo) near Messina, the consul Gaius Duilius beat a Carthaginian fleet, and a column decorated with the Carthaginian *rostra* was set up in the Forum to celebrate the victory.

That this was not simply beginner's luck seemed to be amply proved by another and much greater Roman sea victory, fought off Ecnomus, in which 30 Carthaginian ships were sunk and 64 taken for a Roman loss of only 24. The way now seemed clear for a Roman invasion of Africa. Accordingly in 256, a vast armada set sail, under the command of the consul M. Atilius Regulus, bearing 20,000 infantry and 500 cavalry. The consul was, however, completely outmanœuvred by Xanthippus the Spartan, leader of the Carthaginian mercenary army, and the Romans suffered a disastrous defeat. Only 2,000 of them managed to escape to their fortified base. But worse was to follow. The rescuing Roman fleet was caught in a storm and 284 ships were lost. The Carthaginians took fresh hope and returned to the fray. Again they were lucky: another Roman fleet was caught in a storm and 180 ships lost.

Realizing that the sea was not Rome's natural element, the Senate now pinned its faith on land operations in Sicily. On the whole they were successful but, like Pyrrhus before them, the Romans were brought to a halt in front of the Carthaginian fortress of Lilybaeum. They laid siege to it in 250, but soon discovered that the city could not be starved into submission as long as the Carthaginians could provision it by sea. Lilybaeum stood on a headland near modern Marsala and the harbour entrance was surrounded by shoals, which only the Carthaginian pilots knew how to navigate.

34 The triumphal column of Gaius Duilius in the Roman Forum, decorated with the prows of ships captured from the Carthaginians; an engraved reconstruction. Note the *rostra* used for ramming (see Ill. 133).

After a year's siege, in a desperate attempt to break the deadlock, the Romans built another fleet. The commander was Publius Claudius Pulcher, son of Appius Claudius the Censor. He seems to have inherited the family eccentricity but not the brains, and from the start things went against him. When the auspices were taken before the battle, the sacred chickens refused to eat, whereupon Claudius Pulcher ordered them to be thrown into the sea 'so that they might drink since they would not eat.' Still, victory seemed certain as the Carthaginian fleet was bottled up in the harbour of Drepanum (Trapani). Claudius Pulcher, however, had neglected to put a guard on a secondary entrance to the harbour, thus allowing the Carthaginians to escape and attack the Romans in the rear, an action which resulted in the destruction of the entire Roman fleet. This was one of the few occasions upon which a Roman commander was tried for high treason. Claudius Pulcher was condemned and died not long afterwards, probably by his own hand.

The siege of Lilybaeum dragged on for another nine years, during which blockade-runners kept the city supplied. Famous among them was a certain Hannibal, nicknamed the Rhodian, who made the run from the African coast constantly, evading the watching Romans in his fast quinquereme. At last, by a ruse, they forced him to fight and captured his ship. This the Romans examined with interest for, although it was capable of great speed, they found that it was of remarkably solid construction.

In 242 it seemed to the Romans that the war would never end. During 22 years they had poured out men and money but to no avail. The last census had shown a drop of over 46,000 men and the treasury was empty. Private enterprise now came to the rescue. A group of well-to-do citizens got together and decided to build their own fleet. Between them they managed to produce enough money to build and equip 200 quinqueremes, using Hannibal the Rhodian's captured ship as a model. Those who fathered the enterprise did so on the understanding that if all went well they would be repaid. They took a great risk, but it succeeded. The commander of this new fleet, Gaius Lutatius Catulus, was a disciplinarian and his crews were well trained. The Carthaginians evidently did not know what they were up against and at the battle of Aegates they were soundly beaten. 50 of their ships were sunk and 70 captured, together with 10,000 prisoners. The Carthaginian leader in Sicily, Hamilcar Barca, sued for peace and in 241 the First Punic War ended in a Roman victory.

After 23 years of anguished watching and waiting, the citizens of Rome now reaped their reward. All Sicily, except the domains of Hiero of Syracuse and his allies, became a Roman province – it was the first. Carthage had also to give up the Lipari Islands and agree to pay a war indemnity of 2,200 talents of silver in 20 years. This did not, however, satisfy the assembly of the people, who insisted that the figure should be raised to 3,300 talents and that it should be paid in ten years.

During the long struggle Rome had changed considerably. Greeks from southern Italy were thronging into the city. Many were the slaves of rich families, who employed them to teach their children. One of them, Spurius Carvilius, made history. After he was freed he stopped teaching children privately as a *grammaticus*, and in 250 set up the first primary school in Rome. Secondary education was also now in the hands of Greeks: boys in their teens were taught at home by a *litterator* in the art of correct speaking and the

interpretation of Greek poetry. Roman education had obviously changed and broadened considerably since the days of parental instruction. Greek influence was not confined to the schoolroom, however, and Carvilius was not the only slave to be manumitted and to make a career for himself. His achievement was eclipsed by that of Livius Andronicus of Tarentum, who wrote the first play to be performed in Rome. This was an adaptation of the old Roman mimed scenes which were accompanied by *saturae*, satirical words and songs. Andronicus provided these with a plot and thus wove them into a comprehensive whole. His play was performed at the Ludi Romani in the first year of peace.

The Romans may have been beginning to enjoy the lighter side of life – another new play, the first by the Roman poet Ennius, was performed in 235 – but they were far from idle in the years following the First Punic War. The victory year of 241 saw the beginning of a new road along the Tyrrhenian coast, connecting Rome with what is now Pisa. According to custom, this was called after the Censor, C. Aurelius Cotta, who built it. The Via Aurelia was no doubt useful for the expeditions which wrested Corsica and Sardinia from Carthage in 238 and 237. Carthage made warlike gestures and nursed a deep resentment, but the islands – Sardinia was particularly important for its iron and lead mines – were added to the growing list of Roman provinces. In 221 Rome acquired a second circus, the Circus Flaminius, named for the Censor, Gaius Flaminius Nepos, who later completed the Via Flaminia, linking Rome with her colony at Ariminum on the Adriatic.

When at the end of the First Punic War, Hamilcar Barca had marched out of the Sicilian fortress of Eryx with all the honours of war, Rome no doubt believed that she had heard the last of the Barcide House. Even Hamilcar's success in carving out a state for himself, far away in Spain, may not have interested the Romans overmuch, except that the silver mines he captured there enabled Carthage to pay the war indemnity. Hamilcar died in 228 and, such was the Romans' confidence in his son-in-law and successor, Hasdrubal, that they negotiated a treaty with him, by which Spain was divided into zones of influence – that of the Romans to the north of the Ebro, Hasdrubal's to the south. In 221 Hasdrubal was murdered by a slave and Hamilcar's son Hannibal, then aged 26, was proclaimed general in his stead. Whether or not the tale is true that when Hannibal was 9, Hamilcar had made him swear undying enmity to Rome, this was in fact to be his life's mission. His monument was the fear that he alone among all men managed to instil into the Roman mind, so that as long as Rome is remembered Hannibal will not be forgotten.

On his accession to power Hannibal was quick to put his plans into effect. His first moves were made in secret, but rumours that something was afoot evidently reached Rome. The Senate thought, mistakenly, that they could overawe this young man and offered to arbitrate in a dispute which had arisen at Saguntum; the town was south of the Ebro and was therefore strictly Hannibal's affair. The Senate also sent a commission to New Carthage (Cartagena) to warn Hannibal not to cross the Ebro, and the commission then proceeded to Carthage itself to repeat the warning. Hannibal's reaction was prompt. In the spring of 219 he laid siege to Saguntum and after ten months it fell. Rome protested, but did not help Saguntum. After its fall, however, an ultimatum was sent to Carthage ordering her to liberate the city and hand over Hannibal. The Carthaginians protested that all this was no affair of the Romans and that in any case Hannibal had not violated the treaty with Rome because he had not crossed the Ebro.

35, 36 *Opposite* General view of Saguntum in Spain, captured by Hannibal – seen, *above*, on one of his coins – in 219 BC. It was this act which led Rome to declare war on Carthage.

Rome now declared war on Carthage and dispatched one army to Sicily, under Tiberius Sempronius Longus, preparatory to attacking Africa, and another, under Publius Cornelius Scipio, to defend the Ebro frontier. Scipio marched up the Via Aurelia to Pisa and then made his way into Gaul, intending to cross the Rhône at what is now Tarascon. Hannibal had, however, moved a great deal faster. Four days before Scipio reached the Rhône, Hannibal had crossed it going in the opposite direction, and disappeared into the mountain fastnesses to the east of the Rhône. Scipio guessed correctly that Italy was Hannibal's goal, but he was wrong in his estimate of how long the march would take. He could be forgiven for this, as no one had as yet taken the measure of Hannibal, and the only known land route into Italy was by the pass through the Alps which we now call the Little St Bernard. This is over 7,000 feet high and it was already October when Hannibal crossed the Rhône. Scipio sent his brother Gnaeus on to Spain, and returned to Italy by way of the coast. He believed that he had plenty of time to make his dispositions before Hannibal could get over the Alps, encumbered as he was with an army of nearly 60,000 men and war elephants.

But Hannibal had laid his plans well in advance. His agents had previously made contact with a Gaulish tribe, the Allobroges, who lived in what is now Savoy. They had promised to guide him over the then unknown pass of Mont-Genèvre. Through either treachery or mistake, Hannibal failed to find the correct route, and the way by which he crossed the Alps remains to this day one of the most hotly debated questions of military history. The horror of that journey and the driving force of the leader who accomplished it are best illustrated by the fact that less than half of Hannibal's army survived, together with perhaps six or seven of his elephants.

Thus Scipio was greeted upon his arrival at Placentia (Piacenza) from Tarascon with the news that Hannibal had already crossed the Alps, defeated the Taurini in the area of Turin, and was on his way south. Scipio had fewer men than Hannibal but he advanced to the Ticinus, was worsted and wounded in a cavalry engagement, and had to retreat to Placentia. Scipio's wound was severe and he owed his life to being rescued by his 17-year-old son, also named Publius Cornelius Scipio. Scipio remained in Placentia, recovering and awaiting reinforcements. He was soon joined by Tiberius Sempronius Longus, who had travelled with remarkable speed, coming by sea from Sicily to Ariminum, then marching with his army across Italy. Although it was winter, Sempronius now insisted upon giving battle, contrary to the warnings of Scipio who had a better estimate of Hannibal's capacities and knew the strength of his Numidian cavalry. The result was Sempronius' defeat on the River Trebia, from which he escaped with only 10,000 men. The two consuls now retreated to Cremona and Sempronius returned to Rome to report.

News of the disasters had preceded him and already the name of Hannibal, which few had probably heard of a year before, struck terror into the hearts of the Romans, who expected him to arrive at any moment before the walls of the city. There were some grounds for their apprehensions: the Gauls in the north were only too plainly sitting on the fence, while Hannibal's Numidian cavalry were raiding far and wide through Italy. Sempronius himself had only just managed to slip through and was lucky to have reached Rome in safety. His presence there as the only available consul was, however, essential as he had to preside over the election of the consuls for the coming year. According to Roman law only magistrates invested with the *imperium*, such as a consul, praetor or dictator, could exercise the *ius agendi cum populo*, that is, put the question to the people and receive their reply in the form of the vote at elections. Gnaeus Servilius and Gaius Flaminius were now elected and, according to custom, were due to take up their consular office in March 219 after the completion of the induction ceremonies.

Gaius Flaminius was the particular favourite of the people: he already had a distinguished career behind him, having served as tribune, consul and Censor, but his activities had more than once brought him into collision with the Senate. Now, fearing that the Senate might manage to prevent his leaving Rome to take up command in the field by arranging for contrary auspices – a science at which they were adept – he made the excuse of private business to attend to in the country and left the city. He did not come back, even when the Senate ordered his return. Thus in March, Gnaeus Servilius solemnly went through the long ritual of the consular induction alone, while Flaminius took over command of the legions from Sempronius at Ariminum on the Ides of March, 217.

Horrifying prodigies were now reported to have occurred all over Italy – soldiers were struck by lightning, shields sweated blood and sacred images simply sweated. These horrors were naturally attributed to Flaminius' impious behaviour. Undeterred, however, Flaminius marched to Arretium (Arezzo),

37 An African war elephant, with armed warriors in a 'tower' on its back, decorates this Campanian pottery dish of the third century BC.

and Hannibal, hearing of his arrival there, resorted to the same tactics as had lured Sempronius to defeat on the Trebia. He laid waste the Etruscan country, side, making feints in all directions, until Flaminius left the security of Arre, tium and followed him. Gradually Hannibal drew Flaminius on, until on 24 June he had him where he wanted him, marching unsuspectingly along the northern shore of Lake Trasimene, where the hills come close to the water. It was a misty morning and Hannibal had concealed his troops in semi, circular formation in the hills overlooking the lake. When the Romans had reached the point he desired, a particularly marshy spot, Hannibal sprang the trap he had so cleverly prepared. He advanced the two wings of his army to the lake shore in a pincer movement, thus cutting off the Romans' way of escape in either direction. Flaminius and 15,000 Romans were killed and 10,000 fled. Hannibal's losses were 2,500 men.

Rumours of disaster began to filter into Rome, but still there was no definite news. Men gathered in groups in the Forum and distraught women thronged the streets, asking for news. Finally the crowd surged into the Comitium and, standing before the Curia, called for the magistrates. For long they called and waited in vain; the Senate made no move. Finally at sunset the praetor, Marcus Pomponius Matho, appeared at the door of the Curia and mounted the *rostra*: 'We have been beaten in a great battle', was all he said. There were no further announcements, but the news spread through Rome that Flaminius and most of the army had been killed or taken prisoner.

The Senate sat from dawn to sunset for days debating what to do. With one consul dead and the other isolated at Ariminum, the state, from the constitutional as well as the practical point of view, was like a rudderless ship. Hannibal had now established himself at Spoletum (Spoleto), a mere 70 miles from Rome; he seemed to bestride the Italian peninsula like a giant. In a mere nine months Hannibal's genius had raised him from the status of the unknown young man who had led his heterogeneous force of Carthaginians, Spaniards and Numidians out of Spain the year before. His name had now assumed an almost diabolical significance for the Romans, which, unlike the memory of barbarous Gallic hordes, was never exorcised. Something of the Romans' dread of that uncanny genius still echoes down the corridors of time.

The Senate finally arrived at the decision that their only course was to appoint a dictator, or rather arrange for the election of a pro-dictator, as they could not communicate with the surviving consul and no one else possessed the power to appoint a dictator. Thus it fell to the assembly of the people to elect the man they hoped would be the saviour of Rome. In this crisis some atavistic instinct made them turn to a Roman of the old school – the solid, dour, unshakable Quintus Fabius Maximus, descendant of the sole survivor of those Fabii who had shouldered the defence of Rome against the Veiientines nearly two and a half centuries before.

Fabius was evidently untouched by any modern trend of cynicism about religious duties. In his address to the Senate he attributed Flaminius' defeat to his neglect of proper religious observances, and, before himself setting out to tackle Hannibal, Fabius ensured that the gods received their due. Indeed he went further, reviving the old rite of the Sacred Spring, which included the sacrifice to Jupiter of the natural increase of all herds born that spring.

Hannibal evidently soon learnt that the crucial moment had passed, that Rome, having recovered from her terror-stricken apathy, was now mobilizing a new army, and also that her allies were standing by her, for he crossed over to the Adriatic coast and marched down to Hadria, and from there made contact with Carthage by sea. Fabius was a new factor in Hannibal's calculations and soon showed himself to be a very troublesome one. Whereas all the other Roman generals, even Scipio, had either given battle or been tempted into it, Fabius would do no such thing. He planned to match plain Roman common sense against genius. It was an unequal battle, but Hannibal was also at a

38 The grave of a soldier killed at the Battle of Lake Trasimene in 217 B C.

disadvantage. He was operating in enemy territory and had to live off it – not a thing that endears any commander to an agricultural population, and if peasants are killed off they produce no more food. Hannibal had also to recruit men to replace his losses. Time was therefore Fabius' ally. If he could harass Hannibal continually so that he was unable to collect supplies and rein-forcements, Fabius knew that he could wear out his enemy in the end. These delaying tactics might be unspectacular but they were the only means of avoiding battle against a military genius and, in all likelihood, a débâcle like that of Lake Trasimene.

Fabius was successful for some months. Even when Hannibal crossed over into Campania and applied a scorched-earth policy to what was one of the most fertile parts of Italy, Fabius refused to be drawn. He simply occupied the narrow pass in the Callicula Mountains, thus cutting Hannibal off from his swiftest escape route across the mountain fastnesses of central Italy. But even Fabius had underrated Hannibal. With a cunning that matched Roman ideas of his diabolical character, Hannibal rounded up herds of cattle, tied torches to their horns, and gave orders to some of his men to light these as soon as night fell, then to drive the herds over the mountains bordering the pass. Seen from the valley, the flaming torches on the mountain-side looked like an army making a forced night march over difficult country. The Romans rushed to intercept, leaving the pass practically unguarded, Hannibal slipped through, and Fabius became a laughing-stock. Hannibal again settled not far from the Adriatic coast, at Gereonium, for the winter; Fabius followed and, after establishing his camp near by, returned to Rome to face the music.

Luck was still against the pro-dictator. In his absence his master of horse, P. Minucius Rufus, who had already been chafing at Fabius' delaying tactics, fought Hannibal and was not actually defeated. Encouraged, the popular party opened a campaign against Fabius. His speech in the Senate was coldly received and, bowing to public opinion, he appointed a consul to take the place of the dead Flaminius, thus providing for a return to normal govern-ment and arranging for the expiry of his own office. Fabius then left Rome to avoid being present at the impending debate on his own command and on his way back to Apulia he received orders from the Senate that he was to share it with Minucius. The moving spirit in the cabal which had brought this about was the ex-praetor, Gaius Terentius Varro, a butcher's son who had climbed the administrative ladder as a popular agitator.

The campaign for the consular elections was particularly hard fought and resulted in G. Terentius Varro's becoming the plebeian consul, Lucius Aemilius Paullus, a violent opponent of all Varro stood for, the patrician one. It was indeed an ill-matched pair who set out for Apulia in the spring of 216 to command an army estimated at over 80,000 men in the coming battle which would decide the future of Rome.

Hannibal's own situation was far from promising. He was short of both supplies and funds, and his mercenary army was becoming restive. A swift and decisive engagement was therefore essential. Hannibal resorted to his usual tactics of feints and ruses to draw the Romans out of their fortified camp. Paullus' caution prevented their falling into one of his traps, but according to custom, the consuls exercised command on alternative days, and unfortunately Varro had the army behind him. Hannibal retreated south, Varro followed

39 The site of the Battle of Cannae, fought in 216 B C, is marked today by a fragment of an antique column.

him until, at Cannae, the Carthaginian found the ground which was perfectly suited to his purpose. Hannibal's army probably numbered little more than half the Roman one, but on the field of Cannae, on 2 August 216 he inflicted upon the Romans one of the most disastrous defeats they ever suffered. The entire Roman army was encircled in a vast pincer movement by the Carthaginian cavalry.

Historically Hannibal's action at Cannae is the classic example of this manœuvre. By nightfall, L. Aemilius Paullus lay dead on the field together with some 80 ex-magistrates and Senators. Ancient historians estimated the Roman casualties at 50–70,000 men.

It had taken close on three hundred years for the Roman Republic to rise to the status of a Mediterranean power. Now that power seemed to be shattered. Inevitably the whole of Rome had known that a trial of strength was at hand. Days passed and no word came; the silence of death seemed to have settled upon Apulia while Rome echoed to the wailing of distraught women. Crowds gathered in the Forum; everyone, including the Senate, believed that Hannibal would now attack the city. But in this unparalleled crisis the old Roman spirit found its voice in Fabius Maximus. It was the voice of quiet common sense which, without recrimination, suggested that certain practical steps should be taken to restore order and to discover what the situation really was.

Thus action replaced the apathy of despair. At Fabius' suggestion, picked riders were sent out as scouts to scour the countryside along the Via Appia and other ways leading south to search for survivors and bring in any news they could gather. The Senators themselves went out to restore order in the city, for such public officers as remained were not enough. The crowds were cleared from the Forum, mourning women were forbidden to wander in the streets and the people in general instructed to stay in their homes.

In Apulia, Fabius' son, together with young Publius Cornelius Scipio, Appius Claudius Pulcher and another military tribune, had taken the situation in hand and succeeded in rallying the scattered Roman survivors at Canusium. Here they were helped by a rich Apulian woman called Busa, who gave them food and money. So great was the general chaos, however, that it was some time before the young officers discovered that the consul, Varro, was still alive, having escaped with a few men to Venusia. These young men had no reason to love Varro, either for his antecedents or his actions, but punctiliously they informed him of the number of troops at Canusium and asked for orders. Varro's answer was to join them, bringing such forces as he had with him. Thus some semblance of order was re-established, and in a few days Varro was able to write to the Senate stating that he was at Venusia with the remainder of the army – some 10,000 men – and that Hannibal was prepared to ransom the Roman prisoners.

After further bad news had arrived in Rome that the Carthaginian fleets were now attacking Sicily, the sense of doom and tragedy seems to have created a religious hysteria in the city. There followed one of the rare occasions upon which Vestal Virgins were convicted of breaking their vows of chastity, and in this instance there were two of them – one committed suicide, but the other was condemned to be shut in an underground chamber, there to await her death.

Although the penalties had been exacted to the full, it was evidently felt that the wrath of the gods had not yet been sufficiently appeased. Quintus Fabius Pictor, the earliest historian of Rome, was dispatched to Delphi for oracular advice and the Sibylline books were consulted. Apparently the deaths of the Vestal Virgins had not yet satisfied the jealous gods, for what Livy describes as 'a most un-Roman rite' was now performed. Quite simply it was a human sacrifice: two Gauls and two Greeks – a man and woman of each race – were buried alive in a walled enclosure in the Forum Boarium.

The victory at Cannae had given Hannibal control of southern Italy. Not very surprisingly the Samnites rallied to him, together with some of Rome's lesser allies and the cities of Magna Graecia. Hannibal now advanced and entered Capua; but he failed to take the important port of Naples. He also failed to detach any of Rome's principal allies from their allegiance. However, his star was very much in the ascendant among other Mediterranean powers. The Romans discovered this in the summer of 215, when one of their ships patrolling in the Ionian Sea captured a strange vessel. A Carthaginian was found on board who had in his possession a treaty concluded between Hannibal and King Philip of Macedon. The actual terms were vague, but the preamble revealed that many states in the Greek and Carthaginian spheres of influence were involved. Most serious of all, however, was the indication that Hieronymus, the successor of Rome's old ally, Hiero of Syracuse, intended to change sides.

40 Marcus Claudius Marcellus. He conquered Syracuse, brought to Rome the first Greek statues that the city had ever seen, but was finally surprised and killed by Hannibal.

In the Italian peninsula Fabian tactics now held sway. The Roman army was divided into small forces, one led by Fabius himself, the others commanded by men who appreciated the lesson he had taught. In Syracuse, where Hiero's descendants had not inherited the sagacity of the old King, two Carthaginian advisers were installed by Hannibal. During the thirteen months of young Hieronymus' short reign, for one reason or another all his relations were put to death or died. In the end he himself was murdered. Syracuse was now undisguisedly a Carthaginian stronghold. Events had moved so quickly that when the consul, Marcus Claudius Marcellus, arrived to take up the Sicilian command in 214, he was confronted with this *fait accompli*.

The strength of the fortress of Syracuse was legendary in the ancient world and Marcellus mustered every ship, every man and every device he could think of in an attempt to take it by storm, but he failed. Geographically the site was a natural fortress, but it was also one defended by engines of war invented by one of the greatest mechanical geniuses of all time. Archimedes had been Hiero's master of ordinance and he was still in Syracuse.

Syracuse now became the key to ultimate victory in Sicily, as Lilybaeum had been in the First Punic War. While Roman armies marched and fought in Italy, in Spain and against King Philip of Macedon in Epirus, for 28 months Marcellus grimly hung on at Syracuse. At last he had his reward. He had discovered that one of the towers in the city wall was badly defended and on the evening of the feast of Artemis, when the Syracusans had feasted and drunk their fill, Marcellus seized the tower, then the great Hexapylon (six-door) gate and, finally, captured the entire quarter of Epipolae. The Carthaginians exerted every effort to save Syracuse, but plague broke out, a relieving fleet was delayed and at last Syracuse sued for peace. Nevertheless Marcellus had to fight his way into Achradina, the most heavily defended part of the city, which was held by mercenaries. Either there or on the island of Ortygia, Archimedes was killed. Marcellus was greatly grieved by Archimedes' death and perhaps it was he who built the tomb that Cicero saw in Syracuse 137 years later, neglected and forgotten.

Considering that he was a tough and businesslike soldier, Marcellus evidently possessed a remarkable aesthetic sense, one, if we are to believe Plutarch, which was much more highly developed than that of the Roman patricians of the old school. This was all the more remarkable because the Rome in which Marcellus had grown up was, according to Plutarch – admittedly a prejudiced Greek – still 'filled with blood-stained arms and spoils of barbarian tribes, and crowned with the monuments and trophies of victorious campaigns'. It seems that the glories of Greek art which Marcellus found in Syracuse came to him as a revelation and he realized that here were treasures more precious than gold and silver and the usual loot and trophies of war. Not only did Marcellus insist upon taking many statues back to Rome, but he had them conspicuously displayed in his ovation procession. For Marcellus was denied a triumph on the pretext that the war in Sicily had not yet ended and it might

41 The death of Archimedes (shown seated at his work-table), portrayed in a mosaic of the second century AD.

arouse jealousy. Marcellus' statues, the first masterpieces of Greek art to reach Rome, apparently earned him the disapproval of stalwart old warriors like Fabius. He remained undeterred, however, maintaining that he had 'taught the ignorant Romans to admire and honour the glories of Greek art'.

About the same time as Syracuse fell to Marcellus in 212, the Roman forces besieging Capua had accomplished a more mundane task but one, nevertheless, that was to provoke one of the most extraordinary incidents in the whole war. Hannibal decided to march on Rome. Ten days' rations were served out to a picked body of troops before they crossed the Volturnus. In the course of their advance they laid the surrounding countryside waste with fire and sword. Coming by way of Casinum, Aquinum and Anagnia, Hannibal encamped eight miles from Rome. Then, following the River Anio he advanced to within three miles of the city.

Since a messenger had ridden night and day from Fregellae to warn Rome, the news of Hannibal's advance had preceded him and the non-combatant population gave way to panic. Hannibal rode right up to the walls of the city with 2,000 of his cavalry. Peering from the walls, the Romans saw him clearly, mounted upon his coal-black charger: he appeared to be surveying the Porta Collina. The nightmare that had haunted Roman minds for years had now emerged into the broad light of day; Hannibal was finally at the gates of Rome. With hindsight it is easy to ask why he had delayed so long; after Trasimene and Cannae the road to Rome had lain open before him, but Hannibal had not struck the blow which, if successful, would have meant the end of Rome. Possessed as he was of immeasurable confidence and daring, nevertheless Hannibal could not have achieved what he did without an equal measure of cold calculation. If after Trasimene and Cannae he did not attack Rome, it was because he was not equipped to storm or lay siege to a city of this size. Instead he relied upon a war of movement and devastation to bleed Rome white and alienate her allies and thus bring her to her knees. Hannibal might have been successful but for Fabius. The time Fabius bought enabled Rome to hang on and to organize; the results of that organization had become evident at Syracuse, and were now even more threateningly apparent in the Roman stranglehold on Capua. Paradoxically, it was the situation at Capua that had brought Hannibal to Rome: if by the speed and daring of his advance he could shake Rome's nerve, Hannibal could relieve Capua and regain the initiative.

In Rome at first Hannibal's appearance provoked hysteria. Some Numidian cavalry deserters, who were now in Roman service, were seen crossing the city and the rumour spread that Hannibal's army was already within the walls. Every man who had ever held magisterial rank was invested with military powers in order to quell the panic, while Roman forces engaged Hannibal's army outside the walls. One of Rome's characteristically violent storms of rain and hail now came down, blinding the combatants, so that the engagement was broken off. Roman sang-froid evidently returned, for Livy ascribes Hannibal's decision to withdraw at this juncture, not to any military cause, but to the report that the land upon which he was encamped had just been sold by its Roman owner at what would have been its normal price. Moreover, in spite of his presence, the Roman reinforcements for the Spanish garrisons were leaving according to schedule.

Whatever the cause, Hannibal withdrew and his exotic African army, with its Numidian horsemen and towering elephants, disappeared into the mountain fastnesses from which it had so abruptly come. The incubus was lifted from Rome, but not from Capua – Hannibal's gesture had failed, for no Roman troops had been withdrawn from the investment of Capua even when he was at the gates of Rome, and in that same year of 211 Capua surrendered.

Attention was now focused upon the war in Spain where, for the last seven years, Publius Cornelius Scipio and his brother Gnaeus had been fighting Hannibal's brother Hasdrubal. The two Scipios had died and it was feared that Hasdrubal might now see his way clear to come to Hannibal's aid in Italy. Fortunately the fall of Capua had freed a large number of men to reinforce the Roman army in Spain, but there remained the question of who was to lead them. No candidate came forward and neither the Senate nor the assembly had anyone in mind. Suddenly into this void stepped a young legionary tribune, who said that his only grounds for seeking the command was that he was the son of Publius Cornelius Scipio and nephew of Gnaeus; in fact he was the Scipio who, as a boy, had saved his father's life on the Ticinus and later rallied the survivors of Cannae. Publius Cornelius Scipio was apparently unanimously elected for the Spanish command. By such a freak of fortune did young Scipio set out in 210, at the age of 25, to command the army in Spain with the rank of proconsul.

In 209 Fabius Maximus captured Tarentum, by treachery on the part of the Carthaginian commander. The loot was enormous – 30,000 slaves, 3,080 pounds of gold and an immense quantity of silver, but Fabius refused to include Greek works of art among his spoils; 'Let us leave the Tarentines their angry gods,' he said. He did, however, make an exception for Lysippus' colossal statue of Hercules which he set up on the Capitol, placing a bronze equestrian statue of himself beside it.

Marcellus, who had beautified Rome with the statues from Syracuse, now found that his generalship was being attacked, especially by the tribune, Gaius Publicius Bibulus. Although Marcellus was himself a plebeian, the cry was raised again that the war was being prolonged by the patricians while the common people suffered. As a result it was decided to hold a mass meeting in the Circus Flaminius in which the whole conduct of the war was studied. Marcellus made a speech giving an excellent account of his actions and carried the meeting with him. The attack upon him seems, however, to have upset his usual sense of judgment and caution, for upon his return to the front in Apulia he and his fellow consul, Crispinus, were surprised by Hannibal while on a reconnaissance. Marcellus was killed and Crispinus died of his wounds. Thus Rome was bereft of both consuls, a thing which had never previously occurred in time of war. Fortunately, before he died, Crispinus had appointed a dictator to preside at the consular elections and Gaius Claudius Nero and Marcus Livius Salinator were duly elected.

The new consuls were a strangely assorted pair. Nero possessed all the brilliance and perversity of a Claudian, fortunately allied, however, to independence and determination. Marcus Livius was also eccentric and difficult, the complexities of his character increased by the fact that after his consulship in 219 he had been condemned for dishonesty during the Greek campaign and had since lived as a recluse. All in all, they did not appear to be a very promising

42 Hasdrubal Barca, on a coin of *c.* 209 BC.

team with which to confront two of the most brilliant generals the world has ever seen. For young Scipio had been unsuccessful in his attempts to pin Hasdrubal down in Spain and the Carthaginian was known already to be in Gaul with a large army, waiting for the Alpine snows to melt before crossing into Italy. The spring or summer of 207 would, therefore, inevitably witness the decisive battle of the whole war. As the weeks passed, it became evident that the personal relationship between the consuls was far from happy. In addition prodigies were reported from far and wide, producing their usual dismal effect upon Roman morale: stones rained upon Veii, temples were struck by lightning, and a monstrous child of indeterminate sex was born. Etruscan soothsayers were called in to pronounce upon this last horrifying event and the poor child was drowned far out at sea. Heaven did not even seem to approve of other, more attractive, propitiatory rites. While 27 virgins were gathered together, studiously learning the words of a propitiatory hymn written by Livius Andronicus, which the priests had decreed they should sing walking in procession through Rome, the Temple of Juno on the Aventine was struck by lightning. This, the soothsayers decided, was an indication that the goddess must be propitiated by some gift from the married women of the community. Thus, all the matrons of Rome and those living within a 10-mile radius of the city were summoned to the Capitol. They volunteered a gift of money from their dowries, and from the proceeds a golden bowl was presented to Juno.

These rites completed and every available man having been called up, the consuls left Rome to take up their commands: Gaius Claudius Nero going south to Bruttium to deal with Hannibal, Marcus Livius Salinator marching north to confront Hasdrubal. Hearing that his brother had already crossed the Alps, Hannibal advanced to Apulia, Claudius Nero keeping pace with him at a respectful distance. News reached Hannibal that his brother was besieging Placentia; aware that this would cause considerable delay, he stopped at Canusium and waited for further indications of his brother's movements and, above all, for a message telling him where they were to meet. Hasdrubal had discovered that Placentia was too tough a nut to crack in the time at his disposal so he hurried on, sending in advance a letter to Hannibal to meet him in Umbria.

The letter was carried by a party of four Gallic and two Numidian cavalry-men who managed to ride the length of Italy unobserved but, on their arrival in Apulia, failed to connect with Hannibal and reached Tarentum by mistake. Here they were captured, together with Hasdrubal's letter, and sent under guard to Nero. No sooner had the letter been translated and Nero realized that he possessed the most vital intelligence secret of the whole war, than his mind was made up. Ignoring all rules about consular provinces, he determined to join Marcus Livius at once at Sena Gallica (Senigallia) on the Adriatic coast south of Ariminum. In doing so, Nero was taking a risk of almost un-imaginable proportions; Sena Gallica was 250 miles to the north and he proposed to march there hot-foot with the pick of his army, leaving only a rearguard behind to watch Hannibal. When Nero's letter telling them of his intentions reached the Senate, there was an uproar as great, Livy says, as when Hannibal was at the gates of Rome. But by then Nero was well on his way. In fact he reached Sena Gallica in five days' forced march and entered Marcus Livius' camp under cover of darkness.

43 A Numidian horseman; reverse of a coin of the Car-thaginian ally Syphax (see Ill. 44).

Hasdrubal had also advanced along the Adriatic coast, coming from the north and had already reached the Cesano river, a short distance from the Roman camp. Some intelligence or rumour evidently now reached him of the junction of the consular armies, for he retreated to the Metaurus river and, being unable to cross it owing to floodwater, retired further inland along the south bank, still unable to cross the river. The two consuls soon arrived at his halting-place and the battle was joined. In the ferocious struggle that followed, the final decision was achieved by Claudius Nero's daring move in detaching his forces from the battle, marching across the Roman rear and driving home a surprise attack on Hasdrubal's flank. Realizing that the battle was lost, Hasdrubal rode into the thick of the fighting and was killed. The Roman victory was overwhelming: 60,000 men were killed or taken prisoner, the loot including the whole of Hasdrubal's treasure. That same night Nero left for Apulia. He took with him Hasdrubal's head, which was flung down outside the outposts of Hannibal's camp. It is said that Nero also sent two of his African prisoners into Hannibal's camp to tell him of his brother's defeat and that in his anguish Hannibal exclaimed, 'Now at last I see the destiny of Carthage plain!' Shortly afterwards he retreated into Bruttium.

Rome had waited in a state of anguish ever since the arrival of Nero's letter. During those seemingly endless days the Senate sat from dawn to dusk while officials and crowds alike filled the Forum waiting for news. When at last a courier arrived from the camp commander bearing a letter, he was nearly torn to pieces before the Senate were able to have his victory message read first in the Curia, then from the *rostra*. The joy it brought was so overwhelming that some still refused to believe it until official confirmation was received from the consuls themselves. When news arrived that dispatch-riders from the consuls were approaching Rome, the people rushed to meet them and crowds lined the whole way from the city to the Milvian Bridge, where the Via Flaminia crosses the Tiber. In the Forum the dispatch-riders were besieged with questions and, throwing all normal official discretion to the winds, they shouted back the glad news that the Carthaginian army was destroyed, Hasdrubal dead, the legions intact and both consuls safe. The dispatches were then read aloud, first to the Senate, then to the assembly.

The two consuls who were responsible for the victory were summoned to Rome by the Senate in the autumn. The outcome on the Metaurus had healed their differences and they agreed by letter that, as they had fought together, so they would enter Rome together. After travelling from the opposite ends of Italy, they met again at Praeneste and from there sent a joint edict summoning the Senate to a meeting in the Temple of Bellona three days later. After the consuls had made their report to the Senate, they asked that thanks should be given to the gods and requested permission for themselves to enter Rome in triumph. Naturally this was granted but, contrary to usual practice, they asked to celebrate a joint triumph. This request posed some problems of procedure. In the end, however, it was agreed that, as the battle had been fought in Livius' province on the day that he was in command and his legions were now present in Rome, so he would drive in the triumphal chariot and Nero ride on horseback. Nero's unselfishness in this matter won him the special affection of the crowd and even Livius' legionaries included his name in the ribald songs which it was their privilege to sing as they marched with their commander in a triumph.

In describing all this rejoicing, Livy, in a few lines here and there, gives a glimpse of the other side of the coin, especially of the devastation of the Italian countryside resulting from twelve years of war. He says that in the spring of 206, 'Before the consuls left Rome they were instructed by the Senate to do all they could to put the people back on their farms. . . . Surely it could not be right to take more trouble over the cultivation of Sicily than Italy . . . nevertheless it was by no means easy for the people themselves. Many free farmers had been killed in the war, slaves were scarce, cattle had been carried off and farmhouses destroyed or burned.' The war had in fact created a revolution in the life of Italy which was to be reflected in that of Rome. Vast numbers of smallholdings had gone out of cultivation which, even if redeemed, were no longer economically viable. Increasingly, large estates replaced the smallholdings and destitute peasants in search of work thronged the city.

In 206, however, Hannibal was still in Italy and Scipio was fighting another of his brothers, Mago, in Spain. This third Barcide brother was, however, no match for Scipio. Even before his army had won the second battle of Baecula, Scipio was forming plans to rid Italy of Hannibal and come to grips with him in Africa. Evidently he already saw that this was the only way to bring the war to a successful conclusion. Like his father and uncle before him, Scipio had made contact with Syphax, chief of the Massaesyllians of Mauretania, and with the Numidian chief, Masinissa, who was the cavalry commander of the Carthaginian forces in Spain. Scipio even went to Africa to see Syphax, but found that the Carthaginian leader, Hasdrubal Gisconides, had arrived before him. Syphax actually invited Scipio and Hasdrubal to dine with him together. Scipio now determined to return to Rome but before leaving Spain he arrived at a secret understanding with Masinissa. Mago also went to Italy, landing in Liguria, evidently with the hope of joining Hannibal.

44, 45 The North African leaders Syphax, *top*, and Masinissa, depicted on their coins.

On his return, though received somewhat coolly by the Senate, Scipio was elected consul by the enthusiastic people. He now outlined his plan for an African campaign. This was bitterly opposed by Fabius Maximus and a number of Senators, but, after considerable political juggling, Scipio got his way. The Senate agreed to his going to Africa provided he was willing to undertake the campaign with a volunteer army and not one raised by the usual conscript levy. Scipio was more than willing and so were men from all over Italy to follow him. In 204 he sailed with a great armada from Lilybaeum and landed safely near the Cape of The Beautiful One (Cape Bon) where he made contact with Masinissa.

In the same year occurred a singularly significant event in the history of Rome, the introduction into the city, actually within its confines this time, of Cybele, the Idean Mother of the Gods, from Pessinus in Phrygia. This was due to what Livy calls 'a wave of superstition' that had swept the city. No doubt this religious hysteria was partly the result of the slackening of tension after the victory on the Metaurus, following upon years of acute strain. Probably, too, there was a feeling of disillusionment abroad because the war still dragged on. The situation had been dealt with in traditional fashion by consultation of the Sibylline books. The result was a heartening prophecy that if a foreign enemy invaded Italy, he would be defeated and driven out so long as Cybele was brought to Rome. Happily, this appeared to confirm a previous pronouncement of the Delphic Oracle.

There was a marked difference between Cybele's installation in Rome and that of Aesculapius 87 years before. On that occasion there was a logical connection between the plague and the introduction of the god of healing; but then, although his rites were decorous and unexceptional, Aesculapius was carefully relegated to the Tiber Island. Cybele was borne in triumph to the Temple of Victory on the Palatine.

Trojan associations would have provided an added excuse for the elaborate ceremonial accompanying Cybele's arrival and her establishment as the Magna Mater on the Palatine. But the mere fact that the Roman establishment felt called upon to introduce such a goddess in the first place – their capacity for manipulating augury and the machinery of state religion is a commonplace – and that they did so in such a spectacular fashion, argues that they felt strong measures were necessary to combat some spiritual malaise among the people which the state religion was apparently ill adapted to appease. The troubled times had evidently revealed signs of a craving among the masses for some greater or more emotional religious satisfaction; a state of affairs which was ultimately to have momentous results in Rome. Thus the arrival in Rome of the block of stone from Pessinus was, in its way, as historic an event as those then taking place in Africa.

Scipio had achieved complete surprise in his landing a few miles north of Carthage and proceeded without loss of time to lay siege to Utica, to draw the Carthaginians out. They mobilized a large army and relieved the town, whereupon Scipio retired to winter on an impregnable headland almost encompassed by the sea. Syphax now tried his hand as peacemaker; Scipio smiled and played the game, making frequent visits to the Carthaginian camp, ostensibly for discussions of peace terms. Scipio had not wasted his time: when spring came he cut short the peace discussion and attacked the camp, of which he knew every detail, and won a resounding victory. Syphax and Hasdrubal Gisconides mustered another army and again tried to beat Scipio. The battle was fought at the Great Plains in the upper Bagradas valley, and again Scipio won. The only course now open to Carthage was to summon Hannibal and play for time. To achieve this, the Carthaginians accepted Scipio's humiliating peace terms. A Carthaginian peace delegation arrived in Rome, much to the perplexity of the Senate, but wisely they decided to leave matters to Scipio. He had got what he wanted: in 203 Hannibal left Italy to defend Carthage.

Adopting Hannibal's tactics, which had resulted in his victories at Trasimene and Cannae, Scipio laid waste the fertile lands of the Bagradas valley, to force a rapid decision. Hannibal now did an astonishing thing: he asked Scipio

46, 47 The great mother-goddess from Asia Minor, Cybele, was worshipped in Rome in a temple on the Palatine hill (*above*, its foundations). Her distinctive attributes included lions, shown *opposite* drawing her cart; she wears the 'mural' crown and carries a tympanum and patera, or drum and flat dish.

for a personal interview. Scipio agreed, providing he could choose the place; he chose the only well-watered spot in a dry land. Hannibal advanced and the two men met in the open space between their respective armies – alone except for their interpreters. Hannibal was 43 and Scipio 34. The last time they had been within measuring distance of each other had been by the Ticinus 17 years before, when Scipio had saved his father's life. Although this was their first meeting, probably no other two men of their time understood each other better. For years they had watched each other's careers and gradually the war had narrowed down until it resembled a game of chess in which they faced each other across the board, and now Scipio was calling check to Hannibal.

Both men fell silent when they met, but afterwards they talked together for a long time. No one knows what they said for they both spoke Greek and had no need of interpreters. Later they said no agreement had been reached between them, but they had much in common and they knew well that it was quite possible that neither of them would survive the coming battle. In such circum-stances men are unlikely to lie to one another and each emerged from the encounter with a warm regard for his opponent.

Scipio's victory of Zama, which followed, is as famous as it was undecided up to the last moment. In the end Hannibal was defeated by the cavalry pincer movement which had so often brought him victory. If the battle had been delayed for a few days Hannibal might have won; his cavalry reinforcements arrived too late. But he survived the battle and escaped.

The peace terms put forward by Scipio were surprisingly liberal. Carthage was to preserve her autonomy and keep her lands, but she was to be deprived of her fleet, all except ten ships. Nor was she to be allowed to keep or train war elephants. In fact, Carthage was not in future to be permitted to make war without Rome's consent. Masinissa's lands were to be guaranteed to him and all Roman prisoners of war, deserters and fugitives returned. A war indemnity of 10,000 talents was to be paid and 100 hostages sent to Rome.

On Hannibal's advice the terms were accepted and a Carthaginian delega-tion left for Rome. There was some debate in the assembly of the people about the terms' acceptance, but the decision to make peace won the vote and Scipio was appointed Rome's plenipotentiary for the conclusion of the treaty. Follow-ing the Senate's orders, ten Roman envoys set out for Africa, taking with them 200 Carthaginian prisoners who were to be released when the peace treaty had been concluded. Among the party were the Fetial priests, whose traditional task it was to draw up the actual treaty of peace. Before leaving Rome they received the time-honoured instructions, that each should take with him a flint knife and a bunch of the sacred herbs. The flint knives indicate the anti-quity of this tradition, which also required that the herbs should be plucked on the Capitol and include that humble little wayside plant, *Verbena officinalis*.

Thus the representatives of all the might and majesty of Rome set out to dictate peace to vanquished Carthage, carrying with them posies of what must have been very withered and dusty weeds and leaves by the time they reached Africa. But these were sanctified in Roman eyes because they were part of Roman tradition and because they grew on the hill that centuries later was to be called Caput Mundi. The surrender of Carthage was the first step in the process which was to make this come true – Rome's conquest of Italy was behind her, that of the world had just begun.

48 This coin of *c.* 105 BC is thought to show Scipio Africanus.

Fortune grants Rome world dominion

Seventeen years of war against Hannibal had left a devastated Italy and an exhausted and strangely altered Rome in its wake. Nevertheless, the Senate realized that there was one more account to settle. Although the First Macedonian War had ended four years previously in an uneasy peace, the Senators had not forgotten King Philip V's treaty with Carthage or the threat that he and his Macedonian army represented to Italy's eastern seaboard. Furthermore, King Antiochus the Great of Syria, at whose court Hannibal took refuge, had recently reminded the world of his warlike Seleucid forbears and their Macedonian origins by reconquering the entire Seleucid realm, reaching from Persia to the Mediterranean, and contracted an alliance with Philip. In order to counter this threatening situation, Rome had entered into diplomatic relations with several of the Greek city states, while Egypt had, for the same reason, aligned herself with Rome.

Philip now invaded Greece and, meeting with little opposition, had reached Attica by the time Rome's allies appealed to her for aid. In the assembly of the people the weary Romans at first voted against the project of war with Macedonia, but then, realizing that to fight now in Greece might in the end spare Italy further horrors of war on her own soil, they finally gave the Senate the mandate for war.

No decisive result was achieved until the war was in its third year and Titus Quintius Flamininus took over the command in Greece. His first step was to arrange a meeting with Philip in Epirus. In doing so Flamininus displayed his political acumen by stipulating that the basis of discussion should be the restitution of their liberties to the Greek states. Philip professed himself willing to come to an agreement until the consul made it clear that he included Thessaly – which had been annexed to Macedonia by Alexander the Great's father – among the Greek states that were to regain their freedom. Flamininus' object was to avoid becoming enmeshed in Greek political rivalries and bring the war to a decisive end, and he realized that this could only be accomplished by defeating Macedonia in the field. He achieved the first step towards this goal when Philip left the council table in a rage, swearing that he would not give up lands which he had inherited. The King retreated into Thessaly and, using a little-known route over the mountains, Flamininus followed, taking Philip by surprise. The Macedonians retired into the impenetrable Gorge of Tempe and by autumn the whole of the rest of Thessaly was in Roman hands.

According to normal procedure, in the following spring the command of the Roman army in Greece would have passed to one of the consuls elected for that year. However, two tribunes proposed that, as Flamininus had begun so well, he should be confirmed in his command and allowed to get on with the job. This was finally agreed, and Flamininus was faced with the immediate

49 Gold *stater* of Flamininus. His victory at Cynoscephalae ended the Macedonian threat for a time.

50 The Macedonian defeat was commemorated on this silver *denarius*, where a Macedonian helmet appears behind the horse's tail.

prospect of trying conclusions with the military machine that enjoyed the highest reputation in the ancient world. For the first time the Romans were to fight the Macedonian army, whose training and traditions dated from the days of Philip II and Alexander.

The Roman and Macedonian armies first made contact near Pherae at the southern end of the ridge of hills, called Cynoscephalae, that traverse the great plain of Thessaly from north to south, and the result was a Roman victory which ended with 8,000 Macedonians dead upon the field and 5,000 taken prisoner. The invincible phalanx of Macedonia had at last been beaten by the new, mobile form of warfare which the Romans had first learnt from the hill tribes of Italy and perfected during their long struggle against Hannibal.

The Roman victory at Cynoscephalae not only put an end to hostilities in Greece; it also halted King Antiochus, who had advanced into Asia Minor to come to Philip's aid. Antiochus' action had confirmed the Senate's suspicions that he, too, would have to be dealt with at a later date; in the meantime they pursued a highly diplomatic course in dealing with Macedonia and the Greek states. The Romans concluded a treaty with Philip similar to that made with Carthage. Following Flamininus' urgent representations, it was agreed that at the Isthmian Games he should be empowered to make the astonishing announcement that all the Greek states' independence and liberties were restored to them and all Roman garrisons would be withdrawn.

Some members of the Senatorial commission which had been dispatched to Greece to supervise the settlement proceeded to Asia Minor where they encountered Antiochus encamped beside the Dardanelles with his army and a fleet. The Romans had already warned Antiochus' representatives in Greece that he must not cross the straits or meddle with the liberty of the Greek cities, and this warning was now repeated to the King in person, in emphatic terms. Nevertheless, two years later he landed in Greece at the invitation of the Aetolians, posing as a liberator. His expedition was not a great success, as no other Greek state made him welcome. Antiochus was beaten by the Romans first at Thermopylae in 191 and again decisively at Magnesia in Asia Minor in 189. As a result Antiochus was forced to withdraw beyond the Taurus and, although they retained internal independence, the states of Asia Minor became Roman protectorates.

After the battle of Magnesia, the victors, Scipio Africanus and his brother Lucius, were attacked on the grounds that Lucius had been bribed by Antiochus to effect a conciliatory peace. Lucius was condemned and only saved by his brother's high-handed action. As for the charges of malversation of public funds laid against Africanus, he simply rebutted them by reciting a eulogy of his own actions which resulted in his receiving a popular ovation on the Capitol. Nevertheless, disgusted with the ingratitude of his countrymen, Africanus withdrew to his villa at Liternum and died there in 183 at the age of 50, refusing to leave his bones in Rome. Hannibal did not survive him long; two years later he committed suicide in Bithynia rather than fall into Roman hands.

One of the key figures in the Roman victory at Thermopylae had been Marcus Porcius Cato, who was then 43 years old and had a distinguished military and administrative career behind him. This might have been supposed already to have reached its peak when he was elected consul in 195, but in fact the next 42 years of his long life were even more remarkable.

Although he came to regard himself as the champion of the old patriarchal Rome, Cato was not born in the city or in the purple; he came of hardy country stock and grew up on the family farm in the Sabine hills. To the effects of this austere upbringing was added his hero-worship of Manius Curius Dentatus, the conqueror of Pyrrhus, whose simple cottage still stood near Cato's home. Since childhood, Cato had been a frequent visitor to the place – the scene of the Samnite ambassadors' encounter with Manius Curius while he was cooking turnips for his supper.

Cato was 17 when he first served in the army, and in the years that followed he saw Italy laid waste by Hannibal. He also saw the luxury of great Greek cities such as Tarentum, and observed how contact with this world was, in his view, corrupting the Romans, especially members of great aristocratic families such as the Scipios. As a result, Cato believed it to be his mission in life to fight all foreign influence and to prevent it from corrupting Rome; he pursued his aim with that fiery singleness of purpose so often associated with men of his type – he had red hair, piercing grey eyes and was possessed of a biting tongue.

It must be admitted that Rome in the second century BC provided many ready targets for Cato's wit and indignation. As at other periods in history, when two devastating wars have followed one another in quick succession, it was not only the vanquished country that had changed out of recognition; Rome and the Romans of 188 were already a very different place and people from those that had witnessed the beginning of the First Punic War only 76 years earlier, and the process of change was to accelerate rapidly as the century advanced.

There were many reasons for this state of affairs. The most obvious was, of course, war casualties, which had been very heavy indeed. Another will have been the introduction into the citizen body of numbers of men who were made, not born, Romans: probably many of them were slaves who had served in the army and thus earned their freedom. Slave legions were raised and are said to

51, 52 Statuettes of characters in Roman comedy: a potter, *above*, holding a pot in his right hand and possibly a ham in his left, and a slave, *above right*. The slave, who wears a mask (through which the actor's own mouth can be seen) and a garland like those worn at banquets, has taken refuge on an altar – a standard escape when a plot had misfired.

have fought well under the consul, and later Censor, Tiberius Sempronius Gracchus, but as many of these slaves would have been prisoners of war and not of Roman, and in some cases perhaps not even Italian origin, their admission to the roll of citizens represented a dilution of Roman stock. In addition to this, refugees from the devastated countryside had flocked into the city and remained there because work was easier to find. The extent of this migration, and its effect in depleting the surrounding areas of manpower, is illustrated by the fact that in 187 and 177 numbers of Latins were expelled from Rome because the Latin authorities had found that the consequent decline in their own city population made it impossible for them to provide their quota of men for the military levies, required by their treaties with Rome. The Romans who had come back from the war were also, inevitably, different. Thousands of them had, like Cato, been called up as boys; since then they had fought in Sicily, Spain, Africa and Greece, and had seen the luxury and riches of cities such as Syracuse, Tarentum, Carthage and Corinth but, unlike Cato, did not at all despise their gayer and more comfortable way of life.

Just as the life-and-death struggle against Hannibal had resulted in the importation of the Great Mother goddess to assuage the public need for an accessible and emotional cult, so too the Roman authorities had evidently realized that more public entertainment must be provided to offset the grimness of the war years. Thus, apart from the Ludi Megalenses – the Games of the

Great Mother which became an annual event in 194 – the beginnings of two other annual games date from this period. These were the Ludi Plebei, instituted in 216 and celebrated between 4 and 17 November, which were second in importance only to the Ludi Romani. There were also Ludi Ceriales, the Games of Ceres, originating probably in 202, and celebrated between 12 and 19 April. To them, in 173, were added the Ludi Florales, the Games of Flora, that lasted from 28 April to 3 May.

Contrary to modern popular ideas, gladiatorial displays did not form part of the *ludi*, or games. These *munera* or shows, which were exceedingly rare under the Republic, originated in Etruria as a form of blood sacrifice performed at the tomb of a chief. The earliest recorded in Rome were given in 264 in the Forum Boarium by D. Junius Pera in memory of his father, and in 216 by the sons of Marcus Aemilius Lepidus in the Forum. Even in 65, when Julius Caesar put on 320 pairs of gladiators, he did so, ostensibly at least, to commemorate his father who had died 20 years before. Nor, before 169, were there animal shows or fights in Rome, with the exception of the curious custom of loosing foxes into the arena with torches tied to their tails during the Games of Ceres and the hunting of does and hares on the last day of the Games of Flora.

The Ludi Romani and Ludi Plebei, which shared the pomp of an opening state procession and cavalry parade, ended with five and three days' chariot racing respectively, which in the other games was limited to the last day. The

53 In this scene from a New Comedy play, the son (right, in naturalistic mask) returns home drunk from a party, supported by a slave and heralded by a girl playing the flute. His irate father – another stock character – rages in front of his house, indicated by an ornate door. The various masks identify traditional types of character.

54 A fragment of the walls of the Porticus Aemilia, a great market-hall or warehouse some 2,000 feet long, built in 193 BC and rebuilt in 174 BC.

rest of the entertainment was theatrical. When these Ludi Scaenici were first introduced in 362 they would have taken the form of broad pantomime accompanied by the *saturae* that Livius Andronicus later wove into plays based on Greek plots. The new drama was evidently a popular success, for some years later Naevius was also at work adapting Greek plays for Roman audiences. Naevius, who was probably born in Campania, had served in Sicily and been present at the victory of Zama. He wrote an annalistic poem of the history of Rome and a play about Romulus, but his principal work was to provide Romanized versions of the Greek plays, including tragedies of the Trojan cycle.

Not all the historical plays performed in Rome at this time were Greek. Ennius, whom Cato had brought back from Sardinia in 204, further developed the Roman historical drama originated by Naevius, adopting as his protagonists contemporary generals as well as ancient heroes. Although he became a Roman citizen, like his predecessors Ennius came from southern Italy – he was a Calabrian probably of Greek extraction, but such was his mastery of Latin that later generations called him the father of Latin poetry and Virgil quoted lines from his poems in his own compositions, while for centuries most young Romans first learned the history of their country from Ennius' *Annals of Rome*. His best-known play was the *Ambracia* written to celebrate M. Fulvius Nobilior's conquest of the Aetolian city of that name, probably to be performed at his triumphal games in 187.

Contemporary with the development of historical drama and tragedy was that of Roman adaptations of the Attic 'New Comedy', with broadly farcical situations produced by the adventures of rascally slaves, intriguing courtesans, scapegrace young men and the new rich. Such adaptations had already been

begun by Andronicus and Naevius but the evergreen master of this genre was, of course, Titus Maccius Plautus, whose plays were still, rather surprisingly, read by St Jerome in his cell six hundred years later. Like Andronicus and Naevius, Plautus was not Roman-born; he came from Umbria and, like his fellow playwrights, he was absorbed into the increasingly cosmopolitan city and identified himself completely with the life of Rome.

Plautus had evidently travelled and traded abroad, but he also knew the seamiest side of life in Rome and, although his plays were ostensibly set in Greece and the plots were Greek, his characters and dialogue were richly and typically Roman. Plautus' first play, the *Menaechmi*, which has much in common with *The Comedy of Errors*, was given in 212, the *Miles Gloriosus* probably in 204. Such comedies would have been good morale-raisers in those grim days, while a reminder of how large a proportion of the audience were former or serving soldiers is afforded by the number of Greek words with which the dialogue is sprinkled. Thus, originating as military slang or drawn from a canteen vocabulary, Greek terms such as *catapulta*, *machina* and *barbarus* passed into Latin, while from the Punic came the immemorial salutation *Ave*.

One of the principal butts of these new comedies were the new rich, of which there were plenty in Rome. The conquest of Sicily and the victories over Carthage, Macedonia and Syria had opened the eastern Mediterranean to trade with Italy. The rich vulgarian was a natural, and safer, target for ridicule, but in actual fact the great patrician families had also been not slow to take advantage of new means of acquiring wealth. In 219 a law had been passed by the assembly of the people which prohibited senators and their sons from owning ships with more than 300 amphorae capacity – in the ancient world not only oil and wine were shipped in amphorae but also dry goods such as wheat.

55 The civic improvements of 179 BC included the first stone bridge in Rome, the Pons Aemilius. Only one arch now survives, known as the Ponte Rotto or 'broken bridge'.

The boom, especially in overseas trade, was reflected in Rome in 194 in the building of a new riverside port. At this Emporium, the lighters into which cargo had been transshipped at Ostia and towed up the Tiber were off-loaded. Near by rose the Porticus Aemilia, a spacious warehouse called after the aediles, M. Aemilius Lepidus and L. Aemilius Paullus, who built it. Although this was a purely functional building, it was designed with elegance; its fifty barrel-vaults were carried on arches and it was surrounded by arcades. In both its materials and design the Porticus provides an excellent illustration of the striking change which was to take place in Roman architecture and the general aspect of the city centre during the second century BC. Until then, with the rare exceptions already mentioned, aesthetic efforts had to all intents and purposes been limited to religious buildings. The aftermath of the wars did, of course, result in many new votive temples being built, and the new Hellenistic influence was evident in these. That influence was most clearly seen in the Romans' desire to embellish their city with fine civic buildings and to create a monumental city centre. Increasingly also, consuls and other members of the oligarchy, who had come to the forefront of national affairs during the wars, contributed to this development as a means of acquiring personal prestige.

This motive gave rise to one of Rome's most characteristic contributions to architecture, the triumphal arch. The first triumphal arches were built in 193 (or 196) by L. Stertinius from the proceeds of his Spanish campaigns. Two stood in the Forum Boarium and one in the Circus Maximus; little is known about their design except that they supported gilded statues.

The first basilica, which made its appearance in 184, was a more sober monument. Although Cato, one of its sponsors, might not have cared to admit it, the basilica is believed to have been evolved from the Hellenistic portico, but he would have gloried in the fact that it has ever since been regarded as a peculiarly Roman contribution to architecture. Little is known of Cato's Basilica Porcia except that it stood on the west side of the Comitium, but in all probability its basic design was similar to that of the Basilica Aemilia that was built in 179 and of which the ruins still stand on the north-east side of the Forum.

Originally, basilicas were used as a general meeting-place and also as a stock exchange. This commercial aspect was particularly marked in the Basilica Aemilia, part of whose site had been occupied by the *tabernae* of the bankers and money-changers. A row of such *tabernae*, opening on to a portico, was incorporated into the Basilica on the side facing the Forum; their gilded shield trade-signs can still be seen hanging on the columns of the portico in a coin minted to record the Basilica's restoration in 79.

The Censorships of 184 and 179 were particularly important in the development of Rome. Apart from the work already mentioned, the public fountains were paved and the Cloaca Maxima cleaned, restored and extended at a cost of 24 million sesterces. Two *atria* were also built, and these would have been for public use like the Atrium Libertatis, originally built by Appius Claudius in 312 as the record office of the Censors. One of the outstanding public works of 179, apart from the Basilica Aemilia, was the building of the Pons Aemilius. This represented a great advance upon the old Sublician, the only other existing bridge in the city, as the piers were of stone.

56 The Basilica Aemilia, like the Pons Aemilius (Ill. 55), was built in AD 179; this coin commemorating its restoration shows its two-storeyed colonnades.

It might have seemed after the victory at Magnesia that Rome would settle down in a world at peace. But three years later, in 186, Roman society was shaken by the discovery that with the returning armies a strange new cult worshipping Bacchus had come to Italy and that this might operate almost as a secret society, bringing widespread debauchery in its train.

By whatever means the Senate discovered the truth about the Bacchic orgies, they were horrified at what appears to have been the deliberate corruption of young initiates, who had to be under 20 and, once having taken part in such criminal practices, were no longer free agents. Although they believed this to be a deliberate attack upon the moral fibre of Rome, the Senate could not proscribe a religious rite, so they declared that this depraved form of Bacchic worship constituted a conspiracy against the state. It was a dangerous precedent but only on these grounds could the consuls be empowered to take emergency measures as if the state itself were really in peril – a concept that had hitherto applied only to a military threat. Later, Roman historians claimed that 7,000 people were involved in the Bacchanalian scandal. This is probably an exaggeration, but certainly there were numerous summary executions of guilty men and it would be difficult to ascertain how many women were condemned and put to death in private by their families. It was decreed that in future no more than five people could gather together at one time to worship Bacchus and that express permission must be obtained from the urban praetor.

It is scarcely surprising that, when in the aftermath of this affair, Cato, the advocate of ancient Roman virtue, stood for the Censorship, he was elected, in spite of all that the rich and powerful – and no doubt luxurious – could do to prevent it. But Cato on the *rostra* would have been a draw in any age and the Romans' appreciation of his sarcastic comments is all to their credit. How many politicians today would have the courage to stand up and refuse the electorate the rations they were clamouring for in terms such as, 'It is difficult, my fellow

57 A Bacchanalian dance, portrayed on a fresco from the Villa Pamphili in Rome. In the centre is a figure garlanded with vines, who holds a large amphora of wine. Around him are dancers, accompanied by a musician playing on the double flute. Astonished onlookers watch from the background.

citizens, to argue with the belly, since it has no ears,' or 'The Roman people are like sheep: you cannot budge one of them on its own, but when they are in a flock they all follow their leaders as in a single body. In the same way when you come together in the assembly you allow yourselves to be led by men whose advice you would never think of following in your private affairs.' To those who indulged in fashionable luxuries Cato was merciless: he once refused an invitation to dine with an epicure, saying that he could not spend his time 'with a man whose palate was so much more highly developed than his heart.' Not that Cato's own heart was soft in any way, as the advice he gave in his agricultural treatise, to sell off slaves when they were old and past hard work, shows only too clearly.

In carrying out their Censorial duties Cato and his friend and colleague, Valerius Flaccus, spared no one. Several members of the Senate, whose private lives were not above reproach, were expelled from that august body, including ex-consuls and the brother of Flamininus, the victor of Cynoscephalae. One unfortunate Senator was expelled because he was known to have embraced his wife in daylight in the presence of his daughter.

In his efforts to reduce luxury, Cato devised an ingenious system of taxation. All clothing, carriages, plate, furniture and women's jewels were assessed and each 1,500 drachmas' worth in any family was rated at ten times its value and taxed accordingly.

Cato's Censorship made a profound impression upon Rome. When the people erected a statue in his honour in the Temple of Hygieia, the inscription commemorated not his campaigns and triumph but instead recorded the fact that 'when the Roman state was sinking in decay he became Censor and through his wise leadership, sober discipline and sound principles, restored its strength.' Similar reactions were represented in subsequent legislation. In the year 181 a law was passed against bribery at elections, and those convicted were to be debarred from standing for office for 10 years. In the same year a limit was set on the number of guests who could be invited to banquets. In 180 the *lex villia annalis* laid down the minimum age at which men might stand for the various offices of state and stipulated that an interval of two years must intervene before re-election. This was strongly supported by Cato who hoped thus to put a brake on the careers of ambitious young men. In general a man embarking upon a public career – the only one worth while in Roman eyes – would begin at 17 with 10 years' military service, after attaining a minor command at 25 he would stand for the quaestorship, then the aedileship or tribuneship, followed by the praetorship. If he was really successful, he would achieve the consulship; thus automatically he and his family were ennobled. Those who had held the quaestorship were qualified to enter the Senate, of which the lists were drawn up by the Censors, who had the right to select members and expel them.

The Third Macedonian War broke out in 171. Twenty-five years of peace had restored Macedonia to prosperity; she had also reformed her army and patched up her relations with the Greek states. Thus Philip's son, Perseus, believed himself able to challenge Rome. After a year's indecisive campaigning, Perseus offered to make peace on the same terms as those concluded with his father, but the Senate replied that they would accept only his unconditional surrender. The war dragged on inconclusively for three years, but by the time

Aemilius Paullus took command the situation was already prepared for decisive action. At Pydna, the Macedonian phalanx once again confronted the Roman legions and in the space of a single, terrifying hour the superiority of the mobile Roman system was definitively established. This time Macedonia did not recover; in 168 she was divided into four republics.

The partition of Macedonia was a portent, and a sinister one, in Roman policy. Hitherto, although they did not enjoy the special terms granted to the Latin and Italian allies, states forming the outer perimeter of Roman conquests had been allowed to preserve their identity and independence; only their foreign relations and power to make war were limited. But from now on the policy was reversed. Rome's demand for unconditional surrender was followed by a dictated peace, the alternative being destruction. In some ways it is possible to see how this came about. In the case of Macedonia a conciliatory peace had led to another war 25 years later. In 149 a revolt followed the partition, this was quashed and in 148 Macedonia became a Roman province. The internecine jealousies of the Greek states had also led to Roman domination.

It is perhaps understandable that Rome did not pay much attention now to Greek affairs, but the upshot of this was that the Achaean League defied her and tried to force Sparta to join them. Rome intervened and defeated the League; Corinth, the leading city, was stormed and sacked in 146 by L. Mummius, and the League dissolved, its members becoming client states of Rome. The case of Carthage was different and more dreadful because it was a legacy of the fear engendered by the war against Hannibal. Like Macedonia, Carthage had recovered with incredible speed. According to tradition, when Cato went there on an official mission and saw the city's commercial power and wealth, he was convinced that she might again threaten Rome. Accordingly, Cato concluded every speech he made in the Senate with the words: 'I consider Carthage ought to be destroyed.' He was laughed at, but in the end

58 Romans fighting Macedonians at the Battle of Pydna (168 BC), which brought the Third Macedonian War to a triumphant close. This relief is from the monument of the victorious general, L. Aemilius Paullus.

the Senate listened to him and Rome's persecution of Carthage began. It culminated in a demand that the city should be dismantled and rebuilt several miles inland. Since Carthage existed on maritime trade, she had no alternative to resistance. The Romans besieged the city for three years and in 146 it fell among the most appalling scenes of carnage. The very site of the city was ploughed over, and the Carthaginian lands became the Roman province of Africa. The conqueror of Carthage was one of Aemilius Paullus' elder sons, who had been adopted by the son of Scipio Africanus. He had taken the name of Publius Cornelius Scipio, to which the cognomen of Africanus was now added.

In Spain trouble had been endemic since 154. A stiff-necked people, who had accepted a fair settlement from the consul, T. Sempronius Gracchus, 23 years earlier, were now in a sporadic state of rebellion against incompetent Roman administration. The situation came to a head in 143 and 10 years were to pass before Scipio Aemilianus finally quelled resistance at Numantia; Spain was ultimately divided into three Roman provinces.

The first Roman province of Asia was acquired not by conquest but because Attalus, who died in 133, bequeathed his kingdom of Pergamum to the Roman people. Thus in the space of 16 years Rome became the ruler of domains stretching from the shores of Africa to Asia Minor and what is now Castile.

59 Excavated remains of the Punic necropolis at Carthage, destroyed by the Romans in 146 B C.

6

Rome pays the price – the great change

From a material point of view the results of these conquests benefited Rome enormously. The people enjoyed more triumphs, more booty and more splendid temples and public works. For the first time marble was used in a Roman temple in 149; it was dedicated to Jupiter Stator and was surrounded by a spacious portico which was subsequently replaced by that of Octavia. Nine years later a new aqueduct, the Aqua Marcia, was completed. For the first time use was made of the inverted syphon; nevertheless the underground channel that brought the water from the Sabine hills was 50 miles long and for a further six miles the aqueduct was carried on stately arches right into the heart of the city, there to discharge its water on the Capitoline hill.

But there were other aspects of Roman expansion and these boded ill for the future. Material progress had not been matched by the improvement of moral standards – quite the reverse. In 149 it was found necessary to legislate against the corruption of provincial governors. Rome had come a long way in the hundred years since the day when Manius Curius Dentatus had told the Samnite ambassadors that he was not interested in money, but in power. The law of 181 against bribery at elections shows that power could already be bought in Rome, and the imposition, 25 years later, of the death sentence for those convicted of political bribery indicates how ineffectual the original law had been. Most Romans, rich and poor, were now far from indifferent to money, because there were so many things that they could buy with it to make life more pleasant. Moreover, the conquest of Greece and Macedonia had not only opened the eyes of cultivated Romans like the Scipios to the marvels of Greek art and thought; others had also taken to Greek vices and luxury. Cato said quite openly that in Rome a handsome boy cost more than an estate and a jar of Pontic caviar fetched a higher price than a yoke of oxen. But Cato himself departed from the tenets of his model, Manius Curius Dentatus, where the profit motive was concerned.

Somewhere about 168 Cato had written his *De Re Rustica*. This was no cultivated gentleman's dissertation on agriculture; the book was based on a Greek translation of a Carthaginian treatise and where money was concerned Cato was quite prepared to follow Carthaginian methods. His book was in fact an exposition of new business-efficiency methods and these were even less squeamish in the second century BC than they are today. When asked what was the best way to make money in land, Cato replied: 'Own a good ranch.' And his answer to the question of the second, third and fourth ways of making money in land was the same: 'Own a ranch,' be it good, bad or indifferent.

It will be recalled that ownership of land in Italy was a prerequisite for becoming a Senator, also that limitations had been placed upon the size of ships which might be owned by Senators and their sons, so that they, personally, could not even trade on a large scale in the produce of their lands. They were also debarred from taking state contracts. Thus, if Senatorial families were to preserve their political importance and live in accordance with their station, they had to own very large areas of land indeed, especially as a great deal of the profit on the produce inevitably passed into the hands of middlemen.

During the conquest of Italy, Roman colonies had been set up in different areas and the colonists given part of the cultivated land; of the rest, part was returned to the original owners and part became the *ager publicus* or property of the Roman state, while uncultivated land was free for anyone who was willing to work it. Over the years much of the *ager publicus* had, by right of usage, passed into the hands of the Roman and provincial nobility though, until the war against Hannibal, large areas had also been farmed by native smallholders or the descendants of Roman colonists. These were the men who supplied the rank and file of the Roman armies and many of them never returned from the wars; those who did often lacked the money to salvage a derelict farm and were forced by debt to seek work in the cities. There was little hope for their prosperity when they returned to a countryside dominated by huge estates: the *latifundia* of absentee landlords worked on ruthless profit-making lines with gangs of foreign slaves. In fact the smallholder, Roman or Latin, could only eke out a livelihood at subsistence level by working as a labourer at harvest time on big estates. Even so, a succession of bad years might spell disaster and, leaving his land to the moneylender, the smallholder was forced to go back to the city in search of a livelihood. Thus, in spite of the triumphs and flood of new wealth, it is not surprising that Rome in the middle of the second century was, for the poor, a place of discontent and often outright tragedy.

At the other end of the social scale there were the great families, whose members enjoyed what was practically a monopoly of the chief offices of state. It has been calculated that, in the century preceding 134 B C, 159 out of 200 consuls came from 15 families, 99 from 10 families and 23 from that of the Cornelii Scipionis, or Scipios, alone. Also at the end of the century, the great Roman fortunes were concentrated in the hands of some 2,000 persons. This was largely due to the fact that in Rome, as still in many Latin countries today, marriages were arranged, and among the nobility they resembled the political alliances of European royalty at a later date.

The relationships existing at this time between the families of the great Publius Cornelius Scipio Africanus, Lucius Aemilius Paullus and Tiberius Sempronius Gracchus, provide a striking illustration of the results of constant intermarriage in these circles. In this particular case the situation was further complicated by adoption, a practice which was later to become increasingly frequent in order to prevent the extinction of such families. Thus Scipio Africanus' wife Aemilia, who was Paullus' sister, was both the aunt and grandmother by adoption of Scipio Aemilianus – Paullus' second son who had been adopted by Scipio and Aemilia's own son. Of Scipio Africanus and Aemilia's two granddaughters, both named Cornelia according to the customary usage of a woman taking the feminine of their gentilitial *nomen*, the elder married P.B. Scipio Nasica Corculum, who was her father's second cousin, and had a son, P. Scipio Nasica Serapio. The younger Cornelia married Tiberius Sempronius Gracchus and had 12 children of whom only

three survived infancy; these were Tiberius and Gaius, the future tribunes, and Sempronia who married Scipio Aemilianus, who was both her cousin by adoption and her second cousin by blood relationship.

The Scipios were well-to-do (though according to Polybius not rich by Roman standards). The two Cornelias, for instance, each received a dowry of roughly 1,250,000 sesterces and, as a result of intermarriage, these large sums remained within the family circle. For one reason or another large families were exceptional, thus there were few heirs to inherit. The adoption of relatives produced the same result – Scipio Aemilianus was the obvious heir to Aemilia's fortune, which he ultimately inherited.

After the death of Scipio Africanus the dominating figure in this circle, and indeed in Rome, was Scipio Aemilianus, or Africanus the younger as he is usually called. If he lacked the panache of his adoptive grandfather no one could ever have questioned his administration of public money. He seems to have inherited the old Roman austerity of his real father but also its concomitants of cruelty – he had deserters and runaway slaves thrown to the beasts – and frigidity. Perhaps the most revealing thing we know about Scipio Aemilianus and the Rome he lived in, is that his personal ambition was to excel all his contemporaries in morals and ideals and that his friend, the Greek historian Polybius, who recorded this, also commented that it was not difficult to achieve in the Rome of that day, as all restraint had lapsed after the battle of Pydna.

However, if Scipio Aemilianus owed his moral attitude and military capacity to Paullus' inculcation of stern Roman precepts at an early age, his other activities reflected the influence of his subsequent education by what a modern historian, Professor M.L. Clarke, has described as 'a whole army

60 Sarcophagus of L. Cornelius Scipio Barbatus, one of the twenty-three consuls drawn from the Cornelius Scipio family.

61 A relief thought to show the great Greek historian Polybius, friend of Scipio Aemilianus, present with him at the conquest of Carthage.

of Greek tutors . . . grammarians, philosophers, rhetoricians, teachers of sculpture and drawing and experts in hunting', and it may be added, the care of horses and dogs. This balance between mental and physical exercise was, of course, a Greek ideal and Scipio Aemilianus was in fact a product of both Greek and Roman civilization.

One of the results of the war in Greece was the development of Roman education into something approaching modern university standards, with the arrival in Rome of the *rhetor*, or teacher of rhetoric. At first *rhetors*, like philosophers, had a mixed reception in Rome: Crates of Mallus' demonstration of the art of rhetoric so enthralled the young that they deserted their military exercises to listen to him, causing consternation in the Senate. The arrival of Epicurean philosophers provided an even greater shock: preaching that pleasure was the aim of life was thought to be going too far. In 151, both philosophers and *rhetors* were expelled from Rome by order of the Senate. Crates had to stay, however, as he had injured himself by slipping in the opening of a sewer on the Palatine. Although the Senate remained adamant about philosophers – the Athenian ambassadors of 155, Diogenes, Carneades and Critolaus, had also demonstrated their gifts too freely and were hustled out of the city – gradually it was borne in upon upper-class Romans that, as rhetoric was the art of persuasion, it could be exceedingly useful to men in public life; it had indeed already formed part of the education of a man like Scipio Aemilianus. In fact Scipio Aemilianus was destined not only to provide Cicero, a hundred years later, with his picture of a model Roman, but he also anticipated the Italian Renaissance patrons of the arts, for the men who belonged to the Scipionic circle included Polybius, the great historian of the age; Panaetius, the Greek philosopher, whose interpretation of Stoic philosophy was to provide a sheet-anchor for the troubled Roman soul for two centuries to come; and, by way of complete contrast, Lucilius, who fathered poetical satire and whose work may well reflect the opinions and the wit of this remarkable circle. The greatest literary figure in it was, however, the Carthaginian ex-slave, Publius Terentius Afer – Terence, whose plays are as well known as those of Plautus. But as their language and treatment indicate, they were composed for a much more sophisticated audience. The plays are closer to Menander's Greek originals and in them the rather clumsy Plautine *cantica* have been dropped; moreover, Roman society had evidently changed so much that Terence could even present courtesans in a favourable light, which Plautus had been unable to do 40 years earlier.

Rome had indeed changed, when Polybius, a Greek philosopher, who was also a hostage, and Lucilius, a Campanian of non-Roman origins, and Terence, a Carthaginian freedman, could become the intimate friends of a nobleman like Scipio Aemilianus. But already Rome's perennial capacity for absorbing and Romanizing foreign talent is evident. In 160 the funeral games of L. Aemilius Paullus, the victor of Pydna, were celebrated by his two sons with a gladiatorial display and performances of Terence's *Adelphi* and *Hecyra*. To us the staging of two of the latest comedies as a respectful tribute at the death of a father seems strange indeed but, apart from rare occasions such as this when gladiatorial combats were also given, at this time theatrical performances normally formed part of funeral games. With Paullus something of the old austere Rome had disappeared. Livy records that this man, at whose

62 Iberian warriors; relief from the period of Roman occupation found at Osuna in Spain.

triumph the gold and silver alone were valued at 120,000,000 sesterces, died leaving only about 1,480,000 sesterces.

Two years before Paullus' death, his great-niece Cornelia had borne a son who was called after his father, Tiberius Sempronius Gracchus. Cornelia was left a widow some 12 years later, but she was a woman of such outstanding character and so devoted a mother that she did not remarry even though one of her suitors was King Ptolemy of Egypt. Young Tiberius Gracchus embarked upon his career at an early age. He was present at the siege of Carthage in 146 and was said to have been the first to reach the top of the city wall in the attack on Megara; probably, as was the custom with young men of aristocratic birth, he was attached to the staff of Scipio Aemilianus who was in command. But even before this, Tiberius Gracchus was evidently regarded as an exceptional youth. He had already been elected as one of the nine augurs, and at the banquet held to celebrate the occasion, Appius Claudius, Princeps of the Senate and generally considered to be the most distinguished man in Rome, had offered Tiberius his daughter's hand in marriage.

In 137 Tiberius was elected as one of the eight quaestors of the year and left Rome to take up his duties, which corresponded roughly to those of pay- and quartermaster, with the army in Spain. His journey took him through Etruria, where he saw the countryside divided into great estates cultivated by gangs of foreign slaves and almost completely deserted by its native inhabitants. The dismal impression made by this sight was reinforced when Tiberius arrived in Spain and found a discontented and badly organized army – the result of 17

63 A procession of *equites* on the way to a sacrifice, led by musicians playing on the harp and double flute, appears on an alabaster cinerary urn of the second to first century BC from Volterra.

years' mismanagement in Rome and on the spot. Corruption and bad leadership had already in 151 and in 138 led veterans to resist yet another call-up, with the tribunes' support. During those 17 years there had been a state of intermittent war in Spain, and as both Roman citizens and Latin allies were liable to be called up during 16 years of their lives for periods of six years at a time, discontent was rife. Whereas during the Second Punic War no one could doubt that Rome was fighting for existence, now the smallholders, who were the backbone of the army, felt that they were being sacrificed to incompetence and the interests of the rich.

Such was the army with which Tiberius Gracchus was to serve under the unlucky consul, Gaius Hostilius Mancinus. After a series of reverses in the grim mountains of Castile, Mancinus and his forces were encircled by the Numantines, and the consul sent envoys to request a truce and arrange peace terms. The Numantines, who remembered Tiberius' late father, replied flatly that he was the only Roman with whom they would treat. Thus, at the age of 23, Tiberius found himself responsible for the fate of the whole army. He succeeded in coming to an agreement which saved the lives of 20,000 soldiers and the camp-followers as well. The Romans were forced, however, to abandon their supplies and camp and, too late, Tiberius realized that he had left his account books behind. With a few friends he returned to Numantia and asked the magistrates if he could have his ledgers back, so that he could not be accused of being unable to give a proper account of his administration when he returned to Rome. The Numantines invited Tiberius into the city and he courageously accepted; not only was he treated with the greatest friendliness, but his account books were returned to him.

On his return to Rome, Tiberius was given a very different reception by the Senate, who took the view that Roman armies conquered or died and that the treaty should not be ratified. The people, who were naturally overjoyed to know that their relations and friends serving with the army were safe, put the blame for the whole affair upon the consul, insisting that he should be sent back to Numantia in chains, but they were vociferous in their gratitude to Tiberius. Scipio Aemilianus used his influence to a certain extent to back Tiberius, but he did not intervene in favour of Mancinus or the ratification of the treaty. This produced a coolness between the two men and in 134 Scipio Aemilianus left Rome to take command in Spain. He captured Numantia in the following year.

Although he had made such a sensational return, it might have seemed that Tiberius would now settle down with his family in Rome and pursue a normal career, for he was as gentle and composed in appearance as he was in manner and not given to an extravagant way of life. The Rome to which Tiberius had returned was not, however, an easy place in which to settle down. The aristocracy, even such great families as those from which Tiberius was descended, were divided among themselves. Most of the older generation and others of a conservative turn of mind, who were known as the *optimates*, were fighting hard to preserve their own privileged world, in which they controlled the Senate and, by means of their clients, the voting in the assemblies as well. In the same class there were, however, enlightened men who realized that things could not go on as they were, for Rome had expanded and changed too fast: they were called the *populares*. There was yet another group, the *equites*, who until now had not wielded much power. These were not necessarily knights in the military sense, though the term originated with the class recruited for military service as cavalry, but landed gentry and the growing body of businessmen and *publicani*. In this sense the *equites* are usually described in English as 'gentlemen outside the Senate'. If these three groups were rivals in the increasing struggle for power in Rome, theoretically at least, power itself lay in the hands of the thousands of under-privileged citizens who formed the bulk of the 'Sovereign People of Rome'.

This state of affairs had come about through the gradual evolution, over a considerable period, of the tribal assemblies of the people. Their exact origins and early development as voting bodies are not clear but, for long, two forms of tribal gatherings had existed: one, representing the whole people of Rome presided over by a consul or praetor, was known as the *comitia tributa*, or assembly of the people. In the other, the *concilium plebis*, or council of the plebs, patricians were excluded and the plebs met under their tribunes (and sometimes plebeian aediles). In both assemblies, which are often both loosely referred to as the assembly of the people, the citizens voted in tribes and, irrespective of the numbers in it, the vote of each tribe had equal value. Both tribal assemblies voted on laws and crimes against the state punishable by fines and, at elections, the *comitia tributa* voted to elect curule aediles, quaestors and lower officers, the *concilium plebis* to elect tribunes and aediles of the plebs. In 289 the *lex hortensia* had recognized that any measure or *plebiscitus* voted by the *concilium plebis* constituted a law binding to the whole state, even without Senatorial sanction. The city tribes meeting in the assembly and council still numbered four, as in the original Servian classification, but the number of the rural ones had gradually been increased to 31. These new rural tribes had been created when the Roman colonies were formed on conquered Italian lands and included some enfranchised local inhabitants. Thus the members of a tribe were not of common stock nor did they necessarily inhabit a geographically united area. Different sections of the Cornelian tribe, for instance, were distributed as far apart as Umbria and Apulia.

The growth of these popular assemblies had not, however, entirely eclipsed the activities of the older ones: trumpets still sounded along the walls at dawn to summon citizens to the assemblies of the *comitia centuriata* in the Campus Martius. In 241 the 170 centuries of foot soldiers, who formed the overwhelming majority of the *comitia centuriata*, had been re-formed on tribal lines and into junior and senior age groups. The men in them were still also classified according to property, which gave the richer classes a preponderant vote among their peers. They were, however, overshadowed by the 18 centuries of *equites* who served as cavalry in war and included the richest men in the state. At the other end of the scale came the five unarmed centuries. By the second century B C the chief functions of the *comitia centuriata* were the election of consuls and praetors (magistrates possessing the *imperium* who commanded armies in war), confirmation of the Censors' powers, and voting on declarations of war and crimes against the state punishable by death. But in fact the tribal assemblies had by now outstripped the anachronistic *comitia centuriata* in legislative and political power, as it had long ago ousted the archaic *comitia curiata*, though this last maintained a shadowy existence and still confirmed the *imperium* of consuls and praetors and powers of lower officers of state.

Although the *comitia centuriata* and the *comitia tributa* had different powers and places of assembly – the latter met in the Comitium and Forum, on the Capitol and once at least in the Circus Flaminius – their assemblies had certain features in common. In both, a consul or praetor presided over meetings of the whole people and consultation of the auspices was essential. This rite was carried out by the presiding magistrate who had to go, between midnight and dawn on the day the meeting was to be held, to the place of the assembly. He and his attendant seated themselves in the *templum* or consecrated area, such as the *rostra* or the porch of the Temple of Jupiter, where during the day he was to preside over the meeting. They watched the heavens and the magistrate then asked his attendant if there was silence; then, if the latter agreed he addressed a prayer to Jupiter asking for a sign. If all went well, the attendant then duly reported that he had seen one. Inevitably, in course of time this ritual became a mere formality but a convenient one if, for any reason, it was considered impolitic to hold the assembly. Moreover, even when the meeting was in session, it could be interrupted practically until voting had begun, if anyone declared that he had seen or heard an adverse sign, such as distant lightning or thunder. These are not uncommon phenomena in Rome at any season and the presentation of a controversial bill or candidate could result in extraordinary meteorological sensitivity in the opposing party. By declaring that he had 'heard thunder' Pompey blocked his enemy, the younger Cato's election as praetor. Thus it is easy to understand how the bulk of legislation had in time come to be enacted in the *concilium plebis*, where the auspices were not consulted and under tribunes proceedings were more informal. In fact after 287 much of the legislation passed by the plebs was inspired by the Senate, and relations between it and the tribunes were cordial as the tribunate was now but a step on the ladder which led to Senatorial rank. This happy state of affairs changed, however, after the middle of the second century B C when ambitious men who were at odds with the Senate, tried to use the office for pushing through a popular and anti-Senatorial programme.

Another characteristic feature of all Roman assemblies was the practice of drawing lots. It was introduced into the *comitia centuriata* in 241. Lots were drawn to decide which of the centuries should vote first; the winning century was known as the *centuria praerogativa* and its vote was regarded as an omen. Lots were also drawn to decide the order in which tribes should vote on legislation in the other assemblies. Lots were drawn by inscribing the names of tribes or centuries on pieces of wood or wooden balls and putting them into an urn filled with water. The urn was then apparently whirled round and the lots poured or shaken out. If there was any doubt about the result an augur was consulted.

The interruptions which could be caused by 'hearing thunder' or other contrary signs, together with hazards of drawing lots and consultation with augurs, indicate that numerous opportunities existed in Roman assemblies for influencing the results. But even if proceedings were conducted with scrupulous impartiality, their very form did not admit of anything approaching the modern conception of responsible democratic government. The people could not meet unless convened by a magistrate and then could only vote on measures proposed by him; he also possessed the power of terminating the assembly at any time on the grounds of disorder. It is true that the magistrates were elected, but not necessarily by the greatest number of voters, as the group voting system did not take into account the number of voters in each group. In addition to this, if only five or fewer members of a tribe were present, the magistrate directed men of his own choice from other tribes to fill the gap. Furthermore, in the *comitia centuriata*, which elected the consuls and praetors, even after the reforms of 241, the system of voting was heavily weighted on the side of the well-to-do. Consuls were answerable at law for their actions, but within these limits they exercised their *imperium* as they saw fit during their year of office. By the middle of the second century the nobles, which meant families – either patrician or plebeian – whose members had held the offices of consul, dictator or, earlier, consular tribune, really controlled the consulate and the Senate. The one restriction on the nobles' power was the tribunes' veto, but by the second century the tribunes were also usually members of the nobility. This is the political background against which Tiberius Gracchus' and later his brother Gaius' attempts at reform must be viewed.

After his return from Spain, Tiberius had a choice of two offices for which he could stand. These represented the next step on the political ladder, or career of honour, which it was the custom, and indeed generally considered to be the duty, for a young man of his class to follow. The alternatives were the aedileship, an administrative job, and the tribunate, which was a key position in politics and legislature. Tiberius was elected tribune of the plebs in 134 and probably assumed office on 10 December as, since 153, the consular year began on 1 January instead of 15 March, and the tribunes took up their duties some weeks beforehand. According to Plutarch the people had left Tiberius in no doubt as to what was expected of him. Unknown hands, as in Rome today, had been at work 'inscribing slogans and appeals on porticoes, monuments and the walls of houses, calling upon him to recover the public land for the poor'.

Immediately after taking up office, Tiberius presented his bill for land reform to the council of the plebs. He was only 29, but the bill's apparently simple clauses were in fact based upon a profound knowledge of the complicated land laws. Plutarch says that Tiberius had been advised by P. Mucius Scaevola, who was elected consul in the same year, and his father-in-law, Appius Claudius; he was also encouraged in his plans by the Stoic philosopher, Blossius of Cumae. Briefly, the bill proposed that the *lex licinia* of 366 B C, which laid down that no one could hold more than 500 *jugera* (about 310 acres) of state land (*ager publicus*), should be re-enacted; it had fallen into disuse but never been repealed. The regained land was to be distributed as small-holdings and the present holders recompensed. In support of his bill Tiberius made a speech whose echoes reach us still. He said: 'The wild beasts that roam over Italy have their dens and holes to lurk in, but the men who fight and die for our country enjoy the common light and air and nothing else.' His words were never forgotten and a century and a half later they were reinterpreted as: 'Foxes have holes and the birds of the air have nests but the Son of Man has nowhere to lay His head,' and 'The sun shines on the just and the unjust.'

Quite obviously, when Tiberius' bill was put to the vote, it would be passed and in any case its contents were already known, as custom required that bills should be publicly posted 24 days before voting took place. The only way to prevent its becoming law was to persuade another tribune to apply the veto. By dint of pressure and persuasion the powerful opponents of the bill finally got their man, Marcus Octavius, to utter the fatal word *intercedo* – 'I forbid' – and stop the reading of the bill. Thus faced with the veto, Tiberius withdrew his bill. He may well have expected the veto in any event for he now produced another much harsher bill that contained no provisions for compensating the holders of state land. The battle of speeches for and against the bill continued day after day. Tiberius even offered personally to recompense Octavius for any losses he would incur if the bill became law. Octavius refused, and in the consequent period of tension it appears that all business of state was interrupted. The treasury was closed, the courts ceased to function and no magistrate could take action. The opposition paraded about the Forum in mourning and Tiberius let it be publicly known that, as there was a plot to murder him, he went armed.

The whole dismal process was unrolled against a background of events which should have served as a warning to the party of reaction and purely financial interest. In Sicily in 134, the slaves had rebelled against the terrible conditions of their lives on the great ranches of the new-rich landlords. The two protagonists of the struggle were Eunus, a Syrian, the leader of the slaves who had proclaimed himself king, and Damophilus, the ranch owner and his wife Megalis, both of whom were murdered. 'King' Eunus now reigned over most of Sicily.

Veto or not, Tiberius proceeded to summon the people to vote on his land reform bill. The urns were produced to draw lots to decide which tribe should vote first, but they were seized by the opposition party. Tiberius' followers were preparing to take the urns back by force when two respected Senators intervened, begging Tiberius to reflect. Asked what they proposed, the two Senators had no advice to offer other than that the matter should be referred to the Senate. Tiberius agreed. The Senate deliberated, but the parties of reaction

64 *Opposite, above* Terracotta figurine of a Roman slave, scantily dressed and heavily laden with amphora, wine-skin (in his right hand) and basket strapped to his back.

65 *Opposite* The Roman system of land division, still visible around Lugo near Ravenna. The large square divisions are *centuriates*, of about 800 × 800 yards, originally separated by ditches and walls. Within them the fields are divided into small strips.

and reform were so equally balanced that no decision was reached. This was the crucial moment in the whole affair. Until then the struggle had been conducted according to precedent within the framework of the constitution, but apparently there were not sufficient statesmen among the Senators, men capable of realizing the dangers of the situation and insisting that a definite decision must be made. Resolution to proceed with the reform would have launched Rome on a new path, beset no doubt with political difficulties especially with the Latin allies, but it might have preserved her unity. It is also possible that a firm 'No', accompanied by a statesmanlike handling of the situation, might have given Tiberius himself pause to reflect. Although tradition prescribed an interval of years before he could stand for re-election as a tribune, he was young enough to wait and gather his forces, whose strength would probably grow, and try again in accepted Roman fashion. But the Senate had failed in one of its chief functions, which was to advise, and thus the responsibility for taking a decision rested with Tiberius.

It was at this juncture that, rightly or wrongly, Tiberius decided to defy the constitution. At the time this probably appeared to him as an isolated act

taken to ensure a worthwhile end, but its ultimate consequences were incalculable. Tiberius propounded the revolutionary idea that, if two tribunes disagreed, the only solution was that one should be deprived of office by the vote of the council of the plebs. This proposal ran contrary to all Roman republican tradition. Since the fall of the kings, all magistrates, from the consuls down, had existed in pairs or larger numbers, precisely to prevent any single man – with the exception in the past of a dictator acting in an emergency – from exercising power alone. This also ensured that if a matter were in doubt, no action should be taken or, at least, that time must pass before it could be reconsidered. The tribunes' veto was the quintessence of this concept, and Tiberius now planned to abrogate this basic constitutional rule by a simple vote of the council of the plebs. Evidently Tiberius had qualms, for he repeatedly urged Octavius to recant, right up to the moment before the vote was taken, but Octavius refused to give way. Inevitably, in the circumstances, Octavius' powers were revoked and equally inevitably Tiberius' land reform bill became law.

The Senate now refused to vote the funds for the implementation of the reform, for which a commission had been appointed, consisting of Appius Claudius, Tiberius and his brother Gaius. Again Tiberius resorted to unconstitutional means. King Attalus of Pergamum had just died, bequeathing his kingdom to Rome. Like all foreign affairs, the responsibility for dealing with the matter lay with the Senate, but Tiberius carried a measure through the council of the plebs whereby funds from King Attalus' treasure were to be allocated for the expenses of the land commission. Finally, as time was running short, Tiberius flouted tradition by announcing that he would stand for election as tribune the following year.

Rome was plunged into election fever. Sarcastically, a Senator announced in the Curia that Eudemus, who had brought Attalus' will from Pergamum, had also brought a crown and purple robes for Tiberius, as he would soon be King of Rome. The leader of the opposition to Tiberius was his own cousin, P. Scipio Nasica Serapio, son of his mother's sister, the elder Cornelia. As Pontifex Maximus, an office held for life, Nasica wielded very considerable influence. Even popular opinion was now divided over Tiberius' action and his intention to present himself for election. The situation was so threatening that Tiberius' friends advised him nevertheless to stand, so that he might at least have the protection of his office.

Tiberius is now said to have prepared a programme of liberal legislation, admittedly aimed at pleasing the people. He proposed to curtail the period of military service, and that the *equites* should be included in juries, which were normally composed only of Senators, and that there should be a right of appeal against their verdict. The subsequent meeting of the council of the plebs was so disorderly that it was adjourned. On the second day things went better and a message was sent to Tiberius to hurry to the Capitol, where the meeting was in progress, as things were progressing favourably. But when he arrived, disorder had again broken out. With great difficulty Fulvius Flaccus, a friendly Senator, managed to get close enough to Tiberius to warn him that the opposition party in the Senate were gathering forces to kill him. Tiberius told his near-by supporters and they prepared to form a bodyguard. Friends further away could not make out what was happening and as he could not make himself heard, Tiberius put his hand to his head to indicate to them that his life was threatened. At the sight of this gesture an excited body of his enemies rushed to the Senate to say that Tiberius was asking for the crown. There, in the midst of an uproar, Nasica demanded that the consul should take action to protect the state. According to Plutarch, the consul, who was Tiberius' friend Publius Mucius Scaevola, then replied that he would not be the first to use violence and would put no citizen to death without a regular trial, but that if Tiberius incited the people to pass any illegal resolution, he would not consider it to be binding. Whereupon Nasica sprang to his feet and shouted: 'Now that the consul has betrayed the state, let every man who wishes to uphold the laws follow me!'

As Nasica and a group of Senators left the Curia, they were joined by attendants already armed with clubs and staves, from which it appears that the attack was premeditated. Making their way through the fleeing crowds to the Capitol, the Senators picked up the legs and pieces of benches smashed by the frightened people in their escape. The Senators and their following now made straight for Tiberius, battering down all who tried to protect him. Tiberius fled with the rest, someone clutched his toga but he flung it off, then he tripped over some of the prostrate bodies. As he tried to rise, one of his fellow tribunes hit him on the head, another blow followed and another; together with 300 of his followers Tiberius Gracchus was battered to death with clubs and stones upon the Capitol. The hatred of their opponents pur/sued Tiberius and his supporters even after death: their families were refused the right of giving them decent burial and their bodies were thrown into the Tiber.

The measure of how extraordinary these events were is that the consuls had no police or armed force at their disposal to restore order. No such thing existed in Rome because until then there had been no need for it. A reign of terror followed, during which more of Tiberius' supporters were executed without appeal allowed, or banished without trial. Gradually calm returned and a consular commission was set up to inquire into the disorders. Hastily a veil was drawn over the whole affair. Public hatred of Nasica, however, was such that the Senate, fearing he would be murdered, dispatched him on a mission over/seas. He never returned.

It was a very uneasy Rome that Scipio Aemilianus found after his victory at Numantia. Even his triumphant conclusion of the Spanish war carried no weight with the people, when on a public platform he said in answer to a question from a tribune, that if Tiberius 'had intended to seize control of the state he was legally slain'. There were shouts and heckling from the crowd and Scipio Aemilianus rounded on them in a fury, saying: 'Be quiet, you who are not children but stepchildren of Italy.' Even this did not silence them, where/upon, evidently recognizing some freedmen in the crowd, Scipio Aemilianus said that he himself had brought them to Rome in chains. The results of the incident were unfortunate, for hitherto Scipio Aemilianus had represented a moderating influence, capable of bridging the gap between the extremes of conservative and popular opinion; but of that there was now no hope. More/over, as he had foreseen, Rome's relations with her Italian allies also degenerated as a result of quarrels over the land reform. The allies complained that their land was being filched from them, and Scipio Aemilianus was influential in having such cases judged by the consuls. Distribution was slowed down. It was practically his last official act. Mysteriously in 129, at the age of 55, Scipio Aemilianus died. An inquiry was held, but the findings were never made public. Many suspected political murder, while whispers, more scandalous still, accused Sempronia and Cornelia, her mother.

In 125, Tiberius' brother Gaius returned to Rome from Sardinia where he had been serving as quaestor for a year. He was 30, but little had been heard of him since Tiberius' death. Subsequent events, however, indicate that in the intervening period Gaius had been preparing for the role he was determined to play as the avenger of his brother's death, and as a reformer who would amplify and complete the legislation that Tiberius had begun. In order to further his aims, Gaius had undertaken an arduous training in oratory which, in the classical world, enjoyed a renown unheard of in the present day. For obvious practical reasons, in addressing the electorate and for legislative and legal purposes, public speaking had always been important in Rome, but now, under the influence of Hellenistic rhetoric, oratory was coming to be considered the chief aim of all education and Gaius' demonstration of his mastery of the art at the trial of a friend, had reawakened the worst fears of the *optimates*. They exerted every effort to prevent Gaius' being elected tribune in 123, but were only successful in getting him elected fourth on the list instead of first. He soon asserted his predominance, for, Plutarch says, Gaius 'was incomparably the finest orator in Rome.' He knew how to play the gallery; he was the first Roman to stride up and down the *rostra* and to wrench his toga off his shoulder in his excitement, thus electrifying his audience. Gaius could also vary his style from the heroic, when speaking of the sacrosanct character of the tribunate, to the downright bawdy, in order to get his own back on a homosexual who had dared to mention his mother's name. He said, 'You have a nerve to compare yourself with Cornelia, have you borne any children like hers? At any rate everyone in Rome knows you have slept with a man far more recently than she has!' This was the politician's window-dressing; but behind it lay the shrewd and resourceful brain that had planned, probably over a period of years, a vast and intricate programme of legislation which was to affect Rome's evolution for a century to come.

It is unlikely that the Senate entertained any doubts as to the course which Gaius Gracchus would pursue once he was in office; the only thing that might have surprised them were the extra cards he had up his sleeve. Thus his re-introduction of Tiberius' agrarian reform was not a surprise, any more than was his legislation to prevent a recurrence of the consular commission which had condemned Tiberius' supporters. He proposed to re-enact that old guarantee of Roman liberties – appeal to the Roman people, who alone could pass the death sentence on a fellow citizen. Gaius also sought to confirm the legality of Tiberius' actions by a law which declared if two tribunes disagreed one could be deprived of office and that if the people had deposed a magistrate he could not again hold office. This was obviously aimed at Marcus Octavius but, as Cornelia intervened in Octavius' favour, Gaius withdrew the measure and, according to Plutarch, 'this action pleased the people' – matriarchal influence has always held a particular appeal for the Romans.

The rest of Gaius' legislation, however, ranged from measures designed for the relief of the poorest citizens to projects providing a blueprint for the administration of what was now Rome's far-flung empire, in all but name. Undoubtedly the most popular measure was Gaius' recognition of the fact that Italy was no longer Rome's granary. Her wheat supplies now came from Sicily, Sardinia and Africa and were thus in the hands of speculators and, during the stormy winter months, subject to long delays in shipment. He therefore instituted the common-sense system whereby the state bought and shipped large quantities of grain to Rome immediately after the harvest, when prices were low; it was then stored in government granaries and sold to the people at an equitable price throughout the year. He also tried to lessen the burden of military service by raising the call-up age to 17 and making the state responsible for the cost of clothing its armies.

Much of Gaius' other legislation was directed at curbing the power of the Senate, which was no longer to be permitted to allocate provinces to the consuls as it saw fit; in future, selection of the provinces to be allocated to the next year's consuls was to be made before the elections. Tax collection in the new province of Asia was put into the hands of the *publicani*, who were to bid for five-year contracts, as they already did for those for public works. Another law substituted *equites* for Senators on the juries serving in the courts where provincial governors were tried for corruption. Thus some impetus was now given to

66 Riverside warehouses, part of Rome's commercial port on the Tiber, during excavation.

67 A Roman official of the German province being driven in a three-horse carriage with an armed guard.

corporate class-consciousness in non-Senators of the biggest financial group. It is evident that Gaius hoped that this would provide a counterbalance to Senatorial power, as indeed, in time, it did. But that the *equites* were now favourably placed to develop their own system of corruption and abuse of power was apparently something that Gaius did not foresee. Although his legislative programme was no doubt the result of many years' reflection, Gaius had but a single year of office in a time of crisis to push it through. The machinery of government which had long ago been evolved in Rome to serve a city state lagged far behind the real political situation and the only alternative to complete reorganization and reform seemed to be an explosion.

Nevertheless, it is evident that, as far as Rome and Italy were concerned, Gaius did recognize the immediate danger. His plan to found colonies would have absorbed some of Rome's surplus population and given them work, which was hard to find in the city with its slave economy, while his road-building activities greatly benefited agriculture and trade. Gaius' roads were not built to serve strategic military ends but to open up fertile districts and link them with markets. In the pages of Plutarch's 'Life', we catch a momentary glimpse of the

charm and tact that Gaius displayed when dealing personally with contractors and craftsmen as well as with the great. This was completely at variance with his fiery platform personality.

There is no doubt that Gaius was an excellent administrator and it is not surprising that he was re-elected tribune for a second term in 122. He now planned to extend his activities to a wider field – the creation of Roman commercial colonies in Capua and Tarentum and the endorsement of a fellow tribune's scheme for completely rebuilding another great commercial metropolis, Carthage, as a Roman city. But Gaius went a great deal further and with Fulvius Flaccus, who, contrary to all precedent, had been elected tribune after attaining the consulate, he renewed the proposal for giving the Latins Roman citizenship and other Italians Latin rights. The aristocracy were bitterly opposed to flooding the polls with newly enfranchised Latins, who were not their clients and would therefore disturb the delicate balance of the patron-client relationship by which the elections were arranged in the aristocracy's interest.

The Senate had, however, prepared for such an eventuality with a great

68 Remains of the Roman amphitheatre at Capua, site of one of the most famous schools for gladiators.

deal more skill than that which it had displayed in dealing with Tiberius. This time Marcus Livius Drusus, the tribune who vetoed the bill for the enfranchisement of the Latins, was well qualified to be run by the Senate as a rival reformer – rich and distinguished, he came of an eccentric plebeian family and was known to hold advanced views. Gaius accepted the veto on the enfranchisement bill, as this vital issue had even split the *populares*. It had also aroused the fears of the proletariat who did not wish to share their privileged citizenship with anyone, while even the Latins entertained doubts because of the land reform and the prospect of Roman conscription. Gaius now made the strategical error of absenting himself from Rome for over two months, to oversee the rebuilding of Carthage. During this period Drusus captured the popular imagination with proposals for reforms which far outpaced even those of Gaius: for instance, the foundation of 12 colonies for 36,000 of Rome's poor. That such plans had no practical possibility of execution and that the Senate, which Drusus said had inspired his reforms, intended either not to implement them or immediately to repeal them, was something that the mob in its ignorant self-seeking did not fathom.

Too late, on his return, Gaius may have realized that there was some substance in Scipio Aemilianus' claim that the Roman people were Romans no more. The old, dour common-sense breed had been replaced by something new, since Rome's victories had made her a melting-pot of peoples, and this new breed possessed a fickleness unknown to those who had gone before. Drusus, with his extravagant proposals, had captured the popular fancy and Gaius' popularity was on the wane. In vain he resorted to such expedients as moving house from the fashionable Palatine to the popular quarter near the Forum, and tearing down the expensive stands which had been put up in the Forum for ticket-holders viewing a gladiatorial display, so that the people could also see it. Nevertheless, when Gaius stood again as tribune in 141, he was not elected.

Owing to the system whereby only an elected magistrate could summon the people and address them, the 'greatest orator in Rome' was now muzzled. Worse still, his arch-enemy, Lucius Opimius, had been elected consul. An assembly was called by Opimius on the Capitol to revoke Gaius' legislation. At first Gaius refused to go, but, encouraged by the fiery Flaccus, he went with a party of his supporters to watch, though legally they were powerless to intervene. Proceedings opened with the ritual sacrifice and as Antullus, a temple assistant, carried out the entrails of the sacrificial victim, he passed through the crowd of Gracchan supporters. It is said that Antullus used insulting words and gestures; in any event an outraged Gracchan supporter stabbed him with his sharp metal writing-stylus and Antullus died immediately. On learning what had happened, Gaius recalled his supporters to the Forum and there addressed them sternly. A torrential downpour now intervened and all business stopped.

The next day there was a stormy meeting in the Senate, interrupted by Antullus' funeral procession passing through the Forum. The upshot was that for the first time in history the emergency decree was passed, that later came to be called *senatus consultum ultimum* – the last decree. With the phrase 'let the consuls see that the state takes no harm', which was to become ominously familiar in later years, constitutional proceedings were suspended and the consuls vested with almost absolute power to restore order. Opimius now ordered the Senators to arm themselves and decreed that every member of the equestrian order should present himself with two armed servants, the following morning. During the night Gaius' and Flaccus' supporters gathered round their houses to guard them. Flaccus spent the night roistering after he had summoned Gaius to meet him in the morning in the Temple of Diana on the Aventine, the traditional stronghold of the plebs. But when Gaius prepared to leave home next day, his wife, Licinia, guessed that this was probably the last time she would see him and begged him not to go. Reminding Gaius of Tiberius' fate, Licinia said that if Tiberius had been killed in war at least his body would have been returned for decent burial, and she ended her pathetic appeal with the words: 'but as it is, I too may have to pray to some river or sea to yield up yours. What faith can we put in the gods or men when we have seen Tiberius murdered?'

In order to understand what followed, it must be remembered that no such thing as the emergency decree had ever been heard of in Rome before. The *comitia centuriata* could not even be summoned to meet inside the *pomerium* because, although they were unarmed, they were drawn up as an *exercitus urbanus* and the presiding magistrate could not give orders to them inside the city. A man had been murdered, but neither Gaius nor Flaccus had laid a finger on him and in normal circumstances the assassin would have been arrested and tried. Thus Flaccus, who was after all an ex-consul, was justified in what was evidently his belief that any action of the type envisaged by the emergency decree, of which rumours had no doubt reached him and Gaius, was illegal. Furthermore, although Flaccus' intention of taking refuge in the Temple of Diana on the Aventine might seem exaggerated, they could in ordinary circumstances have defended the temple until things had blown over and sanity returned.

Gaius appealed to Flaccus to attempt a peaceful settlement, and Flaccus agreed to send his son to the Senate to negotiate. Opimius, however, replied that he would accept only unconditional surrender. Gaius then suggested that he himself should go, but his friends would not allow this. Flaccus' son was sent again and detained. Flaccus, who had years of military service behind him, was prepared for an attack by a citizen levy, but not for what actually came – a body of Cretan archers who mowed down the helpless defenders of the temple from a distance. Flaccus and his son were killed; others fled in terror. Gaius, who had taken no part in the fighting, took sanctuary in the Temple of Diana and prepared to kill himself, but was prevented by his friends who snatched the weapon from him and urged him to save himself. When Opimius offered an amnesty to the rank and file, many of them deserted. Then, in Diana's sanctuary there followed one of the most tragic scenes in Roman history, when Gaius stretched out his hands to the goddess and prayed to her 'that in return for their ingratitude and their treachery to him, the people of Rome should remain enslaved to their rulers for ever after.' Later generations believed that Diana heard and did not forget, and Rome's subsequent history seems to bear them out.

Gaius escaped from the temple and reached the old Sublician bridge with his friend Laetorius and his faithful slave Philocrates, but on the way he sprained his ankle. Laetorius sacrificed his life to hold the bridge against pursuit until Gaius was lost to sight on the Janiculum. As he limped and tried to run, bystanders cheered him, but none of them came to his aid or gave him the horse he begged for, which might have saved his life. Finally he could struggle no further, and he and Philocrates took refuge in a grove sacred to the Furies. There Gaius and his slave were killed in 121.

Plutarch says that Opimius had offered its weight in gold for Gaius' head and that a former friend of his filled it with lead and took it to the consul. A judicial inquiry followed and 3,000 of Gaius' followers were condemned to death by Opimius and their bodies, like his, thrown into the Tiber. Petty vengeance was even exacted upon Gaius' wife, whose dowry was confiscated. When Opimius' year as consul had ended, he was impeached by the tribune Q. Decius for having Roman citizens put to death without allowing them to appeal to the people. Opimius was acquitted on the grounds that Gaius had aspired to the monarchy and that his own actions were sanctioned by the emergency decree, but he did not escape the avenging Furies in the end.

Death made the Gracchi legendary figures; statues were raised to them and to their mother, which was simply inscribed, 'Cornelia, mother of the Gracchi'. Cornelia herself retired to her villa at Misenum and became the personification of the stoic Roman matron. According to Plutarch, she 'made no change in her normal mode of life. She had many friends and kept a good table which was always thronged with guests.' He goes on to relate how some people were surprised that 'she would speak of her sons without showing sorrow or shedding a tear, and recall their achievements and fate to any enquirer.' Cornelia lived to a considerable age and her villa was famous, eventually becoming an Imperial residence. By some strange freak of fate or poetic justice, the last Roman emperor died there – a forlorn figure, shorn of his titles and his great estate. If the Gracchi had lived, the Republic, which in the fifth century AD still existed in name, might have survived indeed.

69 Plinth of a statue commemorating Cornelia, sister of Scipio Africanus and mother of the Gracchi. A smaller inscription notes that the statue, which has disappeared, was the work of Tisicrates.

7

Rome and the first war-lords – Marius and Sulla

If the Gracchi had been willing to follow precedent and bide their time, would they have been able to carry through their reforms and thereby spare Rome the wars of the next century? The roots of the tragedy seem to lie not so much in the actions of the Gracchi themselves as in the transformation of Rome after the war against Hannibal and the fact that they came upon the scene too late. In any event, the years following Gaius' death were ones of anticlimax; it seemed as if the passions aroused during the two years of his career had spent themselves and that the problems he had set out to solve might in the end just peter out. This period of waiting was, of course, the false calm that preceded the whirlwind to come, but in fact, although the Romans were unaware of it, the first faint stirrings of that wind ruffled the surface of events only two years after Gaius' death.

Few Romans in the year 120 can have taken any account of the election as tribune of Gaius Marius, the son of a provincial family of Cereatae near Arpino. That Marius was a born soldier is evident from the fact that, his undistinguished antecedents notwithstanding, by the time he was 24 he was serving on Scipio Aemilianus' staff at the siege of Numantia, in company with sprigs of the Roman nobility and the Numidian prince Jugurtha. One night at dinner, Scipio Aemilianus was asked who could possibly succeed him as Rome's great general, and, tapping the shoulder of Marius who was sitting next to him, Scipio replied, 'Perhaps this is the man.'

Rough and uncultured as he was, Marius had all the toughness of his Volscian ancestry, and when the test came Scipio Aemilianus was proved right. Shortly after Marius' election, the whole bench of tribunes decided that the secrecy of the ballot was not being maintained and that pressure was being exerted upon voters. By this time, voting by ballot had been introduced into the assemblies for all purposes, except in trials for high treason; it also came into use for the latter purpose in 107.

In Roman elections, after the voters had received the wax-covered tablets upon which they registered their vote, they had to traverse high raised gangways, called *pontes*, on their way to the ballot-box. As a result of this system, voters had to mark their ballots in full view of election officials standing on the *pontes* and might thus be subject to coercion. In order to avoid such a practice the tribunes drafted a bill requiring that the *pontes* should be narrowed. Marius was the tribune delegated to present the bill to the Senate. The consul, L. Aurelius Cotta, procured its rejection on a technicality. Marius was summoned, but far from being intimidated, he declared that the dignity of the tribunician power was being impugned and threatened to have Cotta arrested. Cotta appealed to his colleague, L. Caecilius Metellus Dalmaticus, who, ironically, had been influential in Marius' election as tribune and who was a patron of

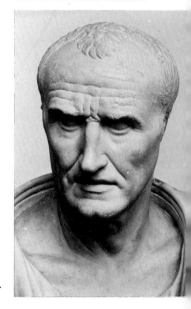

70 Marius; a first-century BC marble bust thought to represent the new leader of Rome.

his family. However, Marius stood his ground and actually ordered Metellus' arrest. Metellus now appealed to the other tribunes, but as they were united in their support of the bill, it was ultimately passed.

This was the first step in Marius' public career. His rising ambition did not, however, lie in politics but in the army and he had no wish to be identified with any particular political group. Thus, with unexpected political acumen, he opposed and stopped a popular measure for providing a corn distribution to the citizens. The outcome of these two actions was that Marius had earned the respect of both conservative and popular trends of opinion and also enjoyed a reputation for independence and strength of character. Nevertheless, when he later stood for election as aedile he was unsuccessful, but, amid general astonishment, he was eventually elected to the praetorship. It is true that he was at the bottom of the poll among those elected and that there were allegations of graft, but Marius assumed his office. Having risen to the praetorship, Marius was made. On his return from governing Further Spain, he married the daughter of the aristocratic Gaius Julius Caesar, and thus in due course became the uncle of another Gaius Julius Caesar, who was born in 100 (or 101) on the 13th of the month which was later called July in his honour.

If on the surface Rome appeared calm during the last decades of the second century B C, one incident alone should have been sufficient to alert the suspicions of any thoughtful observer. Any allegation of unchastity among the Vestal Virgins had, throughout its history, been a sure indication that something was wrong in the body politic of Rome, and that which occurred in 114 was no exception. Moreover, on this occasion it was not one single member, but the whole College of Vestals, that was alleged to be corrupt. An investigation and the Pontifex Maximus' condemnation of one Vestal did not appease public opinion – or rather hysteria.

The following year a tribune succeeded in getting the case reopened and tried before a civil court. Two more unfortunate Vestals were condemned and, torture being employed upon witnesses, the number of their alleged lovers grew. This time the expiation was performed before the catastrophe, not afterwards as at the time of Cannae, for it was in the same year as the scandal of the Vestals that Rome first heard of the Cimbri. Emerging suddenly out of the northern wastelands, this tribe defeated a Roman army at Noreia (in what is now northern Yugoslavia), but distance lessened the shock and no effective counter-measures were taken.

71, 72 Coins showing voting in Rome: *right*, voters cross the raised gangway and are handed a tally on their way to the ballot-box; *far right*, a voter places his tablet in the box.

73 The six Vestal Virgins. Their antique style of dress was shared by brides (see Ill. 102). Marble relief from the Ara Pietatis, first century AD.

Nearer home, but also apparently another peripheral affair, was Jugurtha's successful *coup d'etat* in Numidia (Algeria). In 112 he ousted King Adherbal, his half-brother. Adherbal took refuge in Cirta (Constantine) where there was a settlement of Italian merchants and appealed to Rome for protection. The Senate treated the situation much as it had done that of Saguntum at the beginning of the war with Hannibal, and the commission sent to Numidia was about as effective as that dispatched to New Carthage a century before. The Italian merchants of Cirta, like men on the spot in other countries and periods, were under no illusions as to what help they might expect from the home government, but unfortunately they were not so realistic in their summing-up of Jugurtha. They advised Adherbal to negotiate a peaceful surrender, which he did, but once Jugurtha was in possession of the town he slaughtered the Italian merchants and had Adherbal tortured to death. The news produced a violent reaction in Rome. There had been many changes in the last hundred years and, thanks partly to the Gracchi, the business interests represented by the *equites* now had considerable political power, which had been increased by their recent alliance with Gaius Gracchus. Jugurtha's activities were no longer a question of foreign policy in a remote sphere, for the merchants of Cirta had been the friends and business associates of the *equites*, who sustained a heavy financial loss. As a result, the unwilling Senate was forced to send an army to Africa.

It must be admitted that the Senate had good reason for its unwillingness to fight Jugurtha. Our own generation has witnessed the fate, even of forces equipped with modern armaments, when confronted by Algerian guerillas on their own ground, and in the twentieth century they did not have a leader of genius like Jugurtha. The Senate was well aware that there could be no

```
      ]ALLVVEISQ
C·SEXTIVS·C·F·CN·CALVIN·PROCO
DELIGVRIBVOCONTIEISSALIVVEISQ
L·AVRELIVS·L·F·L·N·ORESTES·PRO·AN·DC
COS·EX·SARDINIA · VI·IDVS·DEC
Q·CAECILIVS·Q·F·QN·METELLVS·A·DCX
BALIARIC·PROCOS·DEBALIARIB·PR
Q·FABIVS·Q·AEMILIANI·F·QN·AN·DC
MAXIMVS·PROCOS·DE·ALLOBRC
ET·REGE·ARVERNORVM·BET·VLTOX·K
CN·DOMITIVS·CN·F·CN·N·AHENOBARBA
PROCOS·DE·GALLEIS·ARVERNEIS·XVI·K
L·CAECILIVS·L·F·QN·METELLVS·A·NN·DCX
DELMATIC·PROCOS·DE·DELMATEIS·III·NC
Q·MARCIVS·Q·F·QN·REX·PROCOS·AN·DCX
DELIGVRIBVSSTOENEIS·III·NONDE
M·AEMILIVS·M·F·L·N·SCAVRVS·COS
DE·GALLEIS·KARNEIS· V
M·CAECILIVS·Q·F·QN·MET
COS· EX·SARDINI
```

74–76 A triumph of Q. Caecilius Metellus, commemorated on a coin and on the Roman Table of Triumphs. The coin bears the head of Roma, *top*, and shows Metellus crowned by victory as he rides in a chariot drawn by elephants. The table records his triumph (in line 6) and those of other members of his family (line 13 and bottom).

peace in Africa so long as Jugurtha was at large, but they had no illusions as to the difficulty of capturing him. However, in an effort to quieten public opinion in Rome, an army was sent to Africa. After several months no decisive action had been fought, nor could the consul, L. Calpurnius Bestia, foresee any such prospect. Jugurtha could not be pinned down; but, as Calpurnius Bestia discovered, he could be persuaded to make a face-saving agreement. Thus Jugurtha 'surrendered', a treaty was concluded, and the consul was free to return to Rome – but unfortunately Jugurtha was equally free to pursue his career in Africa.

The news of this dubious treaty was greeted with fury by the *equites* and the *populares* in Rome. A tribune demanded that the 'vanquished' Jugurtha should be brought to Rome. No one was in a position to force him to come, but come he did.

Gaius Memmius, the tribune who had insisted upon Jugurtha's appearance, now actually produced him on the platform before the council of the plebs. The whole of Rome must have held its breath, for, having served on Scipio Aemilianus' staff, Jugurtha could speak Latin and, if he had really said in private all the things reported of him, he had a pretty turn of wit when it came to describing highly placed Romans' propensities for accepting bribes. But one of the tribunes placed his veto upon Jugurtha's opening his mouth. Jugurtha, however, did not waste his time in Rome: one of his troublesome relations who had sought refuge there was quietly murdered. Jugurtha was dispatched to Africa forthwith, the treaty was scrapped and the war continued.

After months of inconclusive Roman effort, another unfortunate consul returned from Africa to Rome to report failure. During his absence, however, Jugurtha forced a conclusive battle and captured the consul's brother and 40,000 Romans. Not unnaturally, a commission was now set up to investigate the prosecution of the war. Guilty men were found, all leading figures among the *optimates*; they were tried and condemned for having accepted bribes. Foremost among them was Opimius, the man who had condemned the followers of Gaius Gracchus. Like the rest he was exiled, never saw Rome again, and died, bankrupt, in a foreign land.

The war in Africa had become the dominant political factor in Rome, with salutary results. Q. Caecilius Metellus, a man of unquestioned probity, was elected consul to lead the army against Jugurtha. Characteristically, Metellus put military capacity before personal feeling and, although he cannot have felt much enthusiasm for Marius, he selected him as a member of his staff. Marius' behaviour, once he had got the job he wanted, also casts an interesting light on his character. According to Plutarch, he was not only surly to his commanding officer, but went out of his way to injure him. Yet Marius showed himself to be a first-class officer and one, moreover, who was prepared to accept the hardships of the rank and file. He shared their rations, slept rough, and even took a hand in trench-digging. This, as Plutarch shrewdly observed, was what appealed to the Roman soldier – as it would indeed to any other.

The African army's enthusiasm for Marius was soon reflected in Rome, and the conviction spread that he was the man to conquer Jugurtha. Marius was evidently informed of this trend, for he asked Metellus for leave to return to Rome to stand for the consular elections. Metellus, who was by now well aware of Marius' hostility, evidently believed this request to be in the nature of a bad joke, for the consulate had practically become the prerogative of members of a restricted group of families, and it did not seem that a man like Marius stood a chance. Rather bitterly, therefore, Metellus suggested that Marius should wait until Metellus' young son was of an age to stand for the consulate and that they might be elected together. However, Marius continued to press for leave and, finally, twelve days before the elections were due to be held, Metellus let him go. Riding furiously, Marius reached the coast in 48 hours, embarked at Utica, and in another four days was in Rome. This left him only six days for canvassing before the elections – six days for a man of provincial Volscian background to challenge candidates who were members of the most influential families in Rome – with all that meant within the system of client voters. But Marius' election campaign had already been won for him by the news that had reached Rome from Africa, and hard-headed Roman businessmen believed him when he promised that he would either 'kill Jugurtha or capture him alive'. Marius was triumphantly elected consul for the year 107.

Like Scipio Africanus before him, Marius set sail for Africa with a volunteer army, but, whereas Scipio's recruitment of volunteers had been the outcome of a political compromise, Marius' was the result of his own experience while on campaign. The old armies of citizen levies had served their turn admirably during the years of Rome's expansion in Italy. Since then their shortcomings

77 A soldier in the first century BC swearing the oath of allegiance.

78 Sulla triumphant, seated on a high throne with Jugurtha bound behind him and Bocchus kneeling to offer him an olive branch, on a coin issued in his name about 62 BC.

had become evident. The system was in fact out of date; in the much more advanced state of civilization in Rome and Italy in 107, men were not willing to serve, nor was it practical economics for the vast mass of the property-owning and working classes to be liable for military service and absent from their farms and work for years.

The army was Marius' natural calling, and he saw that more men were needed. But he realized, too, that the normal sources of recruitment were pretty well exhausted: he sought his new recruits among the landless poor, a class from which men were ready to volunteer, and having no land to return to, might be expected to serve for longer periods. The ultimate result was the creation of a regular professional standing army. But this introduced a new factor into the delicate balance of power upon which the Roman constitution rested. Like her military system, the Roman constitution had functioned admirably in the more limited circumstances of the past. But Rome was unique among the states which had achieved world power, in that she had no long-term head of state such as that provided by a hereditary or even an elective monarchy. This is well illustrated by the fact that her soldiers had to renew their *sacramentum*, or oath of allegiance, to each new commander, but the men who were called upon to do so were also, if one may phrase it so, part-time soldiers, and, like the consuls and praetors who led them, would return to private life. Once a permanent professional army was created, the *sacramentum* would be sworn, and the soldiers' loyalties directed, not to elected magistrates whose tenure of command was short, but to the successful professional general, who would thus enjoy a continuity of influence and power hitherto unknown in the Roman state.

With hindsight it is easy to see that the creation of Marius' volunteer army was a turning-point in the history of Rome, but equally easy to understand why in the circumstances Marius was given his head. To the man in the Forum, impatient of muddle at the front and smarting under Jugurtha's impudence in Rome, Marius' new model army held out a hope that at last something would be done – military failure and military necessity have a long history as one of the most revolutionary forces in the world. So Marius set to work to enrol his volunteers. Most of them came from the unemployed and the poorest classes: they might have seemed unpromising material, but poverty had made them tough and Marius' training was to make them tougher; they soon earned the popular nickname of 'Marius' mules'. The whole formation of the army was by degrees radically reformed. The maximum strength of each legion was 6,000 men, in which the cohort – a body of 600 men all armed with the *pilum* – was imposed upon the manipular system. It was Marius who introduced the eagle as the legionary standard – his was silver, in Imperial times they were gold. The eagle was also a religious symbol; in camp it was kept in a shrine and sacrifices were offered to it, in battle it was carried in the front rank of the legion. At all times the eagle was the special charge of the *primus pilus*, the highest ranking regimental officer of the legion.

Marius' quaestor was Lucius Cornelius Sulla, of whom, at the age of 32, all that the world knew was that he was a scion of an impoverished noble family, and that during the war with Pyrrhus one of its members had been fined and expelled from the Senate for owning more than 10 pounds of silver plate. Possibly Marius realized that there was more than met the eye in Sulla; in fact, there was a great deal more than even Marius perceived – to his own undoing. For if Marius reaped the rewards of Q. Caecilius Metellus' unspectacular generalship, and himself succeeded in depriving Jugurtha of the water-holes and supply bases in the desert, upon which Jugurtha's whole strategy was based, Sulla turned the tables on Marius. Although he accomplished it single-handed, it was as Marius' representative that Sulla negotiated the surrender of Jugurtha from his son-in-law, King Bocchus of Mauretania, and it was Sulla who was acclaimed by his conservative friends as the man who had succeeded in capturing Jugurtha and sending him prisoner to Rome.

Marius might now have disappeared from history, but for circumstances more forceful than any political party in Rome. In traditional Roman style – which was not to survive much longer – one of the new consuls, Q. Servilius Caepio, was dispatched to Transalpine Gaul to fight the Cimbri, whose erratic wanderings had now brought them there. At Orange 80,000 Romans perished in one of the most overwhelming defeats Rome had ever known. From then on, the Cimbri became in Roman minds a menace in which the horrific tales of the Gauls and Hannibal were intertwined. The Roman people believed that there could be only one saviour from this terrible threat and that was Marius. Thus he was again elected consul in 104, contrary to law and precedent, even in his absence. This time the Cimbri had done his electioneering for him.

Two other circumstances played into Marius' hands. Instead of attacking Italy, the Cimbri made off to Spain, thus giving Marius a chance to continue his army's rigorous training, and in Sicily there was another slave revolt, which brought control of the whole island into the insurgents' hands. In 103 Marius

79 Head of a barbarian warrior, possibly a Cimbrian, of the first century BC. Note his moustache, a fashion unknown in Rome.

80 The Temple of Fortuna Virilis in Rome, of about 100 B C, is a classic example of the Roman temple form as distinct from the Greek: it stands on a high podium, and has half-columns attached to a solid wall behind the portico, rather than an encircling colonnade.

81 The first-century B C 'Temple of Vesta', set above the gorge at Tivoli. It is also often called the 'Temple of the Sibyl'.

was elected consul for the third time, and not a moment too soon, for the Cimbri and the Teutons had returned to Transalpine Gaul, evidently with the intention of attacking Italy. Marius crossed into Gaul and in 102 defeated the Teutons at Aix-en-Provence. His fellow consul, Q. Lutatius Catulus, had, however, been forced back from the passes in the eastern Alps by the Cimbri, who had crossed Europe returning to the region of Noreia. Catulus was not even able to hold the line of the Adige. Marius was now elected consul for the fifth time – the first man in the history of Rome ever to have held the office over a period of years. His colleague, M. Aquillius, was left to deal, successfully, with the slave war in Sicily.

It was August in the year 101 before Marius was ready to meet with the Cimbri. Catulus' men had been stiffened by months of rigorous training and the army had been equipped with a new type of *pilum*, or javelin. These new javelins created havoc among the Cimbri, but Marius' greatest ally on the battlefield of Vercelli was the torrid summer heat to which the Cimbri were unaccustomed. The result was a decisive Roman victory.

In the autumn Marius returned to Rome and became consul for the sixth time. The election took place on the crest of the wave of enthusiasm and relief that followed the defeat of the Cimbri. But, vanity apart, Marius needed office in order to fulfil his promise to his troops, both Roman and allied, that upon their discharge they would be granted an allotment of land. That this represented the simple soldier's dream of security in retirement, was something that Marius no doubt could well understand. But his plans went awry; it may be that, as Plutarch argued, Marius himself had much less aptitude for civilian life and politics than for military operations. Even though the proposal was that the soldiers' allotments should not be from only provincial land, it aroused bitter opposition in the Senate. To counter this, the tribune L. Appuleius Saturninus, who steered the land distribution measure through the council of

the plebs, drafted a special oath which all Senators were to take to uphold the new law on pain of exile. Such an oath would, of course, involve a serious diminution of the *de facto* powers of the Senate. Inevitably a storm followed. Marius was so shaken or so muddled that, after taking the oath, he added the words 'in as far as the laws were really valid', thus nullifying it completely. This action not only alienated Marius from the coalition of *equites* and *populares* that had originally brought him to power, but split the coalition itself, for his leadership had been the unifying factor.

In the next elections Saturninus stood again as tribune, but Glaucia was the *populares*' consular candidate. As rioting broke out and Glaucia's rival was murdered, the Senate passed the emergency decree and it fell to Marius as consul to enforce it. He had no alternative but to proceed against Glaucia and Saturninus, who were arrested on the Capitol and imprisoned in the Curia, and there by unknown hands they were murdered. Though there was no question of Marius having been involved in the crime, it killed him politically as surely as the assassins had killed his erstwhile supporters. After seven years, during which he had enjoyed power, popularity and glory such as no Roman had known before, this would have been hard for any man to stomach, but particularly so for Gaius Marius, whose vanity was such that, as Plutarch said, 'He disliked anyone who outshone him.' In the year 100 Marius left Rome and, like many disappointed men in any age, took to foreign travel. His journey was not entirely aimed at distraction: King Mithridates of Pontus was stirring up trouble and, like an old warhorse scenting the fray, Marius set out for Asia Minor. But the days of *his* conquests were over.

During the first decade of the century, both rich and cultivated Romans, and those of the rising middle class, were able to indulge their varied tastes and enjoy themselves with gusto. Two surviving buildings afford us some idea of the architectural setting of this period of transition. The first, still a familiar land⁄

mark in Rome today, is the elegant little building standing by the Tiber, that goes by the name of the Temple of Fortuna Virilis. The true dedication is unknown, though Portunus, the Roman equivalent of the Greek god of harbours, Palaemon, seems appropriate to the site and style. For the last provides an object-lesson in the adaptation of the Greek peripteral temple to suit Roman taste and usage: an Ionic portico rises from a characteristically high Roman podium, while the semi-columns on the walls simulate the enveloping porticoes of this type of Greek temple.

Even more evocative of Roman life of the period is the Casa dei Grifi on the Palatine. Here stands, practically complete, a rich man's house in what was then the most fashionable quarter of Rome – the kind of house in which the chief protagonists of the dramatic first century B C were born and lived. The main impression is one of sober elegance and richness, the rooms have vaulted ceilings and fine tessellated floors patterned in geometric designs in black and white. In one room the delicate stucco decoration strikes a lighter note, and the motif of affronted griffins gives the house its name. Wall-paintings in another room illustrate the transition between an early form of decoration of this type and a later one, known as the First and Second Pompeian styles. Evidently the house's owner and the artist shared a taste that was *avant-garde* in their day, for the painted panels of rich marbles, typical of the earlier style, are framed by a *trompe l'œil* composition of painted pedestals and columns 'supporting' a trabeation, thus affording the illusion of adding space to the room.

If surviving architecture of this period illustrates the taste of discriminating patrons, what we know of other arts reflects a very different trend, for both in writing and in drama the influence of popular demand was beginning to make itself felt. Rather surprisingly, it was in the field of historical writing that the change first became evident. Stemming perhaps from the popularity of histori- cal plays in the days following Hannibal's war, and certainly influenced by dramatic current events, the Gracchan period had produced in Cn. Gellius a historical writer who achieved wide success. He livened up the old legends and added equally colourful tales of the exploits of famous men. Although he was no stickler about sources, it is presumed that part at least of Gellius' material was culled from traditions handed down orally from one generation to another in historic Roman families. Gellius had many followers, the most successful of all being Valerius Antias whose romanticized history of Rome seems to have stimulated the vogue for popular autobiographies, written by some quite surprising authors: Marius for one, also aristocrats such as M. Aemilius Scaurus, Q. Lutatius Catulus and even L. Cornelius Sulla.

This was not Sulla's first literary composition. All his life he had entertained a passion for the theatre, and like many fashionable young men of his day he had tried his hand at writing Atellan farces. He may have been encouraged to do so by his friend Q. Roscius Gallus – the most famous actor and most handsome man in Rome, who nevertheless introduced the fashion for actors to wear masks, in order to conceal his slight squint. Masks were a characteristic feature of the rumbustious folk-plays that had come to Rome from the small Campanian town of Atella long before. This was because the *dramatis personae* always consisted of stock characters, such as Maccus the glutton and the plump- faced Bucco – immortal characters who lived on in the *Commedia dell'Arte* as Pulcinella and Arlecchino and still survive as Punch and Harlequin. By the

82, 83 *Left* One of the delicate stucco griffins in the Casa dei Grifi in Rome. *Below* The atrium of a Roman house at Herculaneum, with a central pool, a covered upper gallery enclosed by a delicate stucco parapet, and the remains of architectural frescoes on its entrance wall.

84–86 Sulla's striking features may be seen in this marble bust. He surprised his contemporaries by associating with actors, including the famous Roscius, and by writing plays himself. Decorative mosaics found at Pompeii, *opposite*, show a traditional mask like those advocated by Roscius, and strolling musicians in a street.

time Sulla was a young man, the *Atellanae*, as they were called, had become short witty pieces given as comic relief after tragedies. Extempore additions had always been part of the fun and these now often included cracks about the political situation and it is easy to see how pieces of this kind appealed to amateur gentlemen dramatists and actors.

Not all comedies of folk origin were as respectable as the *Atellanae*. The mimed plays – the only ones in which actresses appeared – later became a byword, and few actors had the standing of Roscius, who was once described as 'a man fit to be a Senator'. In general, actors were treated in Rome not as second-rate citizens but hardly as citizens at all – they were subject to many legal disabilities. The fact that, although he was a highly educated man, throughout his life Sulla consorted with them, was evidently regarded as damaging to his character. Another factor that singled Sulla out was his unusual appearance. His square head and thick thatch of fair hair were strange enough, but to this was added what Plutarch describes as 'the terribly sharp and dominating glare of his blue eyes was made still more dreadful by the complexion of his face in which the pale skin was covered with angry blotches of red.' Not an attractive portrait, but Sulla evidently had charm, especially for women. His stepmother left him her fortune because she loved him as if he were her own child; he had four wives, and his amatory successes were notorious, even as a poor young man.

Evidently in his own day, as by most historians since, Sulla was regarded as an enigma. Nevertheless, he seems to have belonged to a type recurrent through history. There have been other clever, daring and ruthless men who disguised their abilities and ambitions under a nonchalant manner. Some of these Sullan characteristics appeared in the medieval Emperor Frederick II of Hohenstaufen, in Cosimo I Grand Duke of Tuscany and in Talleyrand.

Nothing much had been heard of Sulla until, by his daring and diplomacy, he had persuaded the wily and vacillating King Bocchus to surrender Jugurtha. He was evidently too deep for Marius, but someone in the Senate had recognized his capacities. Nevertheless, Sulla was made by the warlike tenor of the times in which he lived. It was the fortunes of war that prevented Sulla from ending as an embittered libertine, cynically making the best of such pleasures as the theatres and boudoirs of Rome had to offer.

Not for the first time, it was a tribune's legislative programme that set in motion the events which led to war. The tribune was Marcus Livius Drusus, the very different son of the Drusus who had been the Senate's catspaw in their dealings with Gaius Gracchus. This Drusus came upon the scene when the uneasy alliance between the Senate and the *equites* was breaking up. The chief cause was the Senate's recognition of the fact that it must regain control of the extortion courts, for if not, its control of the provinces would be severely hampered.

In his programme, Drusus aimed at three things: to strengthen the Senate, to remove the extortion courts from the *equites*, and to extend full franchise to all Italians. To gain popular support for his project, he resuscitated his father's scheme for creating more Roman colonies; to appease the *equites* he planned to include 300 of their order in the Senate, thus doubling its size. Drusus' legislation was passed by the council of the plebs, but a conservative majority of Senators – hostile as always to any dilution of the Roman ethos – succeeded

87 Mithridates VI, 'the Great', of Pontus, portrayed on one of his coins.

in getting it dismissed by the Senate on a technicality. Drusus was murdered and in 91 BC, exasperated and enraged, the Italians revolted against Rome. The ensuing bitter warfare rapidly brought even the most conservative Romans to their senses, and a law was passed which offered the franchise to all Italians south of the Po. Once the cause of the revolt was removed, the Social War came to an end in 89. Sulla had done well in the war. He had had the toughest job, but he had succeeded in winning over the dour Marsi mountaineers and in conquering the Samnites, who had been the leaders of the revolt. The able but unpopular Gnaeus Pompeius Strabo had also done well, and it was under his command that his handsome 18-year-old son, the Pompey of the future, gained his first military experience.

Political rivalry apart, the end of the Social War did not mean peace for Rome. In the same year King Mithridates of Pontus massacred all the Italians in Asia and some of the Greeks joined him. As the *optimates'* candidate, Sulla was elected consul for 88 and allotted the province of Asia as his command. It did not promise to be an easy one, but if he succeeded he would establish himself. And the party which supported him would enjoy influence such as it had not wielded for a long time. The *optimates* were, however, still obsessed with the idea of treating the Italians as second-class citizens and limiting their voting power. To do this they tried to get all of them inscribed on the electoral roll of a small number of tribes. This was opposed by the tribune P. Sulpicius Rufus, who advocated their being fairly distributed among all the tribes. With the support of the *equites*, Sulpicius also tried to get Sulla's appointment in Asia rescinded and Marius nominated in his stead; in addition, he put forward legislation that would have clipped the Senate's wings. Sulla acted promptly. He declared a religious objection to the meeting to vote upon Sulpicius' legislation, but the crowd rushed the platform upon which he was standing and Sulla was hustled into Marius' house, which was near the Forum. Sulla was forced to withdraw his objection, but he was then set free. He left Rome immediately and went to his army's camp in Campania – the same army that Sulpicius proposed to hand over to Marius. There was now no doubt about the issue – it was Sulla or Marius, one of them had to go. Sulla marched on Rome and seized the city, Sulpicius was murdered and Marius declared an exile.

According to Plutarch, the force that Sulla had at his disposal was six legions – some 36,000 men – an insignificant army with which to attack Rome, whose population at this time has been reckoned at about 400,000. That Sulla was able to do so successfully indicates the surprise which he achieved. Rumours and the knowledge of his advance towards Rome notwithstanding, no one could really believe that a Roman army would attack the city. In all her seven centuries of history, in spite of rivalries and upheavals, such a thing was unheard of. Many of Sulla's own officers were horror-struck, but the rank and file obeyed his orders. For this was no longer a citizen army but a professional one, the type of army that had emerged from Marius' activities, with its own *esprit de corps* and the not altogether disinterested allegiance that bound each individual soldier to his commander. True, Sulla was a consul – that his consular dignity had been insulted and violent hands laid on him during the exercise of his office provided at least a pretext for what he did, but the day was not far off when a popular general would have no need for the sanction of consular office for taking action.

Marius, who had unwittingly forged the instrument of his own undoing, now fled from Rome. He took ship from Ostia, intending to go to Africa, but the ship ran into a storm. Marius was rising seventy, yet his subsequent adventures have become a legend. They included a night spent hiding naked in a swamp at the mouth of the Liris, and his capture – still naked except for mud – by the authorities of Minturno, who saw no alternative but to kill him, but could find no one to do it. Finally a slave, who had been a Cimbrian knight, agreed to do the deed. But when he entered the dark room in which Marius was lying, all he could see was a glittering pair of eyes, and a terrible voice roared at him, 'Man! Do you dare to kill Gaius Marius?' The Cimbrian dropped his sword and fled. The Minturnians decided to let the indestructible Marius go. Eventually he found a ship and got to Africa, landing at Carthage. The Roman governor sent an officer to tell him to leave because he was under sentence of exile. This wrung a cry of anguish from Marius that, like the Psalmist's by the waters of Babylon, has echoed down the centuries: 'Tell him that you have seen Gaius Marius sitting as a fugitive among the ruins of Carthage.'

In Rome, Sulla was faced with a crisis in which the wrong decision could reduce him to a fate worse than that of Marius. For the moment he held Rome, but Mithridates now held all of Asia Minor and had three powerful armies in Greece: he could become another Hannibal. The capacity for swift decision was one of Sulla's strong points. He presided over the elections in which Gnaeus Octavius and Lucius Cornelius Cinna became consuls, and left to tackle Mithridates. It was a gamble, but a calculated one, for chances were that the conqueror of Mithridates would also hold the key to Rome.

The Rome that Sulla left behind was in a state of disarray. Cinna and Octavius quarrelled, there was more wrangling about the distribution of the Italian voters among the Roman tribes, the Social War had left a trial of destruction and misery behind, and trade with the eastern Mediterranean was at a standstill. Cinna sought and found support from the *equites*, who knew full well

88 A relief celebrating one of Sulla's victories. Winged Victories flank the Roman eagle, clutching a thunderbolt in its talons and a palm in its beak.

that they would get little from Sulla if he returned. However, Cinna fell foul of the Senate by adopting Sulpicius' policy for the distribution of the Italian voters and had to flee from Rome to Capua, where the garrison supported him. In his absence the Senate revoked his office and appointed L. Cornelius Merula in his place. When news of these extraordinary happenings reached Marius in Africa, he returned to Italy and sent Cinna a message acknowledging him as consul. Cinna received Marius with all honour, offering him the title of proconsul. But Marius put aside the *fasces* and stood glowering in shabby clothes with hair unkempt, having refused to cut it since he had left Rome nearly two years before. At this point Marius' thirst for revenge was evidently all he lived for, but something of his military capacity remained: he seized the port of Ostia, thus blockading Rome from the sea.

Rome surrendered, but Cinna demanded their acknowledgment that he was the rightful consul, and Marius would not enter the city until his sentence of exile was revoked. After them the gates were shut and savage reprisals began. Even before this, Octavius had been murdered on his own tribunal in the Forum by supporters of Cinna and Marius, but now Lucius and Gaius Julius Caesar and Marcus Antonius the orator (grandfather of Mark Antony) were killed. Cornelius Merula and Lutatius Catulus, who had shared Marius' triumph over the Cimbri, were forced to commit suicide. Marius had a body-guard of 4,000 slaves, known as the Bardyaeans, who acted as executioners, killing the victims he selected. Marius was now elected consul for the seventh time. His mind had perhaps been affected by his reversal of fortune and his experiences on his way to Africa, but now even his incredible physique gave way. He could not sleep and was drinking heavily. On 13 January 86 he died of pleurisy.

L. Valerius Flaccus became consul in Marius' stead. This was really only a matter of form; for the next three years Cinna continued as consul, nominating his fellow in office without any pretence of elections. In such circumstances a man of mettle and ability could have gained such a hold on Rome and Italy that it would have been impossible to dislodge him, but Cinna took only one positive action. He sent L. Valerius Flaccus east with Fimbria as his lieu-tenant to see what Sulla was doing.

With little at his disposal, Sulla had forged ahead. He had financed himself and paid his army by seizing the treasures of the Greek temples, besieged and taken Athens, and also defeated Mithridates' two other armies in Greece. After landing in Greece and meeting Sulla, Flaccus and Fimbria crossed the Dardanelles and, following his commander's death, Fimbria defeated Mithri-dates, laid siege to Pergamum and nearly captured the king. Mithridates' action now gave Sulla good grounds to consider himself fortunate. He offered to make peace with Sulla, thus recognizing him as the legitimate representa-tive of Rome, a fact which did not escape the eyes of the world. The treaty completed, Sulla crossed to Asia and spent the winter there. His was so clearly the rising star that Fimbria's army deserted to him and Fimbria committed suicide. Sulla called the representatives of the Asian cities to a conference at Ephesus, and, as a punishment for having sided with Mithridates, fined them 20,000 talents to be paid at once. With his exchequer thus replenished, Sulla returned to Greece and passed an interesting and enjoyable time there, being initiated into the Eleusinian mysteries, taking the waters at Aedepsus and

89, 90 Sulla's conquest of Greece was reflected in Athen-ian coinage, *top*, where the owl of Athene is flanked by Roman legionary standards. His Roman triumphs were cele-brated by the issue in 82–81 BC of a gold *aureus* showing him driving a four-horse chariot.

amusing himself with theatrical friends. He also took possession of the famous library of Apellicon, which included the manuscripts of Aristotle and Theophrastus.

Early in 83 Sulla arrived at Durazzo. In preparation for his return he had written a conciliatory letter to the Senate, but Cinna and his fellow consul would pay no attention to the Senate's attempts at mediation. They were making preparations to fight, when Cinna was murdered by his own troops. Sulla encountered no resistance when he landed at Brindisi and he was soon joined by such outstanding men as Metellus Pius, Marcus Licinius Crassus and the young, handsome and already popular Gnaeus Pompeius, Pompey. With the support of such capable soldiers, Sulla met with little serious resistance until he reached Praeneste, which was held by Marius' son. However, seeing that Praeneste could not hold out, a Samnite army which had sided with the *populares* attempted to take Rome. They were held at bay by a scratch army of citizens until Sulla arrived and, after an all-night battle by the Colline Gate, beat them. By the end of 82 Sulla was in possession of Rome.

What followed has made Sulla's name a byword for cruelty. There were no mitigating circumstances as in the case of the ageing Marius, half-crazed with ideas of revenge. But it must also be borne in mind that Sulla returned to find Italy in a state almost comparable with that following Hannibal's war, and Rome in a situation that had no precedent. The whole machinery of government had broken down and the cherished constitution – once the pride of Rome – was shattered. No consuls existed and the condition of the Senate can be gauged from the fact that Sulla had to remind its members that an *interrex**

---

* Ancient Roman custom laid down that if both consuls were dead 'the auspices returned to the *patres*', in other words the *imperium* was automatically vested in the Senate and each Senator in turn held the *interregnum* for five days. The man who presided at the following election was the *interrex*.

92 A relief of the mid-first century BC thought to show the census. At the left, an official writes on tablets; at the right stand two legionaries.

should be appointed to preside over the elections. The Senate hastened to appoint L. Valerius Flaccus. Thus far Sulla had adhered strictly to republican tradition. Even his next step in suggesting that a dictator be appointed, was unconstitutional only in that he was to be appointed by the *interrex* and not a consul. But where Sulla overstepped the bounds was in his proposal that his dictatorship should not be restricted to the customary six months. In the event, not only was he unconstitutionally appointed 'dictator for the revision of the constitution' for an unlimited period, but he was indemnified by law against any of his acts – past or future. No Oriental despot could have asked for more. Invested with such powers, most men, including Romans, would have clung to them for life, and in other nations have sought to found a dynasty. The way Sulla used his powers shows him not only to have been essentially Roman, but singles him out as an even stranger dictator than he was a man.

Even allowing for his power of swift decision, the speed with which he now accomplished his designs argues that all but the details had been thought out in advance. The first step was the ruthless elimination of his political enemies and anyone who might frustrate his plans. Even Sulla's supporters seem to have been appalled at what he proposed to do and, probably to exculpate themselves, insisted that the names should be put down on paper. Sulla did so without hesitation, and lists with the names of 40 Senators and 1,600 *equites* were posted in the Forum. The property of those proscribed was confiscated and sold by auction, and their children and grandchildren were deprived of Roman citizenship. Some 3,000 Samnites were also slaughtered. To the horror of this mass murder was added the disgusting spectacle of Sulla and his supporters making financial capital out of the blood-bath, by buying up the victims' property at bargain prices. This was not Sulla's first venture of the kind. When Marius had been exiled, Sulla had bought his luxurious villa at Misenum, the same that had belonged to Cornelia, for 75,000 sesterces. Later it was sold to L. Licinius Lucullus for 2,500,000. But even Sulla was shocked at the avarice displayed by M. Licinius Crassus, who at this time laid the foundation of his colossal fortune. According to Plutarch, so flagrant was the cupidity of the Sullan party, that, with savage Roman humour, men said, 'So-and-so was killed by his big mansion, so-and-so by his gardens, so-and-so by his hot water installations.'

About this time Sulla had a brush with a young man of 20, whose name was Gaius Julius Caesar; his aunt Julia was Marius' widow and his wife Cornelia, Cinna's daughter. Sulla suggested that he should divorce her and marry someone more politically acceptable. Caesar refused, and so did not become, like Pompey and Lucullus, one of the dictator's promising young men. Instead he went abroad.

Sulla now put forward his legislative programme for the reform of the constitution, its two basic aims being a return to Senatorial government and the emasculation of the tribunate. This shows clearly that Sulla had no intention of retaining personal power, but it also reveals an almost romantic belief – in a man who otherwise seems to have been so cynical and worldly – that by putting the clock back a new Senate could be created in the image of the old. Inevitably the Senate again gained control of the juries in the extortion courts. But Sulla also enlarged the size of the Senate and broadened the base of recruitment to it by abolishing the office of Censor and making membership of it automatic for the twenty quaestors now to be elected annually. No one who had been a tribune could now, however, aspire to the Senate, as he was debarred from holding any other office. This, and the fact that tribunes could no longer introduce legislation without the Senate's previous assent and the practical limitation of their powers to the ancient function of intervening to save a plebeian's life, ensured that few ambitious young men would wish to stand for the office. Other points in Sulla's legislation were eminently sensible. He saw to it that the Italian voters were fairly distributed among the 35 Roman tribes, and he created a number of new permanent criminal courts. Veterans from his armies received their reward, being settled in colonies mostly on land expropriated where Sulla's forces had encountered resistance, for example at Praeneste.

It was at Praeneste that Sulla set up the chief monument to his victory, the Temple of Fortuna. This was a vast composition of terraces, stairs and ramps, covering the hillside and rising to a spectacular climax in the semi-circular sanctuary that still exists embedded in the Palazzo Barberini. Although scholarly argument continues as to how much of the Temple of Fortuna was built by Sulla, the sanctuary is definitely attributed to him, as well as the extension and rearrangement of the monumental approach. The whole layout has been described as 'a turning-point in Roman architecture and perhaps the most seminal complex in the whole Roman world'* – certainly its influence made itself felt in Rome for centuries, notably in the Renaissance Cortile del Belvedere and in the Victor Emanuele monument of 1885.

* P. MacKendrick, *The Mute Stones Speak*, New York 1960.

The temple of Praeneste is important because from it we can gain an idea of what Sulla achieved and what he evidently hoped to do in Rome. From literary sources and the few of his buildings that survive, it seems that he intended to introduce something of this monumental character and symmetry into the Comitium and the Forum. Among other things, he rebuilt the Curia, the Graecostasis and the *rostra*, and restored the Regia and the House of the Vestals. However, the only one of Sulla's Roman buildings to have survived even in part, and it was completed after his death, is the Tabularium, or Public Records Office. This impressive building, of which the porticoed substructure is still visible, was constructed to fill the hollow between the two crests of the Capitoline hill, thus giving it architectural unity and serving as a backdrop, as it were, to the view of the Capitol from the Forum.

No trace now remains of what Sulla would certainly have regarded as his major work – the rebuilding of the Capitoline Temple of Jupiter, which was burnt down in 83 BC. Religious prejudice forbade any alteration to the size and shape of the building, and the slightly higher new temple was erected on the old podium of 509 BC. Traditional features, such as the hole in the roof above the altar of Terminus, were repeated, and the only change permitted was the use of luxurious decoration and materials: marble for the floor, gilding for the ceiling and pentelic marble Corinthian columns, for which, according to Pliny, Sulla despoiled the Temple of Zeus Olympius in Athens.

93, 94 The grandeur of Sulla's architectural vision appears in the Temple of Fortuna at Palestrina (Praeneste): *opposite*, a reconstruction. His only surviving work in Rome is the arched substructure of the Tabularium, *left*.

Sulla, now officially L. Cornelius Sulla Felix, or Sulla the Fortunate, did not live to see his Capitoline temple completed. After two years of absolute power, he resigned the dictatorship in 79 at the age of 59.

The consular elections now took place in the normal way and Sulla settled down to enjoy himself with his theatrical friends, as before. He even married again. His fourth wife was a pretty young woman, Valeria, the sister of the orator Hortensius, whom Sulla met at a gladiatorial show. She bore him a posthumous child. In 78 he died. On the monument in the Campus Martius, which contained his ashes, was an epitaph composed, probably with relish, by Sulla himself. In effect it stated that he had not been surpassed by any of his friends in doing good or by any of his enemies in doing harm.

Sulla's career was short and his attempt to put the clock back failed. All he tried to do for the Roman state was undone within ten years. But his dictatorship presages the shape of things to come: notably in building and the architectural style, in the dedication of the annual games (Ludi Victoriae Sullae), in which the glorification of a man usurped a privilege hitherto afforded only to the gods, and above all in Sulla's march on Rome, which showed that from now on armies owed their loyalty as much to themselves as to the man who commanded them and only to him because he could repay that loyalty. This was to be a basic fact of life in Rome to the end.

8

Rome and the war-lords continued – Pompey and Caesar

95 Marble portrait head of Pompey the Great, about 50 B C.

Plutarch's vignette of a woman called Praecia casts a revealing light on life in Rome during the years immediately following upon Sulla's death. He says Praecia was witty and beautiful but in other respects 'no better than a common prostitute' and the inference is that at other periods in Roman history, such she would have remained. But in the seventies B C Praecia was a power to be reckoned with in Rome. She used her contacts cleverly to further her friends' interests and had such a hold over her lover, the despicable turncoat and political intriguer Cornelius Cethegus, that it was said of this unattractive pair, 'No public decision was taken unless Cethegus backed it, and Cethegus took his orders from Praecia.' Even Lucullus – to whom Sulla had dedicated his memoirs and given the guardianship of his son – had, when he was elected consul in 74 B C, to win Praecia over 'by gifts and flatteries' in order to get Cilicia as his province instead of Cisalpine Gaul, and with it command of the army against Mithridates.

Both Lucullus and the Senate had good reason to wish for his success as a counterweight to the rising power of Pompey. That popular young man's remarkable military ability had provided all too striking a contrast to Senatorial ineptitude. The oligarchs must have cursed the luck that brought Pompey home from a successful campaign in Spain just in time to snatch further laurels by mopping up the last, but still frightening remnants, of the ex-gladiator Spartacus' army of escaped gladiators and slaves, which had paralysed Italy for two years. It was even more irritating because Marcus Licinius Crassus had already done all the hard work: Spartacus was dead and the main body of the insurgents defeated. And to cap it all, at the end of 71 B C, although debarred by age and station – he was only 36 and a simple *eques* – Pompey proceeded to celebrate his second triumph.

Such meteoric success has never endeared a man to those who have no prospect of sharing it. Thus, although Pompey had been one of Sulla's lieutenants and a supporter of the oligarchy, the *optimates* regarded him with suspicion. Pompey himself had evidently noted a certain coolness among them and was shrewd enough to realize that not even he could afford to ignore it altogether. In their present frame of mind the *optimates* were unlikely to temper their traditionally rigid attitude to land distribution, and Pompey's hold over his army, their votes, and in fact his own future, depended upon his capacity to ensure that his veterans received the land allotments he had promised them.

At this juncture apparently not a single *optimate* had the wit to see which way the tide would turn. Perhaps they counted upon the fact that Pompey had never held magisterial office of any kind, in spite of his two proconsular commands, and, according to the rules, election as praetor was the most he could hope for at the age of 36. But the rules were not made for men of Pompey's stamp, even less for the age that bred them. He now made a deal with the *populares*, and was elected consul for 70 B C with Marcus Licinius Crassus, the great financier and friend of the *equites*, as his partner. No two men could have been more different, and in the past this had led to animosity between them. Ironically, these two, who were now committed to a programme of reform which would obliterate all trace of Sulla's constitution, both owed their initial success in life to him. In times gone by such a situation would have been unthinkable, but sentimentality about old loyalties was as much a thing of the past in Rome in the first century B C as antiquated ideas about political principles, good government, or improving the lot of the common man. Power was the thing that counted in this century of the war-lords, and the thirst for power can make bedfellows as strange as poverty ever did.

Although his father, Pompeius Strabo, had been one of the most hated men in Rome, we hear from the first of Pompey's charm and popularity and his extraordinary good looks: it is said that he owed his nickname Magnus – the Great – to his resemblance to Alexander. Nevertheless, judging from his portraits, Pompey's features appear to have been irregular for a Roman, and it seems likely that his remarkable personal attraction lay more in his expression, the magnetism of his eyes and the way his hair swept up from a fine forehead, 'in a kind of wave', as Plutarch describes it. Given the Roman horror of baldness and grey hair, this aspect of Pompey's appearance would have greatly added to his manly beauty in Roman eyes. Plutarch also describes his manner, when young, as being distinguished by a gentle dignity. Even so, as a very young man Pompey could display keen intelligence, courage and charm. That the capacity to charm is not always associated with steadfast qualities was evident when Pompey agreed to divorce his first wife in order to please Sulla, which Caesar had refused to do. The situation was even less attractive in Pompey's case because he was to marry the dictator's stepdaughter, Aemilia, who was already pregnant by her first husband. That Aemilia died in childbirth shortly after their marriage does not, however, reflect on Pompey, but rather upon the distressing frequency of deaths in such circumstances in Rome. Pompey's attraction for women and his partiality to them is well attested; moreover, Roman ladies were by now inured to frequent divorce and remarriage in the interests of their family.

Pompey himself married five times. He divorced two of his wives and lost two in childbirth, and three of them at least were married more than once. Although marriage in this sophisticated governing Roman circle was usually a political or financial arrangement, love was not necessarily excluded. There could be no better proof of this than Pompey's own adoration, when he was over fifty, of his young wife Julia, whom he had married to cement his political ties with her father Caesar.

As for Crassus, all we read about him reveals a very astute man indeed. Although he evidently had little natural charm, and was jealous of those who possessed it – especially Pompey – Crassus obviously went to considerable pains to cultivate the indispensable *blanditia*. According to Plutarch he was adept at flattery, easy of access and had evidently mastered that peculiarly Roman art of being able to return a greeting at any casual encounter, gracefully calling the man by name no matter what his station. In his entertaining, Crassus preserved the same democratic tone, and 'the people he invited to

96 A coin of Pompey, of 46–45 B C, shows him greeted by Spain as he disembarks.

97 The end of a banquet in a well-to-do Pompeian house. Two guests are leaving, and are wearing their dark outer cloaks. One of them, on the left, is having his shoes put on by a child slave, while another slave offers him a final cup of wine; the other guest, on the right, looks as if he may have to be carried home.

dinner were usually ordinary people and not members of the great families'. But reading between the lines, we can see that this was all simply a means to an end. Nevertheless, that end was usually successfully accomplished: Plutarch's description of Crassus was that 'he was strong because he was popular and because he was feared – particularly because he was feared.'

The fear was, of course, the outcome of the power of money, but money alone would not have inspired it. It takes more than mere avarice to make a millionaire at any period, and Crassus undoubtedly possessed an extraordinary business sense and power of organization. It also seems that he knew how to use his money to gain power, but was never ostentatious about it. In fact, in a totally different way from Pompey, Crassus was also a product of the age in which they lived. In the old days, when simplicity and thrift had been rated high as Roman virtues, Crassus could never have wielded the power he did. But during the previous century the Romans' respect for gentlemanly sobriety with regard to wealth had been transformed into a passion for show and osten-tation. And as a result, especially in such troubled times, practically every man of note in Rome was heavily in debt, and many of them to Crassus. In the circumstances it is not surprising that the stories of this multimillionaire's meanness are legion – it was the one way that witty, but impoverished, young men about the Forum had of getting their own back on him.

Such then, were Pompey and Crassus, the ill-assorted pair who were called upon to patch up their differences and push through the legislation which would undo all that their joint benefactor, Sulla, had enacted. The first step – that of completing the revival of the tribunes' full powers – went through successfully, but there remained the more thorny problem of the reversion of the juries of the extortion courts to the *equites*. Circumstances, however, played into the hands of the consuls and the popular faction. Gaius Licinius Verres, ex-Governor of Sicily, came up for trial on charges of extortion and other malpractices. The counsel for the prosecution was a comparatively unknown man who had been quaestor in Sicily, Marcus Tullius Cicero. After scandalous revelations of corruption and the consequent collapse of the defence, Verres retired into voluntary exile and Cicero's name was made. The upshot was the passage of *lex Aurelia*, which deprived the Senate of its control of the juries in the extortion courts: in future jurors were to be empanelled from among the *equites* and the *tribuni aerarii* (whose interests were close to those of the equestrian classes) as well as Senators; thus these last would be in a minority.

In 70 B C, Gaius Julius Caesar was elected among the twenty quaestors for the coming year. During the twelve years since he had first left Sulla's Rome, Caesar had travelled as far as Bithynia and established friendly relations with the family of its king, Nicomedes IV Philopator. On his return to Rome, Caesar had taken the customary first step for anyone beginning a political career: prosecuting some well-known figure in the courts. Not surprisingly, Caesar lost his case, for the defending counsel included the famous orator Q. Hortensius. Continuing his preparation for political life, Caesar went to Rhodes to study oratory under Cicero's praeceptor, Apollonius Molon. During the voyage, he was captured and held to ransom by pirates – again a not unusual occurrence at this period. Caesar's reaction, however, singled him out, for after he was ransomed, he persuaded a unit of the coastal defence to help him catch the pirates, and, when the Roman Governor of Asia was dilatory about charging them, Caesar himself without any legal authority, had all the pirates crucified.

In Rome again, Caesar found that during his absence another step in his career had been taken for him. This was his election to the College of Pontiffs. Membership of such priestly colleges was one of the political assets that normally came the way of young men of good family. But, as in his case both he and his family had adhered to the old patrician rite of marriage by *confarreatio*, Caesar was qualified to aspire to those priesthoods in the state, for which this was one of the necessary qualifications. Except for his action over the pirates, Caesar's career before 70 B C had pursued the normal course for a young man of his age and station; and his election as quaestor and posting to Further Spain (roughly the part of the Iberian peninsula lying south-west of a line drawn from the Douro to Almeria) was in line with this. Fate, however, took a hand in Caesar's affairs before his departure to Spain. If his Aunt Julia had died a few months later, her remains would no doubt have received a respectful family tribute, but nothing more. With Caesar in Rome, her funeral – and her

nephew – acquired a notoriety not usually associated with the obsequies of an elderly widow. There had been previous but rare instances in which the remains of distinguished Roman ladies of advanced age had received honours almost equalling those of their masculine counterparts. Undeniably Julia's age and station as the widow of a national hero qualified her for such an honour, but Julia was the widow of Marius – a personage that tactful Romans had ostensibly forgotten.

Caesar's wife Cornelia also died before he left for Spain. He seized the occasion for making a funeral oration, which would also have had political undertones, as Cornelia was Cinna's daughter. Caesar's own daughter Julia, now fourteen years old, was left in the care of Aurelia, his remarkable mother, who had herself brought Caesar up. In fact Caesar's formative years had been spent in a family circle composed almost entirely of women, since he also had two sisters and his only close male relative was his cousin Sextus. At the time of Caesar's departure for Spain, both his sisters – Julias major and minor – had been married for years and had families of their own. Thus it may have been with the idea of providing his daughter with a younger companion that Caesar contracted to marry Pompeia on his return. For him the choice was a peculiar one; it brought no political advantage – rather the reverse – as Pompeia was Sulla's granddaughter.

The two questions uppermost in the minds of men in Rome in 69 B C were, for the politicians, Lucullus' conduct of the war in Asia and, for the populace as a whole, the rising price of wheat. The latter was due to the depredations of the pirates, who, as a result of the troubled times, had now come to regard the whole Mediterranean as their sphere of action and the peoples dwelling on its shores as potential slaves or – if a Roman patrician like Caesar – as a good source of ransom. The pirates were well organized, their tentacles reached into the highest places. Caesar's difficulty in getting the Roman authorities to take action against them would not have been an isolated case – Roman officials knew that the pirates' bribes were lavish. Interference with the Roman voters' wheat supply was, however, a very different matter. In 67, a tribune brought before the council of the plebs a proposal that Pompey should be given a

98, 99 The trappings of rank: the bronze seat of honour of a proconsul (first century BC), and the triumphal procession of a consul, the highest rank of all. On a platform, bound prisoners are carried with trophies of captured arms; behind them come musicians, and bulls for sacrifice (Marble relief from the Temple of Apollo, Rome; end first century BC).

special command of three years' duration to rid the Mediterranean of piracy. Pompey received his command and carried it to a successful conclusion in three months.

Such lightning success highlighted even further the difficulties which Lucullus was now encountering in Asia. After his initial victories against Mithridates, resulting in the peaceful settlement of Asia and its financial problems in 71–70, and his subsequent capture of Tigranocerta and the Armenian King's treasures – which made his own fortune – Lucullus' star had waned. Mithridates was now on the offensive, and Lucullus' failure to take Artaxata had given the *populares* their chance to attack him and his *optimate* supporters at home. In 67, Lucullus was replaced in his command by the consul of that year. In 66, Pompey was given the command, at the instance of a tribune. As usual, Pompey was spectacularly successful: within three years Mithridates was dead and the war ended. Acting on his own initiative, without the customary advice and sanction of a Senatorial commission, Pompey now made his own settlement in Asia. He proceeded to create two new Roman provinces – Syria and Bithynia-Pontus – and to extend Cilician territory. He also made agreements with local princes.

Caesar was already back in Rome in 67. He had his foot on the first rung of the ladder – as an ex-quaestor he was now a junior member of the Senate. As an ambitious young man, however, he would have fully realized that the hard part was to come. Twenty quaestors were elected each year, but only four aediles – two patrician, two plebeian – and ten tribunes. There were now eight praetors and, on terminating their year of office, they were qualified to become proconsular governors of provinces. The lucky ones got that far, but only the chosen few reached the top rung of all and became consuls, though this was naturally the goal to which every ambitious young man aspired.

Caesar was just one of the crowd of such young men who thronged the Forum, elbowing one another for a place in this *cursus honorum* – or career of honour – where competition was cut-throat. The rewards could, of course, include riches far exceeding those of modern plutocrats' dreams: Lucullus' name is still the synonym for luxury. Nevertheless, in Caesar's world riches

100 The final act in a gladiatorial combat: the fallen adversary offers his throat to the
victor, while heralds with long
trumpets proclaim the end.
Relief of the last first century B C.

were mainly a means to an end and not necessarily the end itself. In spite of his
arduous campaigns and conquests in the wilds of Armenia, Lucullus was
despised because upon his return to Rome he retired into private life and
devoted his time to the cultivation of the company of poets and philosophers –
and of course his famous gardens. Such a life was stigmatized in Rome as the
vita umbratilis – life in the shade. Shade is synonymous with ease and pleasure
in a Mediterranean country, because the burning summer sun beats down on
those who work and strive, but the sunlight also illuminates their attainments
and their glory – and glory was the Roman goal.

As an ex-quaestor the young careerist already had some experience of public
finance; as aedile he became responsible for certain aspects of city administration and minor police duties. The political importance of the office, however,
lay in the organization of the public games which, if judged successful,
brought him popularity with the voting public that could be decisive in the
praetorial elections. The one difficulty was that most of the vast sums required
to stage the games had to come out of the aediles' own pockets, which usually
meant that of the moneylenders or wealthy friends. Caesar was no exception

to this rule, but he was lucky in that his partner in office, M. Calpurnius Bibulus, was a rich man, who put up the lion's share – and Caesar got the credit. This did not improve relations between the two men, who were in any case diametrically opposed to one another in character as in politics. Bibulus was a sound conservative, and his young wife, Porcia, was the daughter of Marcus Porcius Cato the Younger – Cato the Censor's great-grandson. Nevertheless, Caesar did not get it all his own way. The shade of old Cato the Censor would have relished one of Bibulus' sardonic comments on the situation: he went round Rome saying, 'The Temple of the Heavenly Twins in the Forum is simply always called "Castor's"; and I always play Pollux to Caesar's Castor when we give public entertainments together.'

Still, Bibulus was no match for Caesar when it came to publicity – which, after all, was the political aim of the aedileship. It was Caesar who had the brilliant idea of lining the Comitium, the Forum, basilicas and even the Capitol itself with temporary wooden colonnades, in which the wild animals that were to feature in their games were exhibited. This and the games themselves evidently created such a stir that, when it became known that Caesar now intended to hold funeral games in memory of his father (who had died 20 years earlier), a law was hurriedly pushed through by his political opponents to limit the number of gladiators who might appear on such occasions. For funeral games were still the only occasions upon which gladiatorial combats might be held, although such displays already aroused passionate interest in the Roman crowds.

Restrictive legislation notwithstanding, Caesar staged the greatest *munera* yet seen in Rome. Three hundred and twenty pairs of gladiators fought in glittering silvered armour to dazzle the eyes of the Romans. What it cost Caesar is not known, but the sum would have been phenomenal.

Caesar had, however, still not quite exhausted the opportunities offered by his office. Before his year as aedile came to an end, he had replaced upon the Capitol the Trophies of Marius, which had been removed by Sulla. It would have rejoiced Caesar's heart could he have known that twelve centuries later, when the Marian trophies had vanished, like so many other monuments and memories of Rome's greatness, the fame of the conqueror of the Cimbri still lived. A whole quarter of the city was then called Cimbros (the popular medieval name for Marius) because the ruins of a Severan monument standing in it were believed to be the trophies of the immortal Marius. This was glory as the Romans of Caesar's generation understood it; it was part of their tradition that such glory was the ultimate aim of all their struggles to succeed, to achieve high office, victories and triumphs. It was for this that they lavished fortunes on building temples and monuments – so that their names should not only be famous in their lifetime but above all remembered by posterity. It was the only personal immortality that the majority ever dreamed of, and as heirs to a century and a half of almost uninterrupted conquest and material success, they sought no other. The serious minded – like M. Porcius Cato the Younger – might devote themselves to Stoic philosophy; others carried out functions of the priesthoods, more as a matter of patriotic duty and good manners, than out of religious conviction.

In the year following Caesar and Bibulus' aedileship, Marcus Porcius Cato the Younger was quaestor in Rome. Even his great-grandfather could not have

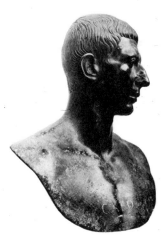

101 Cato the Younger; a bronze bust from Volubilis.

been more assiduous in trying to instil a proper regard for economy in the administration of public funds into the heads of the officials of the public treasury. On moral, as well as economic grounds, Cato made determined efforts to recover for the state the conspicuous sums paid out as prize-money to the men who had actually been responsible for the deaths of those named in Sulla's proscription lists.

In fact, their hatred of Sulla and all his works was the only subject upon which Cato and Caesar were ever to see eye to eye. Nevertheless, this did not prevent Caesar from giving his support – together with Crassus – to the candidature of L. Sergius Catiline (who had been one of Sulla's young men) in the consular elections for 63 B C. Catiline was unsuccessful because he did not get the support he had hoped for from the *optimates*; they gave it instead to the New Man, Marcus Tullius Cicero. It seems that the *optimates* had entertained doubts of Catiline's character and of the soundness of his views on property and finance. In this they were justified, for Catiline had all the recklessness of the ne'er-do-well aristocrat and had squandered the money he made out of Sulla's proscriptions. But the feelings of such a man when he saw Cicero – the provincial outsider – elected consul with the support of his own *optimate* peers, can well be imagined. The blow was all the more bitter because Catiline's hopes of standing for election the year before, had been dashed: he was debarred because of an action pending against him for extortion during his government of Africa.

At the end of 64 B C the prospect of Pompey's return was making itself felt in Rome. Already his friends – but even more his enemies – were making their dispositions. Crassus may have been behind a tribune's attempt to introduce a land bill which would have cut the ground from under Pompey's feet, by preventing the distribution of land to his veterans in the conquered countries, and interfered with his Asian settlement. However, the bill aroused the opposition of the landowning classes in Italy, and Cicero, as the *optimates'* protégé, brought all the power of his matchless eloquence to bear upon the *lex Servilia's* destruction, and succeeded.

In the midst of all this excitement another tribune's bill, that of Caesar's friend (and later companion in arms) T. Labienus, passed practically without comment. It did not seem to be spectacular in any way, for it simply rescinded the restrictive Sullan legislation on the procedure for the election of the Pontifex Maximus: in future, candidates were to be nominated by the College of Pontiffs, but the ultimate decision lay with the vote of 17 out of the 35 tribes. The office of Pontifex Maximus had been vacant since the autumn, and early in 63 three candidates were nominated. They were P. Servilius Vatia, Q. Lutatius Catulus – both ex-consuls and very distinguished men – and Caesar. In the circumstances Caesar's chances of election looked slim indeed. And according to a well-known story, when he left his house in the morning of the election, he kissed his mother goodbye and said, 'I shall return home Pontifex Maximus or not at all.'

The year 63 was in fact an eventful one in Caesar's life, from both the political and the domestic point of view. As soon as he was elected Pontifex Maximus, Caesar and his family moved from their house in the Suburra to the official pontifical residence which stood on the Sacred Way, between the Regia and the crest of the hill now crowned by the Arch of Titus. As the office of Pontifex Maximus was held for life, this now became Caesar's permanent home.

With the exception of the notorious incident that led to its dissolution, little is known of Caesar and Pompeia's married life. They had no children, but the allegations that Caesar was a homosexual seem to have been no more than the usual scurrilous Roman gossip. But equally, no one could have denied that, where women were concerned, Pompeia had grounds for complaint against her husband. Moreover, Roman gossip being what it was, it is likely that Pompeia was aware that at this time Caesar was involved in something more than a transient affair. This was his liaison with Servilia, the only woman who seems to have made a lasting impression on him. And the fact that Caesar was a libertine – the other women in his life included Cleopatra – provides some indication of Servilia's character and charm, for she does not appear to have been beautiful.

In 63, she was about 36 years old and one of the most brilliant and powerful women in Rome, and might well be described as the originator of the political *salon*. At this time Servilia was married to her second husband, D. Junius Silanus, who was to be consul in the following year. Thus the interest of her relationship with Caesar is not confined to the purely personal aspect of their lives. It is in fact of historical interest, because it also affords a glimpse into the intimate world of the circle of great families which, in effect, ruled Rome during the last years before the end of the Republic, and among whose members were numbered the chief protagonists of that epic drama. Indeed, many of the leading actors in the events that were to bring about the fall of the Roman Republic were closely related to Servilia herself.

Servilia was the daughter of Q. Servilius Caepio, who traced his descent from C. Servilius Ahala, a hero of Cincinnatus' dictatorship in the fifth century B C. Her mother was Livia, sister of the tribune M. Livius Drusus, whose murder in 91 had sparked off the Social War. Servilius and Livia had three children; a son called Q. Servilius Caepio and another daughter, also called Servilia, who became Lucullus' second wife. Livia divorced Servilius Caepio and married M. Porcius Cato, grandson of the Censor, and had by him a son, M. Porcius Cato the Younger, and a daughter, Porcia. As both Livia and their father died when Cato the Younger and Porcia were children, they were brought up by their maternal uncle in an affectionate association with Servilia, their stepsister. Servilia herself married twice. By her first husband, Marcus Junius Brutus (who was put to death by Pompey during Aemilius Lepidus' insurrection of 78–77), she had a son, Marcus, known to history as Brutus. Though in actual fact, as he was later adopted by Servilia's brother, Brutus' real name was legally Q. Caepio Brutus. By her second marriage to D. Junius Silanus, Servilia had a son named after his father, D. Junius Silanus and two daughters, both called Junia. The elder Junia married M. Aemilius Lepidus, the triumvir, and the younger, known as Junia Tertia, married C. Cassius Longinus.

Such complicated relationships, resulting from constant marriage and re-marriage within a small circle of families, were the rule rather than the exception in the Roman world to which Servilia belonged. They reflect, even more pronouncedly than the alliances of the Gracchi and the Scipios in the previous century, the role played by the women, whose marriages cemented – as long as it was convenient – the political affiliations of their families. Their marriages formed the links in the chains uniting the various political cabals – as long

102 A detail from the famous 'Aldobrandini Wedding' fresco shows the veiled bride, seated on her couch, waiting for the bridegroom. She is attended by Venus and Bacchus, representative of love and fertility.

as their family interests coincided. When they ceased to do so, the daughters of these noble houses found themselves faced with divorce. Their frequent remarriages, however, suggest that most of them were as politically minded as the men, since for the women divorce involved the loss of their children, who remained with the husband. The majority of the Roman nobility were thus conditioned from childhood to this, to us, coldly unemotional approach to family life. In such a context Caesar and Servilia's liaison, which lasted until his death, comes to the modern mind almost as an emotional relief – it is the epilogue that provides the shock.

In the autumn of 63, Catiline stood again for election as consul and again he failed. Frustrated ambition now drove him to attempt a *coup d'état*. Catiline's plan was to raise an army from the malcontents in Italy – men like Sulla's veterans, who had discovered that life on the land was almost as hard as that in the army and held out no prospect of loot or gratuities. In Rome, too, there was plenty of dissident material ready to hand – dissolute and discontented aristocrats of tarnished reputation that had led to their eviction from the Senate. These were to be the leaders of Catiline's conspiracy – the rank-and-file suborned slaves – and unfortunately the leaders knew that they had little to fear from Cicero's fellow consul, C. Antonius, for he was a man of their own kidney. There was, however, a compensating factor: such men were little more effective as conspirators than they had been in public life. This emerges clearly in Sallust's history of the conspiracy, even more so, perhaps, than the moral decadence which he believed to be the root cause of Rome's ills. There were too many plotters, and among them people who were as lacking in purpose and discretion as they were in morals, including women of high society. Nevertheless it was one of these last – Fulvia by name – who had the wit to see the appalling risks her lover, Q. Curius (an unworthy representative of the family of the austere M. Curius Dentatus), was running as a conspirator. And when Curius turned informer, Fulvia acted as his go-between in warning Cicero of a plan to assassinate him. The deed was to have been done at Cicero's early morning *salutatio*, but by the simple expedient of shutting the doors of his house, and keeping watch together with two distinguished witnesses, Cicero not only saved his life but was able to put the story to the test.

On 8 November, Cicero summoned the Senate and delivered the first of his speeches against Catiline. This opened with the words, 'How long will you abuse our patience, Catiline?' and included the best-known tag of all – 'O tempora, O mores'. Boycotted by his fellow senators, Catiline sat alone, listening apparently unmoved to Cicero's harangue.

Cicero had gained his point: that night Catiline left Rome. But still Cicero had no evidence to prove his case, and he only obtained it by a ruse. Some envoys of the Allobroges (a Gallic people living in what is now Savoy) had been approached by the conspirators and agreed to raise their countrymen against Rome. Then, afraid of what they had done, they told the story to Fabius Sanga, who informed Cicero and, with the connivance of the Allobroges, the trap was set. On the night of 2 December, the Allobrogian envoys were arrested at the Milvian bridge as they were leaving Rome. They had in their possession instructions for an insurrection in Gaul and letters compromising Catiline. These bore the seals of the conspirators, including those of the praetor and ex-consul P. Cornelius Lentulus Sura and Cornelius Cethegus, the former lover of Praecia, and one of the men who had attempted to murder Cicero. Sura and Cethegus were arrested with three smaller fry and Cicero convened the Senate to debate their fate.

For Cicero time was running out, since on 1 January he would cease to be consul and the new magistrates for 62 had already been elected. According to custom it now fell to them to open the debate in the Senate; beginning with the consul designate, D. Junius Silanus, Servilia's husband, who advocated that the prisoners should suffer the supreme penalty. As praetor designate, Caesar's turn came next. At this crucial juncture – when he may well have known himself to be in grave danger, as Q. Lutatius Catulus and C. Piso had tried to persuade Cicero to fabricate evidence of his participation in the conspiracy – Caesar displayed the same cool courage with which he had once confronted Sulla. In the face of a hostile Senate, he appealed to reason. He said that if they voted for the death sentence they would be creating a dangerous precedent, which might in future be abused. Instead, he suggested, the culprits should be imprisoned for life, their property confiscated, and any future proposal for their release declared treason.

Caesar's eloquence and cogent reasoning, and the fact that Gaius Gracchus' law forbidding the execution of Roman citizens without trial was still on the statute-book, swayed the Senate. Even Silanus declared that for Roman senators the 'supreme penalty' meant, of course, imprisonment. It looked as if moderation might prevail, until it was the turn of one of the tribunes-elect to speak. This was Marcus Porcius Cato and, characteristically, he evoked the traditional severity of ancient Rome to enforce his argument. Cato also pointed out the practical dangers of sparing the prisoners' lives: they might escape, and the rebels outside Rome would be even more difficult to quell if an example was not made by passing the death sentence.

If the speeches themselves were as decorous as any which might be delivered today, the same cannot be said of the debate that followed. On such occasions violent personal abuse was no rarity in the Senate, and this was no exception. Because of his former support of Catiline, Cato was convinced that Caesar was a party to the conspiracy and, when a letter was delivered to Caesar during the debate, Cato challenged him to read it aloud, believing it to be from one of the conspirators. Silently Caesar handed the small bundle of waxed tablets to Cato, who was not far from him. Having read, Cato flung the letter back at Caesar with the words, 'Take it, you sot!' The missive was a far from modest love-letter from Servilia to her lover. Again we are reminded how small a circle governed Rome and how, inevitably in the circumstances, the undercurrents of personal feelings and relationships were always present beneath the surface, even in matters of highest policy. For the three leading figures in this momentous debate – Silanus, Caesar and Cato – were respectively Servilia's husband, lover and stepbrother.

In the event, it was Cato's argument that prevailed and the Senate advised the consul that the death sentence should be exacted. Cicero accepted the advice, and with a band of Senators he set out to fetch the prisoners from the praetors' houses, where they had been kept separately for reasons of security. Thus Lentulus, a praetor himself, though now shorn of his office, was brought down from the Palatine to the dread Tullianum, there to be strangled in the sinking gloom of the dungeon by the public executioner. The other conspirators followed. When it was all over, and Cicero returned through the silent crowds, waiting and wondering in the Forum, he called out to them, using the Roman euphemism for death, 'They have lived their lives.' This moment was the triumph of Cicero's life, for, as he and the Senators accompanying him made their way to his house on the Palatine, crowds followed, shouting and clapping and calling Cicero 'the saviour and founder of his country'.

Thus the conspiracy was suppressed in the city, but it was not extinguished elsewhere until Catiline's army was defeated in Tuscany and he himself was killed, fighting with desperate bravery to the end.

By February 62 the Catiline conspiracy was a thing of the past, but it left a troubled Rome in its wake, occupied with the rights and wrongs of the conspirators' summary execution. Nor was this the only dividing factor. There were also mixed feelings about Pompey's imminent return from Asia, and already pro- and contra-Pompey factions were forming; significantly, Caesar had decided to throw in his lot with the former. There was some panic when Pompey actually landed at Brindisi in December, and fears that he might march on Rome with his army. In the event Pompey did nothing more startling than divorce his wife, a not uncommon concomitant of the return, after years of service overseas, of many Roman magistrates.

Caesar was also involved in domestic trouble, and in most unfortunate circumstances that precluded any possibility of its being hushed up. Every year in December a festival was held, in the house of a curule magistrate, in honour of the women's goddess, the Bona Dea. The rites were celebrated at night and shrouded in the deepest secrecy. All men and male animals were excluded from the house, and even statues, paintings and mosaics in which they were represented, were veiled. The participants included the Vestal Virgins and ladies of Roman high society. In 62, the festival was held in Caesar's

official residence, not because he was Pontifex Maximus, but because he was one of the praetors of that year. His wife, Pompeia, was no doubt officially hostess, but his sister Julia (already grandmother to the infant Octavian) was present as well as his mother Aurelia, who, judging from subsequent events, seems really to have been in charge.

Though little is known about its celebration, the Bona Dea festival appears to have been a curious mixture of religious rites combined with a social occasion. There was music, and wine was drunk, though it was referred to as milk – possibly because in early Rome women were forbidden wine – and the wine jug was called a honey-pot. At some stage in the proceedings a sow was sacrificed.

Normally the participants returned home quietly in the early hours and, presumably, the magistrate in whose house the celebration had been held, did the same. In this particular year, however, the husbands of the married partici-pants were wakened during the night to be given the horrifying news that a young man – the notorious P. Clodius – had been discovered in the house disguised as a female harpist, and recognized by Caesar's mother. As far as was known, only the slave-girl who penetrated his disguise and Aurelia had seen young Clodius, who, when the latter ordered him to leave the house, had left at once.

103, 104 *Top* The Tullianum Prison in Rome. *Above* Cicero.

133

105 This rider holding a horn is part of a frieze from Osuna, in Caesar's province of Further Spain.

But why had Clodius ever ventured on this mad and sacrilegious escapade? In his particular case – as in that of any daredevil young buck in a corrupt society – it could well have been nothing more than a prank. But with Clodius, it could also have been an attempt to seduce a woman who would otherwise have been impossible to approach. The house was Caesar's, and Roman gossips assumed that Clodius had seized what appeared to be a unique opportunity to make an assignation with Pompeia.

Caesar divorced Pompeia immediately on the grounds that his wife must be 'above suspicion' – but his reason for this famous dictum was not simply that Pompeia was his own wife but also the consort of the Pontifex Maximus. Inevitably, there was clamour for a trial and, although Clodius' crime was not indictable under any existing law, a case was brought against him. Clodius' defence was that at the material time he was 90 miles away from Rome; in spite of the evidence given by Cicero to break his alibi, Clodius was acquitted. The jury was bribed, said Cicero. Caesar, however, did not seem to take the matter so seriously, for he remained on friendly terms with Clodius. Possibly this was for political reasons, or possibly – as a fellow libertine and man of the world – Caesar saw that the story of 'Clodius among the ladies' was so riotously funny that it would endear the culprit to the Roman crowd, as indeed it did.

Caesar had, in fact, left Rome before the trial took place. In the spring of 61 he departed, somewhat precipitately, to take up office as proconsular Governor of Further Spain. Although as Governor he would have an opportunity to recoup his finances, Caesar's debts in Rome were of such proportions that his creditors made difficulties about his leaving the city. It was only after Crassus agreed to go surety for him that Caesar got away. The governorship of Further Spain was no sinecure; large tracts of it were not yet subdued, and previous Roman governors had been given good reason to fear the warlike proclivities of the inhabitants of the Iberian peninsula. Caesar had, of course, been there before and seen military service there as a young man, but his life in Rome these last eight years – occupied with political and amorous intrigue – had scarcely been of the kind calculated to prepare him for the rigours and responsibilities of a frontier province.

Thus there seemed to be no reason to suppose that his year's governorship would do more for Caesar than enable him to pay his debts. Or, for that matter, that Caesar himself had anything exceptional in his make-up – other than the courage and independence displayed in his dealings with Sulla, his pursuit of the pirates and his recent stand in the Senate opposing the death penalty for the Catiline conspirators. But Spain was to be the watershed in Caesar's life. We do not know if any influences contributed to this, other than Caesar's own discovery that when he was placed in charge of administration and, above all, in command of an army, he possessed a natural genius as a leader. It was an intoxicating discovery for a man to make when he was rising forty. In all probability this was also the secret of that supreme confidence, which from now on Caesar was able to communicate to the troops under his command, and equally probably the source of the famous *celeritas* – his lightning-swift powers of decision and action.

When he returned to Rome in the summer of 60, he was entitled to a triumph; but procedure forbade his entering the *pomerium* beforehand and there was not sufficient time to organize the triumph before the consular elections, due to be held in July. A candidate, on the other hand, had to be present in the city to conduct his campaign, unless the Senate issued a special dispensation permitting him to stand *in absentia*. Caesar asked for this and was refused, because of Cato's opposition. Without hesitation, Caesar renounced his triumph and, entering Rome as a private person, began his election campaign. He hoped to have L. Lucceius as his colleague, but the *optimates*, determined to put a spoke in Caesar's wheel, backed Bibulus heavily and succeeded in getting him elected. Thus Caesar and Bibulus, who had loathed each other as fellow aediles and fellow praetors, now faced the prospect of sharing the consulate.

In the circumstances Caesar needed strong support, if he was to achieve anything, and fortunately for him there were other, and far more powerful, men in Rome who also had their problems. Pompey, for one, was nursing his wounded vanity because the Senate – as it was perfectly entitled to do – had refused to endorse his Asian settlement without a debate: since neither party would give way the settlement had hung fire for two years. Crassus was also in a difficult situation. The *publicani* had asked his help in an embarrassment which had arisen over their tax-farming concession in Asia. In a moment of unwonted optimism they had – or said they had – made too high a bid for their five-year contract. They now maintained that the returns fell far short of their estimate. This might not be strictly true, but the question was not a purely financial one. At the time of the Catiline conspiracy the *publicani* and the equestrian order in general had supported the *optimates*, and the latter could ill afford to lose their goodwill now. With Crassus' support an accommodation of some kind could no doubt have been made, if that 'seagreen Incorruptible', Cato, had not entered the fray and wrecked any possibility of the *publicani*'s petition being granted.

If Cato had been Caesar's best friend, he could scarcely have done him a better turn. Here were two of the most powerful men in Rome – the army's hero and the bankers' friend – disgusted with the turn affairs had taken. If only they could be induced to join forces with Caesar, the three of them would be in an impregnable position. There did not seem to be much hope of this, however, as Crassus and Pompey had always hated each other. Nevertheless, Caesar set to work with infinite tact, and accomplished what was perhaps the most remarkable victory of his career. The result of Caesar's powers of persuasion was not a formal pact, recognized by the three men themselves and the world in general as the Triumvirate, but a personal understanding. In fact, the name was only subsequently given to their agreement; and if Cicero had been willing it would have been a quadrumvirate. In any event what Pompey, Crassus and Caesar agreed to do was to pool their political influence, whether before or after Caesar's election as consul is not certain, and, then during his year of office to obtain, by the same means, endorsement of Pompey's Asian settlement, including land for his veterans, reduction of the price of Crassus' *publicani* friends' tax concession, and a good military command for Caesar when his term of office ended.

Rome had come a long way downhill since Pompey and Crassus were first associated as consuls in 70. Their joint platform then for repealing the constitution of a man to whom – whatever his faults – they both owed much, would have scandalized an earlier generation. But at that time they had at least both been magistrates elected to carry out a political programme. Now they had entered into a secret association with a man whose magistracy was to be used to enable all three to achieve purely personal ends.

In January 59, Caesar lost no time. His first act of moment was the presentation of an agrarian bill which would provide allotments for Pompey's veterans as well as others. It was cleverly drafted: the money for land purchase was to come from the vast sums the State Treasury had received from Pompey's conquests, the land was to be bought in Italy at the recognized market price, and no compulsory purchase would be made for less than that. A board of 20 men and a judicial or executive committee of five were to carry out the purchase and distribution. The Senate's frigid silence when Caesar presented the bill forced him to take it before the assembly. Caesar's colleague Bibulus was attacked when making a speech and three tribunes vetoed the bill. Nevertheless, in the face of this – and Caesar's action was unconstitutional to say the least – he succeeded in getting the bill passed by the assembly. He even included a clause which required senators and candidates for office to take an oath to obey it.

Although in his dealings with Caesar, Bibulus often appeared as something of a buffoon, he was no fool. He now took a step which, although it might seem ridiculous, and certainly did not conform to Roman practice, caused Caesar considerable embarrassment. Bibulus announced that he was going to watch the sky for an indefinite period and that while he was doing so no public meetings could be held. Although watching the sky for an adverse omen formed part of the normal ritual preceding a public meeting, no magistrate had ever before retired to do so for an unlimited period of time. Nevertheless it was more than awkward for Caesar, for by disregarding his colleague's action, as well as the three tribunes' veto, he incurred a grave risk that his legislation might subse-quently be declared illegal. In addition to this it soon became evident that Bibulus was not devoting his entire attention to sky-watching. He had also taken to writing, and the streets of Rome were papered with broadsheets of his composition. These were completely libellous but highly readable. They stopped the traffic while fascinated Romans learnt, among other things, that Caesar 'as Queen of Bithynia . . . once wanted to sleep with a monarch, but now wants to be one'. Subsequently Caesar might conquer the world, but he remained powerless to put a stop to that story.

In the spring of 59 B C however, Caesar pressed ahead with his programme of legislation. A law was passed reducing the amount that the *publicani* were required to pay on their Asiatic tax contract to two-thirds of the original sum. In May a second bill was introduced for the reallocation of leases of state land in Campania. Thanks to its remarkable fertility, leasehold of much Campanian land had long remained the privilege of a limited number of Senatorial families: now some 20,000 persons were settled on it. Some of the former tenants had evidently been friends of Cicero's, and he was much put out. Although normally Pompey's almost slavish admirer, Cicero disapproved

106 Landscape near Ascoli, with a Roman bridge on the right. 'The Campanians', wrote Cicero, 'are inclined to boast of the excellence of their fields and the abundance of their crops.'

of the company that Pompey was now keeping. He made this plain by being rude about all three in a speech he made in the law courts. It was one of his worst mistakes, for young Clodius, who had not loved Cicero since the Bona Dea episode, made it known that he wanted to become a tribune in order to prosecute Cicero for having had the Catiline conspirators executed without trial.

It was, in fact, no easy matter for Clodius to become a tribune of the plebs, in spite of his democratic attitudes (spelling his name with an 'o' in plebeian fashion was one of them – Clodius was really Publius Claudius Pulcher, a member of the Appii Claudii, the family which had produced the decemvir and the Censor). He had his full share of the family eccentricity, but also, unavoidably, of its patrician blood. Caesar had tried to protect Cicero from possible Clodian reprisals and offered him a diplomatic post to get him out of the country, but Cicero refused. Now, however, both Caesar and Pompey were outraged by Cicero's foolishness and, making use of their respective offices of Pontifex Maximus and Augur they enabled Clodius to become a plebeian by sanctioning his adoption into a plebeian family. In July, Clodius was duly elected a tribune of the plebs, an office which could also render him very useful to Caesar.

Well before this, however, the Triumvirate had realized that theirs could not be the ephemeral relationship they had probably originally envisaged. They had obtained much of what they wanted, but their gains might prove to be illusory. Thanks to the tribunes and Bibulus, Caesar could be indicted when he laid down office and his legislation declared invalid. The three could not go back on what they had done and the only way out of the impasse was to go forward together. Pompey's unexpected marriage to Caesar's daughter Julia set the seal on this new development. Fortunately Julia, who was now 25, was charming and attractive, and the marriage a happy one. But the suddenness with which it was decided upon is indicated by the fact that Julia was already engaged and shortly to have been married to another man. Her fiancé may well have been Servilia's son Marcus Brutus.

By the end of May, Caesar's future was assured. He had been allotted his provinces: Cisalpine Gaul and Illyricum for five years (an area roughly corresponding to the whole of Italy north of the Appenines and part of Yugo-slavia), and Transalpine Gaul (roughly France, Belgium and Switzerland) for the same period. A further rush of legislation followed, including Caesar's new law on extortion and his creation of Rome's first newspaper, an official gazette called the *Acta Diurna*, which remained in circulation for centuries.

Foreign policy was not neglected. Rome benignly recognized Ptolemy Auletes (father of the 10-year-old Cleopatra) as King of Egypt, and this cost Ptolemy 36,000,000 sesterces. For nothing – but both he and Caesar were later to pay for it dearly – Ariovistus, a Suebic chief living in Gaul, was recognized as 'a friend of the Roman People'.

Except for the elections of the consuls and other high-ranking magistrates the serious business of the year was over by July. The month was not a dull one, however, for there were alarms about a plot to kill Pompey. For a man who had so often risked his life in battle, Pompey nourished an extraordinary fear of assassination. It was therefore most opportune for the continuing close associ-ation of the three, that the alleged instigators of the plot were not only notable figures among the *optimates*, but ones whose influence might have induced Pompey to desert the Triumvirate. In the event nothing happened. In November Caesar's father-in-law, L. Calpurnius Piso, and A. Gabinius (who as tribune had been responsible for Pompey's command against the pirates) were elected consuls. But the election as praetor of L. Domitius Ahenobarbus, Cato's brother-in-law and Caesar's deadly enemy (also the Emperor Nero's great-great-grandfather), was not so reassuring. Domitius was, however, unsuccessful in the attempt he made with Gaius Memmius, shortly after they took up office in January 58, to interest the Senate in the illegality of Caesar's legislation. Whatever their feelings, the Senators knew that Caesar was beyond their reach – he had only to cross the *pomerium* to become officially an officer absent on military duty, and thus exempt from hostile legal action. Moreover, Cato, who would willingly have led an attack on Caesar, had been persuaded that it was his duty to undertake a diplomatic mission in Crete. Cicero was the most likely person to succeed in detaching Pompey from the Triumvirate during Caesar's absence. Therefore Clodius – who was to be Caesar's agent in Rome during his absence – called for the re-enactment of the law which condemned to exile anyone who had executed a Roman citizen without trial. Deserted by the *optimates*, and even by Pompey – to whom he had appealed in vain – Cicero crossed the Adriatic and went into voluntary exile. His dispositions thus completed, Caesar now left for Gaul.

107 A Gallic warrior. In contrast to the Romans, he has long hair and a moustache as well as a beard, and wears a tunic made of animal skins.

9
Rome before the deluge

It was a turbulent Rome that Caesar left behind him, but if ever a man personified that world in which he lived, it was Caesar's lieutenant, Clodius. A century earlier, Clodius' intelligence and daring would have been canalized in some other direction: he was a good organizer and also seems to have been the tough daredevil type who would have done well in desert warfare. There was no Gracchan high-mindedness about Clodius' activities as a tribune – although he did outdo Gaius Gracchus' cheap corn dole for the Roman populace by giving it completely free – an action which is said to have cost the state 20 per cent of its entire income. Clodius' real function was to hold what in modern Italian parlance would be called the *piazza* – the Roman street mob – for Caesar, and maintain the *populares'* ascendancy in the assembly. He did it in a city that had no police force and in which troops could not be used to quell riots, by galvanizing the *collegia*, or working-men's street clubs and associations, and recruiting from among their members gangs of toughs with which to terrorize opposition. That there was no one capable of quelling Clodius, until a rival organized even more ferocious gangs, illustrates only too well the age of dissolution in which Clodius lived, and of which he was a product. Moral decadence and the Romans' lust for power and money, were, according to Sallust's analysis of the situation, the causes of this state of affairs. Sallust's theme has influenced the opinion of historians of most generations other than our own, and possibly we come nearer to the truth in seeing the causes of the fall of the Republic in the Romans' failure to adapt their institutions to an era of expansion and the wind of change. Still the awkward question remains – why did the Roman establishment fail to do this, if it was not from fear of losing their power and their money?

Nevertheless, this strident, turbulent Rome, which witnessed the death-throes of the Republic, also produced some of the greatest poets of all time. And one at least of them belonged to a group of rebels, of angry young men, revolted by the world in which they lived. Strangely, it was not the establishment – the ultra-conservative society of the *optimates* – that aroused their anger, so much as the pseudo-popular political bossism as represented by Caesar and his friends. Licinius Calvus – a member of a famous Roman family, and leader of the group – had prosecuted Vatinius, who as tribune had introduced the bill which gave Caesar his province of Cisalpine Gaul. This made a young man from Verona – C. Valerius Catullus, who had come to Rome about 62 – admire Calvus very much, and Catullus himself proceeded to attack Caesar in a series of epigrams. Characteristically, the members of this group were also rebels against the established style of poetry of their day: set pieces written in the heroic manner, filled with the names of gods and goddesses, and historical epics written to order to glorify some successful general or leading figure. This group of literary rebels turned for inspiration instead to the unique personal poetry written five hundred years earlier, by Sappho and the Lesbos circle of poets.

Two things singled Catullus out from the rest of this group: his genius and his passionate, searing, and in the end tragic, love for Clodia, Clodius' sister, who was in many ways his feminine counterpart. Their father, Appius Claudius, had been consul in 79, but died leaving his family desperately poor. Clodia was married to Metellus Celer, who became consul in 60, the year after Catullus and Clodia met. Clodia was not only a great lady but one of the most beautiful women in Rome, and Catullus was struck dumb with passionate love for her the first time they met. A few days later he sent her an exquisite little poem to explain his silence. It was an interpretation in Latin verse of a poem of Sappho's on the ecstasy of love and the pain of deprivation. In it Catullus substituted the poetic name of Lesbia for Clodia's own, using it for reasons of discretion and as a delicate compliment.

From the poems addressed to Lesbia we learn a good deal about Clodia and the world in which she lived. In many ways it has an extraordinarily contemporary ring, for the fashionable beauty amusing herself with a group of young *avant-garde* poets was evidently then as much part of the social scene as today. It was smart for a woman of her world to cultivate intellectuals with advanced views, and Clodia was probably not alone in this; but her choice of a genius as a lover has ensured that his tragedy and her way of life have never been forgotten.

When Clodia finally left him for the younger and more dashing M. Caelius Rufus – one of Catullus' own friends – and the poet pictured them 'fondling and loving' at Baiae in a fashionable whirl of gaiety, he voiced his agony in the famous words: 'I hate and love. You ask me why? I do not know, but this is what I feel and it is torment.'

Two years later, in 57 B C it was Caelius who left Clodia. Catullus had meanwhile gone to Asia to join the staff of Gaius Memmius, then Governor of Bithynia. He was sent abroad to make something of his life and earn some money, but within a year he returned, no richer, and to Verona not to Rome.

Catullus had entertained no affection for his chief in Bithynia. Yet he was almost certainly the same Memmius as the one to whom the poet T. Lucretius Carus addressed his great poem *De Rerum Natura* (On the Nature of the World), and apparently at the time when Memmius was actually Governor of Bithynia. It is not certain that Lucretius knew Catullus, though it is possible, but that Catullus could have recommended Memmius to Lucretius as a suitable person to whom to address this poem written to explain Epicurean philosophy is unthinkable. In fact Memmius himself wrote poetry, and one modern authority considers that it was his success as an erotic poet that inspired Lucretius' dedication. Others, however, take the view that Lucretius regarded Memmius as the man most in need of conversion, and one who, if converted, might influence others of his kind.

Of Lucretius himself we know almost as little as we do of his reasons for addressing his poem to Memmius. He is believed to have been born in Rome about 99 and to have died some forty-four years later – certainly before his single surviving masterpiece was completed. To us today the idea of employing poetry as a medium to expound the materialist philosophy of Epicurus and the theory of the atomic creation of the world seems strange indeed. But in putting poetry to didactic use, Lucretius was not only following the Greek philosophers, but also Latin poets such as Ennius, who wrote his *Annals of Rome* in verse. Didactic poetry had originated at an early period when instruction was carried out purely by word of mouth, and poetic rhythm served as a natural aid to memory.

But no such poet had hitherto possessed the genius of Lucretius, or felt the same compulsion to expound his theme. Although nothing is known of any other poetry Lucretius may have written, it seems certain *De Rerum Natura* was not his first work. The resemblance between the poetic imagery of Lucretius' description of outer space and the discoveries of our own day, is as striking as the attraction of materialist philosophy in the troubled world of then and now. It is thought that Lucretius wrote his poem because his discovery of Epicureanism and the atomic theory of the creation of the universe had freed him from the fear of death and he wanted to share his personal experience with others. More particularly he believed it was this fear which provoked men to crime and the lust for power and money. That others shared with Lucretius this desire and means of escape from the horror of the times in which they lived, is borne out by Cicero – who disliked Epicureanism and was grudging in his praise of Lucretius – but who said, nevertheless, that in his time Epicurean philosophy 'had occupied the whole of Italy'.

The year 57 was a momentous one for Cicero. On 4 September he returned to Rome from exile. He reported to his friend Atticus that from the moment of his entry into the city by the Porta Capena – the gate to the Via Appia – he found that 'the steps of the temples were already crowded from top to bottom by the populace; they showed their congratulations by the loudest applause and similar crowds followed me right up to the Capitol, and in the Forum and on the Capitol itself there was again a wonderful throng.'

Even allowing for the fact that Cicero was never inclined to minimize any occasion that contributed to his self-esteem, it is clear that his return was an important factor in the Roman political scene. Although he was no doubt flattered that the great Pompey had participated in his recall, the fundamental fact that made it possible was that one of Cicero's own supporters – the tribune T. Annius Milo – had taken Clodius on at his own game and surpassed him at it, by organizing even more effective gangs of thugs with which to terrorize Rome. Cicero cannot have been quite so pleased when the excitement over his return was eclipsed by the news of Caesar's startling victories in Gaul, and his advance to the Rhine, which was celebrated by the unprecedented honour of a thanksgiving of fifteen days' duration.

Even for the victorious Caesar, however, the news of Cicero's return was bound to be disquieting. Although by now Caesar would have known that if he finally conquered Gaul he would be Pompey's equal as a public figure, and immensely rich, nevertheless, with Cicero in Rome, Pompey's fidelity to the Triumvirate could not be relied upon. Possibly the news that it was as a result of a proposal made by Cicero that Pompey had received a five years' commission to organize Rome's corn supply – with ample means to carry out his task – that decided Caesar to write to Pompey and Crassus, asking them to meet him in Lucca early in 56.

Caesar established his winter quarters at this convenient meeting-place, which was not too far from Rome, but still within the confines of his southern province of Cisalpine Gaul. The meeting was a momentous one, not only for the men concerned, but also for the future of Rome. Caesar had invited many other Roman notables to come to Lucca and Plutarch paints a vivid picture of the scene. Two hundred Senators came from Rome to Lucca to pay their respects to Caesar, and 120 *fasces* of proconsuls and praetors were to be seen at Caesar's doors. It was in such surroundings that the three men planned their future actions, and decided that Pompey and Crassus were to be the consuls for the coming year, that they would ensure indemnification of Caesar's actions when he had been consul, extend his command in Gaul for another five years and increase the number of his legions. Furthermore, it was agreed that after their year of office, Pompey was to have Spain as his proconsular province, and Crassus Syria. In the event there was some difficulty over the election of Pompey and Crassus, but Caesar's victories in Gaul had not only infused new life into the Triumvirate, but also so greatly increased his prestige that in the end the Lucca programme was carried out in full. In 55 the Triumvirate reached the apex of its power.

Pompey also played his part by staging in the Circus Maximus the most magnificent games ever held in Rome until then. A Gallic lynx was shown for the first time in the arena – no doubt a present from Caesar, and a reminder of

108 A battle between Romans and Gauls, portrayed on a Roman mausoleum in southern France; Victory, a winged female figure, appears among the combatants in the background at the left.

his victories – and no fewer than 600 lions and 400 leopards. But the most spectacular item of the games was the elephant hunt, for which 18 of the great animals and trained hunters had been imported from Africa. The elephants' cleverness in seizing the shields of their attackers and throwing them up in the air delighted the crowds. But when the unfortunate beasts stampeded to the barrier, which separated them from the spectators, and raised their trunks and cried, the people were so torn between their fear and their sympathy for these extraordinary animals, that they shook their fists at Pompey. The incident of the elephants was not forgotten, and when Pompey was murdered seven years later on African soil, the Romans saw in his death the elephants' revenge.

The years 54 and 53 were disastrous ones for Rome. In his ill-advised invasion of Parthia, Crassus not only sacrificed his own and his son's life, but practically the whole of his army. Crassus' death also resulted in the dissolution of the Triumvirate and its replacement by a growing rivalry between the two surviving members. There was such disorder in Rome that no elections could be held; but worse was to follow. On the afternoon of 18 January 52, as a result of a chance encounter with Milo on the road near Bovillae, Clodius was killed in a fight between their escorting bands of toughs. Clodius' body was found abandoned on the Via Appia by a Senator returning to Rome, who had it

109 Two lictors, right, carry *fasces* – bundles of rods tied with a red thong, symbols of an official's power to chastise. These were laid down only as signs of mourning or homage, as when 120 *fasces* were laid at Caesar's doors at Lucca.

110 A coin of Caesar shows Vercingetorix stripped and bound, his long hair flying, beneath a trophy of Gallic armour.

placed in his own litter and brought back to the city. Nearly seventy years earlier, the murder of Antullus, and the appearance of his funeral procession before the Senate House, had been the last dramatic incident in the train of events leading to the emergency decree being passed for the first time, and the death of Gaius Gracchus. Now Clodius' supporters carried his body right into the Senate House and burnt it down to make his funeral pyre. Again the last decree was passed; and Pompey was appointed sole consul.

For Pompey, who had feared assassination at the hands of his thugs, Clodius' death in normal circumstances would probably have come as a relief. But murder in the existing political situation was another matter. Pompey took immediate steps to have Milo brought to book. On Pompey's orders the court in which Milo was tried was ringed with soldiers and, although he had Cicero to defend him, Milo was condemned to exile. He seems to have accepted his sentence philosophically, but to have nourished a grudge against Cicero, who had evidently not been at his best in his defence of Milo. For when Cicero sent his client a copy of the elegantly polished version of his speech for the defence, Milo replied that if this had been delivered at the actual trial, he would not have been exiled.

The effect upon Caesar's political position of the murder of Clodius had not escaped the Gauls any more than it had Caesar himself. He emphasizes its importance in this context by describing the event in the opening paragraph of the Seventh Book of his *Commentaries*. In this, the most celebrated of all the Books, Caesar's relation of his life-and-death struggle against Vercingetorix and the rebellion of the whole of Gaul is told with a terseness that raises the impact of the drama to epic heights. In fact this and the *Commentaries* as a whole reveal, perhaps even more clearly than their author hoped, the reasons why Caesar triumphed in the end. For this extraordinary man, who, in the midst of a ferocious campaign was capable of describing it with a limpidity of style that is the quintessence of the art which conceals art, had also forged an army that has seen few equals. For a while Caesar's fate seemed to tremble in the balance. But in the autumn of 52, Vercingetorix surrendered.

It seems that the *optimates* in Rome had failed to appreciate the full significance of these events, or at least that they had not taken the full measure of the man who had made them possible. The Caesar they had known in Rome six years before was very different from the Caesar that had emerged in Gaul. Although they feared Caesar, the *optimates* did not fear him enough to overlook Pompey's past and attempt to attach him to themselves until the eleventh hour. Nor, strangely enough, do they seem to have realized, in spite of their experience of the irregularity of many of his actions during his consulate, that Caesar was not the man to allow a procedural technicality to stand indefinitely in his way when he again wanted to become consul; or that he was even less likely to relinquish his command in Gaul until he got what he wanted.

Nevertheless, there is something intrinsically Roman in the fact that the drama which ended in the destruction of the Republic should have begun with a quarrel over a matter of formal procedure. Caesar wished to be consul in 48, which according to custom meant that he would have to present himself in Rome in 49 to stand for election. However, in giving up his command and returning as a private person, Caesar would risk prosecution for the irregularity of his acts when he had been consul in 59. Therefore he asked for an exception to be made in his favour and to be allowed to stand for election *in absentia*. In 52, the required legislation was passed with Pompey's support, but at the same time, whether intentionally or not, Pompey complicated the issue by getting his own Spanish command prolonged for five years. In 50, the wrangle continued and Caesar's enemies were determined to deprive him of his command in Gaul. This was prevented when the tribune Curio (who had been heavily bribed by Caesar) vetoed the appointment of a new provincial governor. Both consuls elected for 49 were dyed-in-the-wool *optimates*, and so, just before Curio's term of office expired on 10 December, he succeeded in getting the Senate to pass a motion – by a huge majority – which deprived both Caesar and Pompey of their provinces.

By now hysteria was widespread in Rome and rumours were circulating that Caesar was marching upon the city. Gaius Claudius Marcellus, leader of the anti-Caesar faction, went with the two consuls for the following year to see Pompey and, without any authority whatever, commissioned him to take all measures to defend the state, including the raising of troops. Pompey accepted, and mobilization began. Curio now made a lightning dash to Ravenna, where Caesar had established his winter quarters, returning with a letter in which Caesar stated that, if he relinquished his command, Pompey must do the same. Two tribunes, Marcus Antonius (Mark Antony) and Quintus Cassius Longinus, tried to get a hearing for the letter in the Senate, but without result. Instead, a resolution was passed directing Caesar to give up his command by a given date or be declared a public enemy. On 7 January the Senate confirmed Pompey's powers; Antony and Cassius Longinus were warned not to appear in the Senate and advised to leave Rome. That same night they fled to Caesar at Ravenna.

Although it is unlikely that the two tribunes' lives had really been in danger, their flight afforded some semblance of legality for Caesar's action, which was not long in coming. Plans for some such contingency must have been prepared in advance, for Caesar had only one legion – no more than 6,000 men – and a small detachment of cavalry at his disposal. Thus no detail was neglected that could contribute to the maximum surprise of the attack when it came. After giving secret orders to his officers for the advance guard to march, Caesar spent his day in recreation. According to Suetonius, he went to the theatre and then inspected the plans for a school for gladiators which he intended to build. Plutarch says that Caesar passed the day watching gladiators training. In any case, Caesar evidently took care to be seen in public, apparently amusing himself, before he had a bath and joined his guests for dinner.

When dusk fell, after politely excusing himself to his guests for a temporary absence, Caesar left the dining-room. Even then he did not risk using his own transport, but, according to Plutarch, left Ravenna in a hired carriage driving in the wrong direction. Typically, Suetonius tells an even better story: of mules borrowed from a near-by bakery and harnessed to a gig. It was nearly dawn on 12 January 49 when Caesar caught up with his troops and arrived at the Rubicon – the little river that marked the border separating his province of Cisalpine Gaul from the rest of Italy.

This was the point of no return. Once Caesar crossed the river he would be committed; and at the brink he hesitated. Asinius Pollio, who was an eye-witness, afterwards described how Caesar stood for a while in silence. Then he turned to his staff and discussed with them not only the risks of his action, but its possible consequences for mankind. At last, as if abandoning himself to fate, he uttered the words, 'Let the die be cast', and led his troops across to the further bank.

111 Caesar in middle age. He was over 50 when he crossed the Rubicon and began his ascent to absolute power.

10

Civil war

Once across the Rubicon, Caesar moved with lightning speed. Rimini fell the same day, Arezzo followed, and by 18 January Ancona was in his hands. Caesar now held the stretch of mountainous country bordering upon the Via Flaminia nearly halfway to Rome. His moves were not lost upon Pompey, whose troops were not seasoned veterans like Caesar's, and he abandoned Rome, withdrawing to the south. Panic reigned in the city. Domitius Ahenobarbus, who was one of the few *optimates* not to lose his head in the general stampede, prepared to defend Corfinium, but by the end of February Caesar had taken it. Ironically, Domitius had been appointed to take over Caesar's command in Gaul, but Caesar now treated him with courtesy. Corfinium had been the only obstacle in Caesar's way in his pursuit of Pompey, and after its fall Pompey decided to evacuate Italy altogether and retire across the Adriatic, there to collect an army. Accordingly, he made all speed for Brindisi, with Caesar in hot pursuit. But Caesar did not arrive in time to prevent Pompey's embarkation, and as he had no fleet he was powerless to follow. After an unsuccessful interview with Cicero on his way back, Caesar returned to Rome. It was the first time for nearly ten years that he had been in the city, and both for him and for the Romans it must have been a strange encounter.

The majority of the *optimates* had, of course, fled, taking such of their possessions as they could with them. The exodus was apparently led by the consuls, of whom Plutarch relates the shocking fact that they had actually departed 'without even making the sacrifices usual before leaving'. Evidently when they believed their own lives were at stake the *optimates* were not such sticklers for formal procedure. But Caesar's enemies were not the only ones to have joined Pompey; some of his friends had also gone. One of the closest was Titus Labienus, who as tribune in 63 had proposed the bill that made possible Caesar's election as Pontifex Maximus, and had also been one of Caesar's most trusted commanders in Gaul. The defection of Servilia's son Brutus was even more surprising because he regarded Pompey as his father's murderer, and apparently refused to speak to him. But for men such as these, Caesar's crossing of the Rubicon had branded him as a rebel.

Possibly because of his own consciousness of his invidious situation, or from a genuine desire to come to terms, Caesar behaved with great circumspection when he arrived in Rome. Caesar was in any case not vindictive by nature; at no time in his career did he dispose of his opponents by bloodshed and proscriptions, as Marius and Sulla had done. He treated the Senators who were still in Rome with courtesy and deference, and asked them to continue the administration and to try and convince their colleagues in Greece to arrange peace terms. This was a very different Caesar from what they had expected, and from that pictured by his enemies during the last few years. In fact neither the hardships he had undergone nor his victories had altered the charm of Caesar's manner, any more than it had affected the elegance of his appearance. Those who had known him before would have found him surprisingly little changed, while the younger generation might well marvel that this slight, courteous man, with sparse grey hair, had achieved all that he had done. Indeed one of them, the tribune Caecilius Metellus, was misled by this urbanity into thinking he could oppose Caesar's taking control of the State Treasury, which had actually been left behind in the panic following Pompey's departure. Metellus' protests elicited a sharp retort, and were abruptly silenced by the information that Caesar would have no compunction about having him killed. The treasury keys had been lost and the doors were broken open to reveal 15,000 gold bars, 30,000 silver ones and 30,000,000 *sestertii*. Part of the treasure was earmarked as a special fund that had for centuries been held in reserve for use in the event of an invasion by the Gauls. Wryly, Caesar remarked that he was entitled to make use of this, as he had ensured that there would never be a Gallic invasion.

Certainly there was no fear on that count. But Pompey still had to be dealt with, and Caesar could not linger in Rome while Pompey gathered his forces for an attack. Since the army in Spain was still under Pompey's command, Caesar set out for Spain, which he reached before the end of May, and in a campaign of only six weeks succeeded in his plan. Pompey's generals surrendered and most of the rank and file joined Caesar. Marseilles, which had previously resisted, capitulated to him on his return journey. By the end of November he was back in Rome.

Curiously, this second homecoming is the first occasion upon which either of his biographers make any mention of Caesar's family, and this is simply a passing reference by Plutarch to the fact that Caesar's father-in-law, Calpurnius Piso, advised him to send a deputation to Pompey to discuss peace terms. There is no mention whatever of Caesar's wife. This is all the more remarkable because Calpurnia was only eighteen when Caesar went to Gaul and his mother died while he was there; thus, childless as she was, Calpurnia would have been left very much to her own devices. However, that she and Caesar were on good terms, and still hoped for children is evident from the fact that when Caesar made his will in the autumn of 45 the adoption of his great-nephew Octavian as his son and heir was mentioned only as an eventuality, in case Calpurnia had not borne him a male heir.

Personal affairs cannot, however, have occupied much of Caesar's attention during the eleven days he spent in Rome in the winter of 49. In less than a year he had gained control of the whole of Italy, Gaul and Spain, and it was becoming increasingly evident that he would not be easily dislodged. Some interim form of government for these vast territories had therefore to be set up, and the praetor Marcus Aemilius Lepidus (one of Servilia's sons-in-law) obtained sanction from the assembly for Caesar to be nominated dictator, so that the consular elections could be held. Caesar himself stood for office and, not surprisingly in the circumstances, was elected. Thus, finally, he became consul for 48 as he had planned, though the Roman world had been turned upside-down to bring it about.

The Civil War had a disastrous effect upon the Roman economy, and practically no ready money was available. Fear of the future had caused people

112 A war-galley, depicted on one of Pompey's coins struck specially to pay his forces.

113 Marcus Aemilius Lepidus. He was to be one of the Triumvirate after Caesar's assassination.

to hoard what cash they had and the rest had gone to pay the rival armies. Among the chief sufferers were Rome's debtors – always a notable proportion of her inhabitants. In fact, as a modern authority has pointed out, 'a history of Roman debt would at some points be equivalent to a history of Rome itself, and concluded that in a study of this perennial Roman problem, Caesar might well appear 'on a higher humanitarian plane than his critic Cicero'.* Certainly the measures that Caesar took to deal with the situation, in 49 and later, were eminently practical. The hoarding of cash was forbidden and creditors were bound to accept property – either lands, house property or movables – in settle- ment of debts. The value of such property was assessed at pre-war rates by qualified persons appointed by the Praetor Urbanus, and the interest on loans – which had recently risen from 4 to 12 per cent – was deducted from the debt. It is unlikely that this legislation came into force in its entirety in December 49, but at least some order emerged out of the existing chaos and a curb was put on the nefarious activities of the moneylenders.

On 4 January 48 Caesar crossed the Adriatic on his way to deal with Pompey. This was going to be no easy matter, for Pompey had 9 Roman legions and two more were expected from Syria, he also had a large body of cavalry and auxiliary troops, plentiful supplies and a great fleet building in the East. Caesar's 12 legions and small body of cavalry were both tired after the long march to Brindisi, and he was short of transport. Surprise was therefore of the essence – hence Caesar's dash from Rome and risky crossing of the Adriatic in midwinter with only part of his forces, the rest being left with Antony to follow. Short of food, and in appalling conditions, Caesar tried to blockade Pompey in Durazzo. At first Caesar was successful but, acting on information, Pompey struck at the weak point in Caesar's lines and broke through. Caesar thereupon made the daring decision to withdraw inland, hoping Pompey would follow.

Caesar's march through the mountains was appalling. When at last he and his legions reached the plain of Thessaly they were exhausted and, unlike Pompey, had no supply bases near at hand. For Pompey had followed; his advance guard was at Larissa; and in this promising situation he intended, rightly, not to bring Caesar to battle, but simply to wait and watch and wear his forces down. But Pompey had one handicap with which Caesar, at least, did not have to contend. This was the band of 200 Senators who had joined him, and declared themselves Rome's legal government in exile. But as so often in such circumstances, the exiles appeared to have left their common sense at home. Although they were generally at loggerheads with one another, they were united on one point – to push Pompey against his better judgment into making an all-out attack on Caesar.

Cicero was in the camp, having left Rome as soon as Caesar went to Spain, and now, according to Plutarch, 'he made no secret of the fact that he was sorry he had come, he belittled Pompey's military resources and was always criticizing his plans behind his back.' Evidently Cicero found ready listeners, for his sarcastic comments have survived.

Although Plutarch retails several of Cicero's scathing remarks, allegedly made on the field of Pharsalus, Cicero did not in fact take part in the battle,

* Review in *The Times Literary Supplement*, of P.A. Brunt, *Social Conflicts in the Roman Re- public*, London 1971.

which was fought on 9 August 48. Pompey's army was twice the size of Caesar's, but Caesar won the day, largely owing to his unorthodox use of infantry against the cavalry upon which Pompey had counted so much. Caesar ordered his pikemen to strike at the riders' faces when they charged. Apparently he knew, or guessed, that the cavalry were not seasoned troops but dashing young men who would fear disfigurement. And indeed, when confronted with these unexpected tactics, they turned and fled, making havoc of Pompey's dispositions. Thus when Pompey saw the cloud of dust raised by the fleeing cavalry, and Caesar's legions attacking his own on their exposed flank, he knew the battle was lost. Stunned by the shock, Pompey walked back to his camp and sat speechless in his tent. He was roused from his stupor only by the sound of the enemy's arrival, when he recovered sufficiently to change his clothes and escape. Eventually he reached Mytilene, where he had sent his wife and son for safety.

The measure of the confidence with which Pompey and his friends had regarded the outcome of the campaign is illustrated by the extraordinary luxury of their camp. The officers' tents were surrounded by gardens, and their dining-tables were laden with valuable plate. It was at Pompey's own table that Caesar sat down that evening, to eat the dinner prepared for his opponent.

Caesar did not even stay at Pharsalus to see the rank and file of the rest of Pompey's army incorporated into his own. He did, however, see one of his

114 Soldiers prepare to disembark from a galley; a relief from the Temple of Fortuna at Palestrina (see Ill. 93).

erstwhile opponents and had quite a long talk with him. This was Brutus, whose fate had caused Caesar considerable preoccupation, and apparently it was Brutus who told Caesar it was most likely that Pompey would now try to take refuge in Egypt. Recognizing that Pompey still represented the main peril, Caesar immediately set out with a small force in pursuit. Pompey arrived in Alexandria on 28 September and, relying on his friendship with the late father of Ptolemy XIII, he accepted a seemingly friendly invitation and landed practically unaccompanied. But the King was a boy of fifteen and the real power lay in the hands of the palace eunuch Pothinus, who, hoping to curry favour with Caesar, had Pompey murdered as he stepped ashore. The appalling scene, which took place on the day before his sixtieth birthday, was witnessed from their ship by Pompey's wife Cornelia. When Caesar arrived four days later, the Egyptians, thinking to ingratiate themselves with him, offered him Pompey's head and signet ring. Caesar turned away in horror from the head; death in battle was a soldier's risk, but assassination was something Pompey had always feared, and he had been the father of Caesar's short-lived grandchild. Taking Pompey's signet ring in his hands, Caesar wept.

Pothinus thought that he could also dispose of Caesar, but, thanks to the watchfulness of his valet, Caesar was informed of the plot and had Pothinus killed. It was during this period of plot and counterplot that Cleopatra staged her dramatic entrance into Caesar's presence in the palace at Alexandria, concealed in a carpet or sleeping-bag. This story, told by Plutarch, has naturally contributed to the picture of Cleopatra as the Oriental houri of legend. But as a matter of sober fact, she was then 22 – in an age when girls were married at 14 – and a highly cultivated and ambitious woman of pure Greek blood. Pothinus had driven her into exile from court because he feared her political influence – as well he might. There is a statue in the Vatican Museum which with good grounds is believed to be a portrait of Cleopatra – the profile bears a close resemblance to those appearing on the Queen's coinage. The face is that of a woman of marked character, and curiously – in view of her history – of almost austere appearance. Besides intelligence and charm, she is also said to have possessed a beautiful speaking voice. These appear to have been her chief weapons, and the desire for power – not love – to have been her dominating passion.

Caesar's arrival in Alexandria presented Cleopatra with an opportunity of attaching herself to the rising star in Rome, which was by now the arbiter of the fate of all states bordering upon the Mediterranean. With the sovereignty and riches of Egypt at stake, it is not surprising that Cleopatra speedily availed herself of a chance to make Caesar's acquaintance. Nevertheless, during the winter of 48–47 the fate of Caesar and Cleopatra looked extremely doubtful. Young Ptolemy left the palace and raised a faction against them. They were besieged in the palace, and at one moment Caesar escaped death or capture by jumping into Alexandria harbour and making a swim for it. Caesar and Cleopatra were finally rescued from their predicament by a relief expedition led by Mithridates of Pergamum, who defeated Ptolemy's army. The young King died by drowning. Before leaving, Caesar went on a journey with Cleopatra up the Nile and confirmed her as Queen of Egypt, reigning, as was the custom, with her younger brother as king and consort.

Caesar made his way slowly back to Rome by way of Asia Minor. Here, in the campaign of Zela, which lasted only five days, he disposed of Mithridates' son Pharnaces, who had attempted to profit from the troubled times to extend his power. For although after Pompey's death the ultimate issue was scarcely in doubt, the whole Mediterranean world was in a ferment. And in addition the most determined survivors of Pharsalus had reached Africa, where, with the assistance of King Juba of Numidia, they were building up an army. Caesar defeated them at Thapsus in the summer of 46, when, rather than surrender, Cato committed suicide at Utica. Instinctively, Cato seems to have felt that the Roman Republic had in reality perished in the field of Thapsus, and he preferred to die with it.

On his return from Africa Caesar celebrated his victories, and the Romans were treated to a series of spectacles that outshone all those which had gone before. There were four triumphs, held within a few days of each other. The first and most splendid was the Gallic one, during which the axle of Caesar's triumphal car broke and he nearly fell out – surely a very sinister reminder in Roman eyes of the jealous gods. After this mishap, as a sign of humility and atonement, Caesar ascended the Capitol on his knees: an extraordinary spectacle, in a setting of unparalleled splendour, for 40 elephants acted as torch-bearers to light the way. Vercingetorix, who had walked in the triumph, was put to death in the dungeon of the Mamertine prison at the moment when Caesar offered up the great sacrifice of an ox, a sheep and a boar in the Temple of Jupiter Optimus Maximus.

116 Cleopatra (compare her portrait on coins, Ill. 131). The straight nose is a restoration.

There were games of extraordinary variety and splendour. The animal shows alone lasted for five days, and after the lesson learnt at Pompey's games, spectators in the circus were now protected by a canal 10 feet wide, separating them from the arena. A giraffe was shown for the first time – possibly Cleopatra's gift to Caesar – and there was a battle in which armed men in towers mounted upon the backs of 40 elephants, fought each other.

The victory celebrations also included a ceremony dedicated to another aspect of Caesar's activities, one that was to have a more durable effect upon the city. This was the official opening, although neither was entirely completed at the time, of Caesar's forum and basilica. Work on the new forum had begun as early as 54. One of the difficulties of its inception was inherent in its role of relieving the overcrowding in the old forum, thus it had necessarily to be constructed near by, in the heart of the historic city. The chosen site lay to the north-east of the Curia and the Comitium, in an area filled with the mansions of the aristocracy – who asked, and obtained, the highest possible price for them. Thus the site alone cost Caesar a hundred million sesterces, roughly the equivalent of five million sterling. Caesar's forum was designed as a long rectangular porticoed court, with a temple at its north-western end. This was dedicated to Venus Genetrix – Mother Venus – so-called because the Julii claimed descent from her son Aeneas. The temple, like Roman churches today, was a treasure-house of works of art and votive offerings. The cult statue, the work of Arcesilaus, was also not ready for the celebrations, and had to be represented by a clay model. But Venus' breast was covered with British pearls and Caesar presented her with magnificent collections of cameos and engraved gems. Pictures by the celebrated Timomachus of Byzantium were among the temple treasures, which included a gold statue of Cleopatra.

117 The Curia, seen from the Comitium. The marble veneer has disappeared from its brick walls, but its bronze doors are original.

The façade of the temple seems to have been both charming and original. Its decoration included a fountain with reliefs or statues of water-nymphs. This was later much admired by Ovid, who wrote a poetic description of the light-effects of its sparkling waters. In front of the temple stood an equestrian statue of Caesar, the horse a work of Lysippus plundered from a monument to Alexander.

The destruction by fire of the Sullan Curia, after the murder of Clodius in 52, opened the way for the replanning of the whole area of the Comitium. The Curia, which had stood on its north side, was now rebuilt on a new site (the existing one) by the Argiletum, and designed and oriented so as to allow access to it from Caesar's forum as well as from the Comitium. The *rostra* was also transferred from its old site between the Comitium and the Forum, a new and magnificent one being built in a commanding position in the Forum itself. Probably it was more by accident than design, but it is significant that this transformation by the hand of a dictator diminished the size of the Comitium – the original historic place of assembly of the sovereign people of Rome.

On the side of the Forum opposite the Comitium and the Basilica Aemilia now rose the vast bulk of the new Basilica Julia. Built on the site of the old Sempronia, for the use of no less than four courts of law, this porticoed building was completed only after Caesar's death. Time has dealt with it even less

kindly than with many other buildings in the Forum, and today the most durable evidence of the teeming life with which the basilica was once filled are the graffiti in the pavement, scratched by idlers for use as gaming-boards. Not a trace of Caesar's name survives, and perhaps there is poetic justice in this, for his hatred of Q. Lutatius Catulus – whose completion of the Sullan rebuilding of the Capitoline Temple of Jupiter was recorded in an inscription – caused Caesar to have Catulus' name removed and his own substituted.

Caesar's forum, basilica and the rest, were only a beginning – a pilot project, as it were – for his new town plan for Rome, which was codified in a special law, the *lex de urbe augenda*. The overall plan was drawn up by an architect who had never been to Rome before, much to the annoyance of Cicero. In 45 he wrote tetchily to Atticus complaining about such a newcomer's ideas for Rome. The despised architect certainly had grand ideas, for he proposed to divert the course of the Tiber between the Milvian bridge and the Vatican hill, to build over the existing Campus Martius, and to lay out a new one on the agricultural land near the Vatican. Like so many Roman town plans during the next two thousand years, this, the first one of all, was never put into effect, though for a more conclusive reason.

One of Caesar's projects had, however, already been completed and came into operation on 1 January 45. This was his reformed calendar which, with

118 One of the gaming-boards scratched on the steps of the Basilica Julia can be seen here on the topmost step; like modern chess-boards, it has sixty-four squares.

only minor alterations, is the one we use today. It corrected an inaccuracy in the one that had preceded it, that had resulted over the centuries in the official calendar being two and a half months in advance of the actual seasons. Thus the vintage and the harvest festivals, for instance, were celebrated long before the grapes and corn were actually ripe. Nevertheless, at the time this useful measure aroused considerable discontent, epitomized in the comment Cicero made when someone in this hearing remarked that the constellation Lyra would rise the next day, 'No doubt', he said, 'it has been ordered to do so.'

As the year 45 advanced, it became evident that, although the *optimates* had been defeated at Thapsus, Pompey's sons had no intention of abandoning armed resistance. Both of them had succeeded in reaching Spain where, thanks to the bad government of Cassius Longinus, they raised such a following that Caesar was forced to lead an expedition to deal with them. This was in fact to be Caesar's last campaign and, on his own admission, nearly the last of him. When he finally quitted the blood-soaked field of Munda, Caesar told those around him that he had often before striven for victory, but this was the first time he had ever fought for his life. Of Pompey's two sons, the elder was murdered while trying to escape, and Sextus was a fugitive.

Like Marius and Pompey before him, Caesar had considered as one of his immediate concerns the resettlement of veteran soldiers. This, for once, was accomplished swiftly and peacefully by the purchase of land on the open market. Many of the veterans – possibly as many as 30,000 – were settled in colonies in the provinces. An even larger number – possibly twice as many – who were members of the Roman proletariat, also left their native city to settle in places as varied as Carthage, Corinth, Epirus and Fréjus. This policy not only created centres of Romanization in the provinces and relieved overcrowding in Rome, but helped to reduce the numbers who received the very costly Roman corn dole. The figure shrank from 320,000 to 150,000, and all those who laid claim to the bounty had to produce good evidence that they were entitled to it. However, neither Caesar nor any of his Imperial successors ever attempted to do away entirely with this largesse. And Caesar himself, possibly more than anyone else, had been responsible for whetting the public appetite for its concomitant – the extravagant entertainments – which together with the corn dole were in future to be branded by Juvenal in his most biting phrase – *panem et circenses*.

The *collegia*, which had been so useful to Caesar in the past, were firmly and thoroughly suppressed, but his chastening hand was not applied to the working class alone. The new Prefecture of Public Morals enabled him to curb extravagance, and as it carried with it powers similar to the Censorship, it also afforded Caesar considerable control over the Senate. It was most useful at the time, for his planned departure for the East was drawing near. His principal aim was to ensure that during his absence the reins of a stable government should be held firmly in his hands – or at least in those of his trusted deputies. Legislation was thus passed that gave him the right really to nominate men – though the word 'recommend' was used – for office as consul, and for half the other magistracies, among which the numbers of praetors and aediles had been increased. The rest were still elected, but the farce to which elections could be reduced is best illustrated by an incident that occurred at the end of 45. On the last day of the year, Caesar heard that one of the consuls had died, and, wishing to do a man a good turn by giving him the honour of consular rank, Caesar had the entire centuriate assembly summoned to elect his nominee as consul for a few hours. What this travesty of the most honoured Roman institutions meant to a man like Cicero transpires in one of his letters: he wrote, 'This may seem amusing to you, you weren't here. If you had seen it you couldn't have kept back the tears.' It was indeed a new and strange Rome in which to live.

The truth was that Caesar had been away from Rome too long, and now it probably appeared to him as an effete and troublesome city divorced from the realities of life in the great world outside, which had been the stage of the supreme experiences of his own life.

Caesar had in fact the vision to see what the future role of Rome could be, and with true insight he had begun to repair some of her past omissions. The creation of colonies as centres of Romanization was part of this policy; so too were his extensive grants of citizenship – sometimes to whole peoples, as in the case of Cisalpine Gaul – and, very markedly, his extension of membership of the Senate to Gauls and other nonItalians. But the narrow view, which had precipitated the Social War forty-three years before, still reigned in Rome and Caesar's reforms laid him open to the derision of the capital. Thus a verse of one of the most popular songs of the day ran:

> *Caesar led the Gauls in triumph*
> *Led them uphill led them down*
> *To the Senate House he led them*
> *Once the glory of our town*
> *'Pull those breeches off' he shouted,*
> *'Change into a purple gown.'**

Yet honours, human and divine, were heaped upon Caesar by a servile Senate. Thus he was now entitled to wear perpetually the purple robe and laurel crown of a triumphing general. (The latter he adopted with alacrity because it concealed his baldness, of which, like any Roman, he was exceedingly self-conscious.) However, his acceptance of golden thrones in the Senate and on the tribunal, and a raised golden couch in the theatre were less easy to forgive; so too was the renaming of the seventh month, July, after himself. Worse still was the honour – hitherto reserved for the gods – of having his statue carried in a litter in the *pompa circensis*, the ceremonial procession at the opening of the games. It is not surprising that the Romans began to believe that Caesar really did intend to become king: though when the crowd once greeted him with 'Long live the King!' he replied, 'No, I am Caesar, not a King.'

Although Cicero, of all people, had been among the first to propose exceptional honours for Caesar, he was now so sickened by the process that he wrote to Atticus, 'For heaven's sake let us give up flattery and be at least half free!' But it is possible that Cicero had been less than sincere in making his original proposal. Plutarch was later convinced that Caesar's enemies saw in this sycophantic competition to offer more, and yet more, extraordinary honours to Caesar, a useful way to bring discredit upon him and to make him hated. But it was Caesar's friend Antony, who, by repeatedly offering a crown to him during the Lupercalia in February 44, seems finally to have convinced the Roman masses that this was what Caesar wanted.

In reality it was highly unlikely, or at any rate at that particular moment. It is much more probable that the Parthian campaign – the biggest and potentially the most glorious gamble of the lot – was uppermost in Caesar's mind. He was, after all, 55 and his seasoned legionaries were not growing any younger. In a few years it would be too late. This may explain the unconstitutional measures and the iron hand in Rome, but only partly. No man who entertained respect – let alone affection – for the Republic, could have acted thus. Caesar's intimate friend Gaius Matius said that Caesar had no political solution for Rome in mind, but it also seems certain that he had no intention of reviving Republican government. With the hindsight of nearly two thousand years, it is easy to say that Caesar was mistaken in his priorities. No matter how dazzling further conquests might appear to be, to a Roman – and his legionaries – Rome was the real source of power, and until its government rested upon a sure base, anything else was a pursuit of vainglory.

* Suetonius, *The Twelve Caesars*, translated by R. Graves, Harmondsworth 1960.

120 Part of the bronze tablet inscribed with Caesar's *Lex Cisalpina*, of *c.* 48 BC. In it he defined the legal powers of central and local authorities for the province of Cisalpine Gaul, whose inhabitants he had made citizens of Rome.

The only indication – and it is a very tenuous one – that in 45–44 Caesar was looking further ahead than the Parthian campaign, was the interest he had begun to display in Octavian, after the young man had acquitted himself well in Spain. Octavian's place in the Spanish triumph in the autumn of 45 had been that of a favoured lieutenant or a son, and it is worthy of note that Caesar's will – providing for Octavian's adoption as his son and heir if Calpurnia did not have a male child – was made in September of that year. Octavian was also to have accompanied Caesar to Parthia; in March 44 he was waiting at the base camp at Apollonia, filling in time by continuing his studies. That he should serve on his kinsman's staff was normal Roman practice, but neither on this or other occasions do Caesar's two other great-nephews appear to have been singled out for any particular attention. In his will Caesar left only a quarter of his estate to be divided between them. It seems likely, therefore, that Caesar was already aware of Octavian's capacity. And if he had begun privately to think of some future settlement for Rome, involving a successor to his almost unlimited power, he felt that this quiet youth was a likely candidate.

121 A personification of the Roman province of Parthia, wearing the distinctive Parthian cap and leggings, and holding arrows.

During the winter of 45–44 there was not, however, the slightest indication that Caesar contemplated delegating any of his powers, even less of retiring – he said that Sulla was a dunce to have done so – nor did he attempt to conciliate Republican opinion. He was now frequently referred to as the General, or Imperator, more or less officially; and early in 44 his head began to appear on coins – an honour hitherto reserved for the gods or the dead. Such things evidently began to affect not only Caesar himself, but men's attitudes to him. When he came to dinner with Cicero near Puteoli late in December 45, Cicero said that the talk was good and the occasion agreeable, but added on a note of surprise, 'In other words we were human beings together.' But Caesar, the convivial man-about-town, was a thing of the past – Cicero said he was no longer the sort of guest to whom you would say, 'Do come again.'

When Caesar was made dictator for life, the Senate declared his person to be sacrosanct, like that of a tribune. He was also named *pater patriae*, and it was intended that all citizens should take an oath to protect him. Suetonius and

Appian say that the oath was actually administered, though this seems doubtful, but one was certainly sworn to this effect by the Senate. A connection between the seemingly purely honorific title of *pater patriae* and an oath of loyalty seems strange to us. But to the Romans, as father of his country, Caesar could also be regarded as patron of the whole state and its citizens as his clients. Thus the time-honoured bond of loyalty between patron and clients was evoked, whether as a precedent or to gild the pill.

It was a pill that required some gilding. Bit by bit, old Republican liberties and offices were becoming hollow symbols. To Caesar, who in the past had been so adept at manipulating them, this probably appeared as the logical conclusion. But Cicero's anguished words, 'Country, honour, respect and position – things as dear as one's own children – all lost', voiced the feelings of many, and some at least were preparing to take desperate action. They had watched Caesar's dictatorship grow from an emergency measure in 49, until it was transformed into absolute power for life. And shortly it would acquire the even greater horror in the eyes of Romans – to whom personal contact meant so much – of power which would be wielded from far away.

Caesar seems to have been as oblivious of this as he was of the offence that his increasingly autocratic manner was creating among the aristocracy and members of the Senate. On the occasion when a deputation came to inform him that he had been nominated dictator for life and other honours, Caesar was seated in a gold chair in front of the Temple of Venus – apparently discussing further plans for his forum – and he did not rise when the Senatorial deputation approached him. Afterwards, possibly realizing he had gone too far, Caesar excused himself on the grounds that he was not well and that his illness (probably epilepsy) made him feel dizzy when he stood. But it also seems that he was unaware of the impression he was creating; he was a busy man working against time, and ceremony meant little to him. He was conscious of the fact that he had treated many members of the Senate and their friends with extraordinary generosity, pardoning those who had fought against him and afterwards appointing them to important posts. Brutus was a case in point, though the fact that he was Servilia's son would go far to explain Caesar's leniency – but not altogether to the extent of making Brutus Governor of Cisalpine Gaul in 46 and two years later ensuring his appointment as Praetor Urbanus – the most important of the praetorships – and thereby disappointing Gaius Cassius Longinus, who thought he had a better claim.

Although Caesar appreciated Brutus' sterling qualities, he found him hard to understand. Gaius Matius, Caesar's intimate friend, said that Caesar's reaction on first hearing Brutus speak in public was, 'I do not know what that young man wants, but everything that he wants, he wants very badly.' In fact, in the accommodating world of Rome in the first century BC, when so much depended upon personal relationships and favours, Brutus stood out as a man to whom principles mattered more than personalities. Plutarch also makes the point that Brutus 'was opposed to the dictatorship, but Cassius hated the dictator', and, although Caesar himself was not vindictive, he would probably have found Cassius' attitude easier to understand. Caesar did instinctively realize that both men were 'dangerous'; in the case of Brutus, however, he allowed his respect for integrity to outweigh his instinct, though in fact Brutus was by far the more dangerous of the two. It was his reputation for integrity,

122 Marcus Junius Brutus: a coin minted in 43 BC when, after Caesar's murder, the Senate gave him an *imperium* in the eastern provinces.

combined with the magic of his name, that made Brutus a natural rallying-point for Republican sentiment. On the mornings when he went to try cases, he found his praetor's seat covered with writings by anonymous hands, urging him to act like his ancestor the first Brutus, or rebuking him for not doing so, saying: 'You are asleep Brutus', or 'You are no real Brutus.'

This was heady stuff for a man who, even more than most Romans, made a cult of his ancestry; and in fact nothing could have been further from the truth. Shortly after Cato's suicide at Utica, Brutus had divorced his wife and married Cato's daughter Porcia. In the Civil War, Porcia had lost her husband, Bibulus (Caesar's colleague as consul), her brother and all but one of her sons. If there was any woman in Rome who could spur Brutus on to act, surely it was Porcia. But, strangely enough Brutus did not take Porcia into his confi-dence. It was only some time after he had joined Cassius and the other con-spirators, and Brutus' nervous tension and sleepless nights had aroused her suspicions, that Porcia took the initiative. She drove a knife into herself, and when Brutus saw that she was bleeding profusely, she told him that she had wounded herself deliberately so as to convince him of her fortitude. Brutus then told her the whole truth, and the extent to which he was involved with 59 others in a conspiracy to murder Caesar.

One of the conspirators' chief problems was the choice of time and place in which to do the deed. They had debated lying in wait for Caesar in the Via Sacra, where he was bound to pass frequently on the way to and from his house. Another plan was to attack Ceasar during the elections, to push him down from the high platform over which voters had to pass, and then stab him. Although they came to nothing, such plans show only too clearly how vulner-able Caesar really was.

By March 44 time was running out, for on the 18th Caesar was due to leave for Parthia. Thus the announcement that the Senate would be called to meet in one of the halls of Pompey's Theatre three days beforehand, and that Caesar was expected to attend, would have seemed a heaven-sent opportunity to the conspirators. This was especially true because at such a gathering, a large group would be less conspicuous – the conspirators had agreed among themselves that all 60 of them should take part in the crime. On the Ides of March Brutus left the house alone early in the morning, and set out for Pompey's Theatre. It was a day upon which the courts were open, and Brutus was to try cases in the great portico of the theatre. Porcia knew that he had concealed a dagger under his clothes, and as the day wore on and no news came, her anguish was so great that she fainted and the servants believed her dead.

The other conspirators met in Cassius' house. They were able to do this without arousing suspicion, because it was on this day – either by design or lucky chance – that his son was to assume the *toga virilis*. And on such an occasion a large gathering of his friends would not attract attention. They went together to the Forum, and from there to Pompey's Theatre, where they saw Brutus calmly trying a case. As time passed and Caesar did not appear, the tension grew. He had been delayed at home by Calpurnia, who with tears begged him not to go because she had had a dream of evil omen. It was the first time that Caesar had seen Calpurnia upset by superstition and, as he himself was unwell, he was on the point of deciding to stay at home. However, his trusted lieutenant, Decimus Brutus Albinus, succeeded in convincing him that he must not disappoint the Senate, which had been waiting for more than an hour.

Decimus Brutus had good reason to be persuasive, for he also was one of the conspirators. When he and Caesar finally set out, their progress was slow; on the way people crowded round Caesar to present petitions. Among them was a man who slipped a note into Caesar's hand, telling him to read it quickly as it concerned him personally, and not just to give it to one of his secretaries. Caesar was unable to do so because of constant interruptions, and he still held the note, unread, in his hand when he stopped to chaff Spurinna the soothsayer, who had warned him to beware the Ides of March. 'The Ides of March have come', Caesar said, 'Ay they have come, but they have not gone,' was Spurinna's answer. And with the warning that would have saved his life still unread in his hand, Caesar walked into the meeting of the Senate alone. The conspirators had had the forethought to arrange for the herculean Mark Antony, who was accompanying Caesar, to be detained in conversation at the door.

Tullius Cimber and the group of conspirators came forward to meet Caesar, on the pretext of supporting Cimber in presenting a petition on behalf of his exiled brother. After Caesar had seated himself, they pressed round him even more closely, kissing his hands and breast and repeating their pleas, which Caesar had already firmly refused. Finally, in anger, he tried to shake them off by force, whereupon Casca pulled Caesar's toga off his shoulders. This was the signal for the attack, and Casca struck the first blow from behind. Caesar shouted at him, 'Casca, you villain, what are you doing?' and seized Casca's arm and struck at him with his writing stylus. Another blow fell and, as he turned to look for a way to escape, Caesar saw that he was surrounded by a ring of men, daggers in hand. He cried out and tried to defend himself, but of all the hundreds of Senators who had sworn to defend him, only two tried to come to Caesar's aid. Then, recognizing Brutus among his attackers, Caesar exclaimed, 'You too, my son?' and, covering his head with his toga, he fell to the ground. The assassins flung themselves upon him, striking so wildly that they injured one another. Finally – his body riddled with 23 wounds – Caesar lay dead in a pool of blood before a statue of Pompey.

Frozen with terror, the Senators had sat silent throughout the whole terrible scene. But when Brutus came forward and started to make a speech, they rose and fled in a body from the hall. Their wild rush created a panic in the city, people locked themselves up in their houses or ran to see Caesar lying dead, and then fled. In the midst of this chaos Brutus and the conspirators marched in a band to the Capitol, their daggers in their hands, their clothes bespattered with blood. As they went they called out to the people that liberty had been restored, and invited any man of note they saw to come and join them. Their appeal fell flat, and as they had completely misjudged the temper of Rome, they had no plan prepared for such a contingency. Instead of the rejoicing crowds they had expected, people were now either stunned and silent or waiting cautiously upon events. Meanwhile, Caesar's body lay where he had fallen. It was only some time later that three of his household slaves appeared and, in Suetonius' unforgettable phrase, 'carried him home in a litter, with one arm hanging over the side.'

The end of the Republic (44–23 B C)

Although Antony had fled with the rest of the Senate after the murder of Caesar, he recovered rapidly. As surviving consul, acting in concert with Lepidus, Caesar's master of horse, he soon gained control of the situation. When the Senate met on 17 March, its attitude was one of cautious compromise. An act of indemnity was passed in favour of the conspirators, who thus escaped a trial for treason as the murderers of a senior magistrate. But Caesar's decrees were also legally confirmed, subject to Antony's endorsement that they were genuine. Moreover, Antony succeeded in gaining sanction for Caesar's remains to be accorded a state funeral and for his will to be made public. He thus engineered both the occasion and the means for stirring the sympathy of the people. Even if he was an unpredictable character and did not possess the silver tongue with which Shakespeare endowed him, at least on this occasion Antony displayed a shrewd appreciation of the value of propaganda and a lively sense of how to use the material to hand. A dead man who had left three pieces of gold to every Roman citizen and a magnificent park for their enjoy-ment, was not likely to be branded as a tyrant for long. And Antony, as his associate, would reap the benefit.

It was intended that Caesar's body should be cremated in the Campus Martius and his ashes laid to rest near those of his daughter Julia, after the com-pletion of the public ceremony in the Forum. At first everything went accord-ing to plan: the funeral procession made its way through the crowded Forum, and Caesar's body was laid in state on an ivory couch covered with a pall of purple and gold, the blood-stained clothes in which he had met his death displayed beside him. Antony also began his funeral oration quietly, then, as he sensed the rising emotion of the crowds, he – and Shakespeare after him – heightened the pathos until he finished on a note of sheer drama. Holding up Caesar's toga – now rigid with dried blood – for all to see, Antony pointed at the slashes made in it by the murderers' daggers. The crowds went wild, some shouted for the murderers' blood, while others looted neighbouring shops, dragging out tables and benches and piling them up before the Regia to make a funeral pyre, upon which Caesar's body was laid. The professional mourners, who had walked in the procession, dressed in the robes that Caesar had worn at his triumphs, now rent them and threw them on the flames. They were followed by many of Caesar's veterans, who consigned their arms to the blaze. Women, too, were caught up in this frenzy of sorrow and flung their jewels and even the ornaments from their children's clothes upon the pyre. Seizing blazing brands from it, men rushed off to set fire to Brutus' and Cassius' houses. They were repelled with difficulty, and, in their rage, mistaking the unfortunate Helvius Cinna for one of Caesar's murderers, Cornelius Cinna, they killed him.

This was warning enough: Brutus and his supporters left Rome, Brutus retiring to his villa at Lanuvium in the Alban hills, from where he corresponded frequently with Cicero. In one of his letters to Atticus, written at this time, Cicero paints a somewhat malicious picture of Brutus sitting moodily in his garden awaiting events. Its landscape style was evidently as characteristic of Brutus himself as it was appropriate to his present situation. The garden was laid out to evoke a Spartan scene, complete with a replica of one of Sparta's most famous monuments – the Persian porch, built to commemorate the Spartan victory over the Persians in 479 B C. Here Brutus sat brooding while he waited to hear what the Senate would allot to him at the termination of his praetorship. The upshot was most unsatisfactory; the Senate was playing safe and he and Cassius were appointed to minor posts, corn-commissionerships in Asia and in Sicily.

Again from Cicero's letters, we learn not only of the two men's reactions, but of the extraordinary cohesion of a Roman family, even in the strangest and most dramatic circumstances. A family council was now held at Anzio to debate the course of action to be taken by Brutus and Cassius. Cicero was present as friend and counsellor, but the dominant figure was the matriarch, Servilia – the mistress and intimate friend for more than nineteen years of the man whom her son Brutus, and son-in-law Cassius, had murdered less than three months before. When Cicero started talking platitudes, Servilia cut him short, telling him not to talk nonsense, and when Cassius declared his absolute refusal to accept the insulting post allotted to him, the indomitable Servilia said that she would see to it that the Senatorial resolution was rescinded – and she did. She was in a good position to do so, for if one son-in-law, Cassius, was in disgrace, the other, Lepidus, was sharing the government of Rome with Antony, and Antony was also her friend.

Although after the first private reading of Caesar's will, that had actually taken place in his house, Antony was well aware that Octavian was Caesar's heir, he did not publicize the fact. Instead, he seized all Caesar's ready cash in the name of the State Treasury – to which he held the keys – calculating that a poor young man would have no influence. If Caesar's adoption of Octavian came as a surprise to Antony, it would have been even more unpalatable to another of Caesar's friends who had arrived in Rome some months before his death. This was Cleopatra, who, together with her legal spouse – her boy brother Ptolemy XIV – was living as Caesar's guest in a house in his gardens in Trastevere. Cleopatra later claimed that her son Caesarion was Caesar's child, but his putative father had made no provision in his will – drawn up the previous autumn – for any child borne to him by Cleopatra.

Cleopatra stayed on in Rome for about a month after Caesar's murder. Possibly she still hoped to complete the alliance which she had come to negotiate, perhaps she hoped to gain some recognition for the child she claimed was Caesar's, but in such troubled times these would have been slender hopes indeed. Possibly it was mere coincidence, but Cleopatra finally departed only about the time when Octavian arrived in Rome to claim his inheritance. Thirteen years were to pass before she, Antony and Octavian were again to be gathered together.

In the year 44, however, Octavian's arrival was already a most unfortunate event for Antony. He knew something of the young man, and having served

123 Octavian, the future Augustus. He was consul for the sixth time in 28 B C, when this coin was struck to commemorate his capture of Egypt.

with Caesar he could appreciate the attraction that any heir of Caesar's would hold for his legionaries. No doubt Antony hoped that his prompt seizure of Caesar's fortune had spoilt Octavian's chances. If he did, he had certainly not taken the measure of this quiet young man. Octavian sold his own possessions and the rest of Caesar's property, and did his filial duty by paying his adoptive father's donative to the appreciative Romans. Even before he got to Rome, Octavian had already taken another far-seeing step. He had broken his journey to go and see Cicero at Cumae, a tactful gesture from a young man to an elder statesman, particularly from Caesar's great-nephew to an arch Republican, but neither of them had any reason to love Antony. For his part, Antony probably loved Octavian even less when, after the completion of the Temple of Venus Genetrix, the young man shouldered the expense of holding the games celebrating Caesar's victories, which had been an annual event since 46. It was a telling gesture, for Brutus, who as Praetor Urbanus was responsible for the immediately preceding *Ludi Apollinares*, had not dared to appear in Rome. And it seemed that heaven itself approved Octavian's munificence:

each July night during the celebration of Caesar's games, in the limpid Roman sky there blazed the most brilliant comet ever seen. There could have been no better confirmation of the fact that the now officially deified Caesar had become a god.

Caesar seemed indeed to have left much of his famed fortune behind on earth for the benefit of his heir. Antony's swashbuckling pretensions had alarmed the Senate, and to many of its members it seemed as if the murder of one dictator might well have opened the way for another. Their attitude towards Octavian thawed noticeably. Like Cicero they began to feel that this young man might have his uses. This feeling grew when, as a result of a motion of the council of the plebs, Antony received the province of Cisalpine Gaul together with the command of four of Caesar's legions – a sinister-sounding combination in Republican ears. Cicero entered the fray in September when he delivered the First Philippic in the Senate. To this measured censure of his activities, which culminated in a warning allusion to the fate of Caesar, Antony replied with a pamphlet in which he accused Cicero of being party to Caesar's murder.

124, 125 At the state funeral which Antony arranged for Caesar, his body would have been carried in procession, attended by musicians and mourners – as in this sarcophagus relief from Amiternum, first century BC. Not long afterward Caesar was declared a god, and coins were issued by the young Octavian – *opposite* – bearing the inscription *Divi Juli*.

Cicero retaliated with the Second Philippic. This brilliant, scurrilous, attack on Antony was circulated privately, but inevitably Antony was aware of its contents and his hatred of Cicero grew from that moment.

While this propaganda war was raging, young Octavian was making preparations – totally illegal ones – on his own account. As a result of his friendship with the officers of two of the four legions that Antony had summoned from across the Adriatic, and his offers of generous pay, the legions deserted Antony and came over to him. Octavian was also successful in recruiting numbers of Caesar's veterans in Campania. Money allied to the magic of Caesar's name were effective propaganda weapons, and to these – determined at all costs to prevent Antony from becoming dictator – Cicero added all the power of his oratory. The Third, Fourth and Fifth Philippics were delivered during the autumn of 44. Antony arrived in Cisalpine Gaul with only half his army. He was confronted by Decimus Brutus Albinus, who, claiming that his term as governor expired only in March of the following year, refused to relinquish the province. Decimus Brutus retired to Modena and was there besieged by Antony.

The Senate was in a quandary. Neither it nor the consuls, Hirtius and Pansa, disposed of forces sufficient to support Decimus Brutus against Antony. The only person who did was Octavian. The Senate passed the emergency decree against Antony during the first days of 43. As a result of Cicero's persuasion, Octavian's command of the two legions he had filched from Antony was now officially recognized and he was also given praetorial powers. In after years Octavian recorded that 7 January of that year was the day upon which he first accepted the *imperium*. The two consuls and Octavian marched north, and on 15 April Antony was defeated in the grim battle of Forum Gallorum, but Pansa died of wounds and Hirtius was killed in the relief of Modena.

Antony now fled to Transalpine Gaul, there to join forces with Lepidus. His escape had been simplified by the fact that Octavian – on the grounds that Decimus Brutus was one of Caesar's murderers – refused to support his pursuit of Antony.

In doing this, Octavian disregarded orders he had received from Rome, but the moment of truth had now arrived in the complicated series of manœuvres which underlay the alliance between Octavian and the Senate. From the outset both parties had secretly intended to make use of the other as long as it was convenient. Now that Antony was out of the way, a marked coolness developed in the Senate's dealings with Octavian, and he was ordered to place himself and his troops under the command of Decimus Brutus. Octavian appealed to the legions and, receiving their support, he demanded the consulship. The Senate sent desperate appeals to Brutus and Cassius, but they were fully engaged in Asia fighting Antony's supporter – and Cicero's quondam son-in-law – Dolabella. The time had now come for Octavian to drop the mask. He marched on Rome and on the 19th of the month that was afterwards to be called August in his honour, Octavian and his cousin Quintus Pedius, another of Caesar's great-nephews, were elected consuls. Octavian also wrote to Antony and Lepidus suggesting that they should form an alliance. Octavian's adoption was now publicly acknowledged, and he became Gaius Julius Caesar Octavianus. Caesar's murderers were tried *in absentia* and condemned to death.

Antony had not wasted time either. He had won over Munatius Plancus, the other important Caesarian leader in Transalpine Gaul, and recrossed the Alps with a strong cavalry force and 17 legions. Octavian now had 11, and he was not yet twenty years old but he invited Antony and Lepidus to meet him and discuss the situation. Their meeting took place in the strictest secrecy on an island in the River Reno near Bologna. It lasted three days and resulted in the formation of the second Triumvirate. Unlike the first, this commission of three – Antony, Lepidus and Octavian – was subsequently recognized in Rome as the *Triumviri Republicae constituendae* – triumvirs for settling the affairs of the commonwealth – and granted power for five years.

It was not the discussion of knotty questions of policy that had occupied these men for three days on a damp and uncomfortable island in northern Italy in the middle of November, but their trading in human lives. The horror of the bargain they struck – which resulted in the proscription of 300 Senators and 2,000 *equites* – was increased by the fact that, with a few exceptions, these men were not condemned as an act of vengeance and killed in a moment of hot blood. Many of the victims thus selected for execution were chosen because they were rich. The triumvirs had to have the money to pay the legions upon which their power depended, for they knew full well that if they could not pay, the legions would desert them for others who could. Thus in this macabre meeting, the process which had begun in Marius' day – only 64 years earlier – and developed under Sulla, reached its climax in horror. To justify their action, the triumvirs themselves claimed that the results of Sulla's and Caesar's conciliatory policy showed that clemency did not pay. Thus Lepidus agreed to sacrifice his own brother and Antony his uncle, but on one point Antony was adamant – Cicero must die. And in the end Octavian sacrificed the man to whose support he owed the fact that he was there at all.

It was on 27 November that the Triumvirate received official recognition in Rome. The next day posters with the lists of the names of the proscribed appeared in the streets. The luckless victims were hunted down, their heads cut off and produced by their murderers as evidence of their right to prize-money. But heroism and self-sacrifice were displayed by many, and sometimes in the most unexpected quarters. Writing during the reign of Tiberius – itself an age in which terror was not lacking – Velleius Paterculus said that some of the proscribed escaped because 'The utmost loyalty was displayed by their wives, considerable loyalty by their freedmen, a little by their slaves and none at all by their sons.' In fact Antony's own mother put her son to shame, by saving, at the risk of her own life, that of his uncle. Barring the door of the room in her house where her brother had taken refuge, she cried out to the soldiers who had come to kill him, 'It was I who brought Antony, your general, into the world, and you shall not kill Lucius Caesar unless you kill me first.'

It was Cicero's slaves who tried to save him, when, after his escape from Rome, he had given way to despair. They were in the act of carrying him down to the sea in a litter from his villa at Gaeta, in the hope of finding a ship, when Antony's thugs arrived and discovered them. Plutarch describes Cicero as covered in dust, his hair long and disordered, and his face pinched and wasted with his anxieties – so that most of those who stood by covered their faces while the centurion Herennius was killing him. His throat was cut as he stretched out his neck from the litter. He was in his sixty-fourth year. By

Antony's orders Cicero's head and hands were cut off – the hands because with them he had written the Philippics. These were taken to Rome and nailed to the *rostra*.

The time for coming to grips with Brutus and Cassius could no longer be delayed. Antony and Octavian headed for the East while Lepidus remained in Rome. The armies met at Philippi in Macedonia, not far from the modern town of Kavalla. The first battle, in which Brutus was successful, but Cassius was defeated and killed himself, took place on 23 October 42. In the second, fought three weeks later, Brutus was also defeated and committed suicide. When Antony saw Brutus' body, he covered it with his own splendid scarlet cloak. Remembering their friendship, Antony sent Brutus' ashes to Servilia, who was now 56. Brutus' widow Porcia committed suicide.

With Philippi it seemed that the Civil War had ended at last, but Rome was still a tragic, disrupted city when Octavian returned to it. Shortly after the battle it had been decided that Antony should complete the pacification of Asia, while Octavian would oversee the demobilization of 36 legions and the settlement of Italy. Significantly, Lepidus had not been consulted; somewhat as an afterthought, he was allotted the province of Africa. In this division of functions Antony seemed to come off best – probably he thought so himself – with a free hand to take what he could of the riches of the East, which appeared in its most glamorous form as Cleopatra sailed up the Cydnus. Octavian, on the other hand, was faced with the drudgery of striving with an empty treasury, to create order out of chaos, in an Italy still rent by the passions of the Civil War. That his efforts fell far short of success and that he was blamed by everyone, goes without saying. But it was to these patient unspectacular years of work in Italy – to the fact that he had been there and shared those dismal times – that Octavian owed his ultimate triumph.

Octavian's most pressing problem was the resettlement of the legionaries. As a result of the inflation of rival armies during the Civil War, their numbers had assumed proportions hitherto undreamed of. Somehow, 196,000 veterans had to be demobilized and reincorporated into civilian life, and the only solution for the vast majority was to provide them with allotments of land. With the spectre of the Catiline conspiracy, of only twenty years before, present in men's minds, it is not surprising that drastic measures were taken. Sixteen towns had been singled out for their hostility to the triumvirs, and their lands declared forfeit for the benefit of the war veterans. Having become paupers overnight – their slaves and farm equipment were also confiscated – the unfortunate ex-landowners gravitated to the towns to try and find work, and, finding none, many of them drifted to Rome in the hope of qualifying for the corn dole.

If the last hectic years in Rome before the Civil War are mirrored in the life and works of Catullus, by some mysterious alchemy of its own the crucible of the war itself produced a generation of poets even greater. And it is through the eyes of three of these that we see something of the sufferings of the dispossessed, and the longing of a whole people for peace. For Virgil, Horace and Propertius all lost their land or fortune at this time. Virgil was nearly twenty-one when Caesar extended Roman citizenship to all the inhabitants of Cisalpine Gaul, including the region of Mantua where Virgil was born and where his father was a landowner. But Roman citizenship was no protection from

the depredations of land-hungry veterans. Some of them, not content with the allotments given them at the expense of near-by Cremona, also seized Mantuan land, including that belonging to Virgil. In 41 he appealed to the Governor of the province, who, by good fortune, was Asinius Pollio – he who had witnessed Caesar's hesitation on the banks of the Rubicon, but who was also the founder of the first public library in Rome, and the originator of public readings by authors of their works as a form of publication.

Virgil's rising reputation as a poet stood him in good stead. Armed with a letter from Pollio to Octavian, he now went to Rome. Whether Virgil's land was returned to him, or whether he received compensation for it, is not clear, but he joined the privileged circle of Maecenas, who was Octavian's friend and already in a sense his unofficial minister of culture. In any event Virgil's means of livelihood were now assured to him, and he was thus enabled to continue writing the *Eclogues* – the collection of ten short poems in the bucolic genre – which first made him famous when they were published in 37.

The *Eclogues* conjure up in words enchanting landscapes and scenes of the Italian countryside, similar to those portrayed in Pompeian wall-paintings and in the *stucchi* of the Tiberside villa of the Farnesina. This was the style of wall-painting later admired by Vitruvius and described by him as including 'rivers, fountains, straits, fanes, groves, mountains, flocks, shepherds.' Vitruvius lamented that in his own day such landscapes were being replaced by the fashion for what we, and the Renaissance artists who rediscovered them, call 'grotesques'. Vitruvius is believed to have written his *Ten Books on Architecture*

126 The needs of returned veterans (seen in this detail from a mid-first-century BC relief) placed a severe strain on Rome's land resources.

when Octavian had become the Emperor Augustus, and a world at peace could enjoy frivolities such as a taste for the grotesque. But at the time when Virgil was writing the *Eclogues* such a world would have seemed to him and his contemporaries a beautiful dream.

Horace, who was five years younger than Virgil, was the son of a freedman of the little Lucanian town of Venosa. His father made a modest fortune and Horace received a good education in Rome before he went to Athens to study philosophy. There, like many other Roman students, he joined the army that Brutus recruited before Philippi. After the defeat, Horace succeeded in making his way back to Rome, only to find that his father had died and that nearly all his inheritance had been confiscated because he had fought on the Republican side. With what he was able to salvage from the wreck, Horace managed to exist and in his spare time to write the wry caustic poetry of the *Epodes* and the early *Satires* – in fact what one might expect of a man in his situation.

The brilliance of the *Epodes* did not pass unnoticed. Horace became the friend of Virgil, who in turn introduced him to Maecenas.

Horace was tongue-tied at first when confronted by the millionaire descendant of Etruscan kings, and friend of the all-powerful Octavian. But, somehow, as he afterwards recalled, he found himself telling Maecenas all the story of his life from his humble beginnings, and all his aspirations. Maecenas seems to have had a gift for people and a perception that amounted to a sixth sense. Nine months after their first meeting in 38, Maecenas became the friend and patron

127 Painting of a Roman garden from the Empress Livia's
villa at Prima Porta, *opposite*.

128 A portrait of Virgil in a
mosaic from North Africa,
left, shows him with two of the
Muses, holding a scroll of the
Aeneid.

of the insignificant little Quintus Horatius Flaccus – whose surname, Flaccus
(flap-eared), may well have recalled his father's nickname as a slave. Four
years later Maecenas gave Horace a small country estate. Secure now for life
and surrounded by beauty, Horace started to write lyric poetry. The lines

> *The gods watch over me; a heart*
> *That's reverent and the poet's art*
> *Please them. Rich plenty here shall fill*
> *Her horn up to the brim and spell*
> *The harvest's glorious revenue.**

are among the many in the *Odes* that reflect Horace's joy in his Sabine farm.

Thanks to Maecenas, Virgil and Horace freed themselves from the tragic
aftermath of the Civil War. The same could not be said of Propertius, the
youngest of the three, who was also befriended by Maecenas. But owing to the
basic instability of his character, Propertius never seems to have recovered
from the loss of the security that went with the expropriation of his ancestral
lands and the tragic death of a beloved member of his family – possibly his
guardian, since he never mentions his parents. Propertius was born near Assisi
about 50 BC, and the relative he loved was killed during the rebellion and siege
of Perugia between 41 and 40 BC. It was an appalling shock for a sensitive

* Translation by James Michie, Carm. I, 17, *The Odes of Horace*, Harmondsworth 1967.

child. When he went to Rome, however, his precocious genius brought him early fame; his first book of poems was published when he was 20. The rest of the story of Propertius' short life is told in his poems.

Nearly all he wrote were love-poems, and their dominating theme is his tempestuous affair with the even more tempestuous 'Cynthia'. Her real name was Hostia, and opinions differ as to whether she simply enjoyed the life of a courtesan or whether it was actually her profession. But there is no doubt that she was a colourful product of the Roman *demi-monde* of the day, and that it held a fatal attraction for Propertius. When he first knew Cynthia she was the mistress of another man, but she revelled in deceit. She used to climb out of her bedroom in the Suburra and down a rope, to fall into Propertius' arms. The idyllic stage of their relationship did not last long, if they loved passion-ately, they also fought wildly. Cynthia flung wine cups at Propertius, kicked over the table and scratched his face. They both took lovers for fun and to spite each other. The one thing they would, or could not do, if Cynthia was really a prostitute, was to marry. Marriage meant responsibility, respectability – things Propertius could not abide.

The affair ended tragically for both of them. Propertius finally found another mistress, but one of his last two poems shows that she brought him no consola-tion. Cynthia had died, and from the poem it appears that Propertius suspected she had been poisoned and that his own servant, whom Cynthia hated, was implicated.

In 40 BC Antony and Octavian met at Brindisi and agreed that Antony should retain the East as his sphere of influence and Lepidus, Africa. Octa-vian's share was Italy, Gaul, Spain, Dalmatia and Sardinia. It was also agreed that he should lay claim to Sicily, which was under the control of Sextus Pompey, who had been in exile ever since the battle of Munda.

Octavian's situation had certainly improved since the days when Antony had regarded him as a young upstart. Their new relationship was sealed by the marriage of Antony, whose wife Fulvia had died in Greece, to Octavian's sister. This was the same beautiful Octavia whom Caesar had once offered to Pompey and who, at 29, had just been widowed by the death of Caesar's enemy, C. Claudius Marcellus.

At first, politically and domestically, all went well. History does not relate whether Antony told his new wife that she was stepmother to his children by Cleopatra. The couple lived in Pompey's house in his gardens in the Campus Martius, which Caesar had given to Antony. In fact, when Octavian and Antony met Sextus Pompey at Misenum in 39, Sextus said pointedly that he would entertain the other two to dinner on his flagship, because it was the 'only ancestral home' left to him. Nevertheless, the meeting was a successful one and an agreement was reached which secured Rome's corn supply, though Sextus retained control of Sicily. Antony and Octavia then left for Greece where they were to spend the next two winters together, and where Antony began his somewhat dilatory preparations to fight the Parthians, who in 40 had invaded Asia Minor.

In time, however, it became evident that the Misenum agreement could really only be a truce, and that Sextus would have to be dealt with. Octavian started to build a large fleet, but he lost it in a storm in 38. About the same time his relationship with Antony began to degenerate. Thanks to Octavia's good offices, however, the two men met in Tarentum in the spring of 37, patched up their differences, and agreed to cooperate against Sextus. The Triumvirate was also renewed for another five years.

Antony kept his part of the bargain, and sent the ships he had promised to Octavian to help in the war against Sextus. But by the autumn of 37, the legions Octavian had promised Antony for the Parthian campaign had not arrived, possibly because Octavian himself was hard pressed, but also possibly as a deliberate matter of policy. Antony's was a contradictory character: he could be dilatory and happy-go-lucky, but he was also subject to fits of ungovernable rage, and in the circumstances he had good grounds for resentment against Octavian. In any event, he now made the fatal decision of his life – to prosecute the Parthian war in earnest, even without the necessary support from Octavian. Politically the decision was the right one – but only if Antony could have conquered the Parthians unaided. If he could have done this, revenged Crassus and achieved what Caesar had planned, his future might have been very different. But with the forces at his disposal it was not possible. The only alternative was to seek aid elsewhere – and this meant Egypt, or rather Cleopatra. Antony had not seen her for over three years, but he summoned her to meet him at Antioch, and she came. It may have been a meeting of lovers, but they were lovers whose political interests coincided, though, on balance, Cleopatra had more to gain and Antony more to lose.

Octavia, who was on her way from Rome to join her husband, received a letter from him at Corfu telling her to return to her brother and to take Antony's and her own children with her. It was at this moment that Antony is said to have gone through a form of marriage with Cleopatra. The year 36 was in fact the turning-point in the fortunes of both Octavian and Antony. After a disastrous spring, in which Octavian lost nearly the whole of another fleet, and himself narrowly escaped death by drowning, his admiral, M. Vipsanius Agrippa, finally defeated Sextus in the great battle of Naulochus. In that same autumn, Antony and the remnants of his army struggled back across the Araxes after their encounter with the Parthians, and he found that he had lost 20,000 infantry and 4,000 cavalry.

Nevertheless, in the summer of 35 the faithful Octavia set out again with the intention of joining her husband. She brought with her money, men, supplies and, pathetically, presents for Antony and his staff. At Athens she received another letter from him telling her to send the men and supplies but not to come herself. Antony gave as his reason the urgent need to pursue the war against the Parthians. Octavia saw through the excuse – she was already aware of Antony's 'marriage' to Cleopatra, but jurists had advised her that it was not valid because the Queen was not a Roman. However, Octavia obediently sent on the supplies and herself returned sadly to Rome. Octavian, enraged at the insult to his sister, told her that she must leave Antony's roof and set up a household of her own. This Octavia refused to do; she remained at home and continued to care for Antony's children by Fulvia as well as her own. But, as Plutarch points out, her devotion and nobility of spirit did Antony more harm than good, for the Romans were incensed by his treatment of so fine a woman.

In fact the grievously wronged Octavia became one of her brother's chief weapons in the propaganda war he now waged against her husband. For the Triumvirate had degenerated into a duel between the two men. The shadowy Lepidus, after a vain attempt to assert himself, had been relegated by Octavian to forced residence at Monte Circeo. Octavian had telling weapons to use against Antony: the settlement of Italy had made considerable progress, Sextus had been beaten and Rome's food supply was assured, while the pacification of the new province of Dalmatia was now complete. But above all, Octavian was able to play upon the Romans' prejudice against all things foreign and more particularly their detestation of the Oriental world in which Antony was now increasingly immersed.

In 34, Antony at last achieved a victory, the conquest of Armenia, and in order to make capital of it he celebrated a triumph in Alexandria. He followed it up by a ceremony, known as the 'Donations of Alexandria', in which he divided the various provinces of his eastern domain among Cleopatra and her children. These last were little more than infants, but by including Roman provinces, such as Cyprus, among the donations, Antony was guilty of treason, for his official status was still that of a Roman proconsul and triumvir. But Antony also publicly recognized Cleopatra and her – and allegedly Caesar's – son, Caesarion, as Queen of Kings and Mother of Kings. This was, of course, tantamount to impugning Octavian's position because he was only Caesar's son by adoption, and inevitably rumours of the proceedings in Alexandria would reach Rome.

In the following year when Antony made a request to settle his veterans in Italy and recruit replacements there – which he was formally entitled to do – Octavian refused. Antony now tried secretly to get the Senate to recognize his eastern settlement, including the Donations of Alexandria. The consuls of the year 32, to whom he wrote, were his friends, and he had many supporters among the Senators – men with Republican sympathies, who were now opposed to Octavian. In fact they passed a motion censuring him for refusing Antony's request for recruitment and the retirement of his veterans. Octavian retaliated by bringing pressure to bear on them, whereupon the consuls and 300 Senators defected to Antony. When they arrived in Greece and saw the hold that Cleopatra had over Antony they were shocked, and two ex-consuls, Plancus and Titius, so much resented her arrogance that they returned to Rome. Apparently it was they who informed Octavian that Antony's will, which was deposited with the Vestals, contained provisions related to Antony's Oriental settlement and clear indications of Cleopatra's influence over him.

This was just what Octavian needed – proof of Antony's intentions. Once he had got possession of the will, it was easy for him to represent Antony as a renegade with Oriental ideas of despotic monarchy, and thus to underline his own role as the champion of the Roman Republic and all it stood for. Antony's Alexandrian triumph could also be used as evidence of his intention to make Alexandria, not Rome, the capital of his future empire.

In 32, the second term of the Triumvirate came to an end. This was convenient, for Antony was thus no longer invested with a triumvir's special powers; but at the same time it meant that Octavian also had no legal claim to the *imperium*, however he circumnavigated this difficulty by an ingenious expedient. This was a skilfully contrived oath of allegiance 'spontaneously' sworn to Octavian in person by the peoples of Italy and the western provinces.

133 In a naval engagement, galleys with *rostra* projecting below their prows were rowed at each other, while soldiers fought from the decks.

Subsequently this oath, known as the *coniurato Italiae*, was represented as an appeal to Octavian to accept their gift of plenary powers. In fact this oath of allegiance was in future sworn to each emperor on his accession and its anniversaries, in Italy and in all provinces; for the common man it became the chief symbol of the Imperial power. Nevertheless, in the autumn of 32 Octavian tactfully avoided imposing any strain on Roman loyalties when war was finally declared, and, according to the ancient rite, a spear was cast into the ground before the Temple of Bellona – which on such occasions symbolized enemy territory. Cleopatra alone was declared the enemy of Rome; Antony was not even mentioned.

The war was short, ending on 2 September 31, when Octavian and Agrippa won the battle of Actium. The actual tactics of this encounter are a matter of debate, but of the conclusion there was no doubt. Antony was beaten, although Cleopatra and her Egyptian squadron made good their escape and were later joined by Antony. Cleopatra still did not lose courage. When she arrived in Alexandria her ships were dressed as for victory; but Antony was a broken man. Some historians maintain that Cleopatra provoked Antony's suicide by sending him false news of her death, hoping to be free to seduce Octavian. But having failed in this, according to Plutarch, she nevertheless outwitted Octavian in the end by her suicide.

Octavian displayed his customary tact, and gave Antony and Cleopatra honourable burial. He could well afford to be magnanimous, for in all likelihood he regarded the lovers' deaths as having relieved him of an embarrassing situation. Moreover, he had gained possession of the treasure of the Ptolemys that Cleopatra had planned to destroy, and which had played no small part in his own calculations. Still Octavian was taking no chances: Caesarion was put to death, as well as Antony's eldest son Antyllus, and four men who included the last two survivors among Caesar's murderers and Antony's most able and devoted general. Of all the treasures in the palace of the Ptolemys, Octavian is said to have kept for himself only an agate cup.

On 13, 14 and 15 August of 29 BC Octavian celebrated a triple triumph for his victories in Dalmatia, at Actium and Alexandria. With the exception of Actium, they were not the crucial battles of his career – Forum Gallorum and Naulochus had been won by other men – but they were the two cornerstones of his ultimate success.

The crucial date in Octavian's life had been the Ides of March, and by 29 BC he had had 15 years in which to reflect upon the events of that fateful day. Caesar had been murdered by a group of aristocrats who believed that by their act they could save the Republic and the Roman ethos from dictatorship and from the possibility of an even greater peril – the institution of a monarchy of the Hellenistic type. Even after Thapsus and Philippi, the defection of the consuls and 300 Senators in 32 had proved that the Republican spirit was still alive. If he needed one, Octavian had been taught a lesson then, and it was as the champion of Rome and all things Roman that he had ultimately defeated Antony. The *coniurato Italiae* had been well timed, but the success of the propaganda campaign that preceded it owed much to the Roman aristocracy's and the Italian middle class's inherent dislike and scorn of the Oriental world – which was personified for them in Cleopatra. The fact that their feeling for her was also tinged with fear – the same fear that Hannibal had inspired – only added to its strength.

There could, therefore, be no question of Octavian's pursuing Caesar's vision of Rome's future supernational role, any more than there could be of following in the footsteps of a Marius or a Sulla. How long Octavian had taken to make up his mind as to his course of action we do not know, but the Romans received the first indication of his intentions when shortly after his triumphs in 29 he declared that all official acts of the triumvirs would be erased and abolished as from 1 January 28. This was also a step towards wiping the slate clean as far as Octavian himself was personally concerned, for the Triumvirate had been as unconstitutional as the powers of its three members had been despotic. But more indicative still of Octavian's intention to return to Republican normality was his action, undertaken in concert with Agrippa – his fellow consul and Censor in 28 – of purging the Senate of foreigners, freed-men and other unsuitable persons, who had gained entry to it as a result of Caesar's reforms and during the Triumvirate. This action, together with the inscription of his own name as *princeps senatus* – the first on the list of Senators – provided even stronger evidence of the Republican soundness of Octavian's views.

Thus public opinion had been reassured, and to a certain extent prepared, for the dramatic scene in January 27 when Octavian appeared before the Senate and solemnly renounced all his extraordinary powers – retaining only those proper to a Republican consul – and declared that the Republic was restored. In gratitude the Senate voted him the highest civic honours, including the oak wreath, or civic crown, the right to have his door perpetually decorated with laurels, and, most important of all, he was accorded the quasi-religious title of Augustus, the name by which he was always subsequently known and which was borne by all future emperors. And as a perpetual reminder of this, the sixth month was renamed August after him.*

The normal processes of Republican government were now revived. The elections were held and the magistrates resumed their usual functions; the sovereign rights of the popular assembly were also, theoretically at least, re-turned to it. The Senate pressed further powers upon Augustus, but – no doubt with the precedent of Caesar in mind – he refused them. He did, however, finally accept the proconsular power for 10 years, to govern as one enormous province all territories which were not yet entirely pacified and still required military protection. These included Spain – with the exception of the peaceful south – Gaul, Syria and Egypt. Such a command was not contrary to prece-dent; Pompey, Caesar and Crassus had received similar ones, though not over such an extensive area. The fact, however, that all unsettled areas came under Augustus' control also resulted in his being in command of most of the Roman army.

Until 23 B C, Augustus also continued to stand, and was elected annually, as consul, and by then he had held office continuously for eight years. This was, of course, contrary to Republican practice and, also because it halved the opportunities of other aspirants, it aroused discontent. Matters reached a

* Originally the Roman year had two beginnings, the natural one on 1 January and the civil one on 1 March, and the months of the year were numbered from this last.

crisis in 23 with the conspiracy of Murena – Augustus' fellow consul – and, realizing that he must conciliate Republican feeling, Augustus resigned office before the end of his term. He was awarded instead a *maius imperium* over all other proconsuls and the tribunician power for life. Augustus was 40 and the last 21 years of his life would have taxed any man – he was in fact later seriously ill for some time in Spain. In any event, he now left Rome and absented himself for three years, staying in various parts of his extensive province. Thus the Senate was left alone to try its wings afresh in the art of government. It was a gesture well in keeping with Augustus' extraordinary political tact, but not such a bold one as it might perhaps have seemed, for the ordinary people of Rome showed only too clearly their dissatisfaction at his absence by offering him the dictatorship or a perpetual consulship. Thus when Augustus finally returned to Rome in 19 the initial period of adjustment to the new dispensation had been completed.

But how did it all come about? What really caused Augustus to lay down his extraordinary powers and reinstate the Republic? Inevitably the question has aroused speculation throughout the centuries, but it is one to which no one has ever produced the answer. It is possible that Augustus acted with complete sincerity, but it is equally possible – and perhaps more likely – that his foresight had prompted him to act in advance to forestall the criticism and discontent which would in the end inevitably be aroused by his unconstitutional position. In fact the whole transaction had been carefully planned in advance, possibly with Augustus' close friends and collaborators – Agrippa and Maecenas – acting in secret as his negotiators with the Senate. If this is indeed what happened, two factors would have helped to smooth the way: the Senate had been weakened by the loss of much of its best blood during the proscriptions, and years of dictatorial rule had deprived it of its former habit of authority. Nevertheless, Augustus had demonstrated his goodwill during his reform of the Senate as he had selected the best possible men for membership, thus giving a clear indication that he had no wish to rule autocratically like Caesar, but genuinely desired a strong Senate which would take part in the government.

The result was a compromise, a delicate balance and division of powers, to which the term 'diarchy' has been appropriately applied. Ostensibly the Senate returned to its old position, although in fact it had many new functions, but it was Augustus who in reality controlled foreign policy and the power to make war and peace. He also recruited troops and maintained armies. But in Rome itself his chief power was derived from the intangible factors summed up in the word *auctoritas*, signifying the deference which throughout the Republic had been paid to senior statesmen of long experience – the *principes civitatis*, or 'first men in the state', as they were called. Of these, Augustus was now incontestably the greatest, and he came to be known unofficially as the *princeps* – a personage to whose opinion everyone naturally deferred, and whose advice would certainly be accepted.

At first glance this may seem to be a fragile foundation upon which the political future of Rome was to be built, especially a Rome that had only recently emerged from a fratricidal civil war following upon the collapse of the political institutions that had served it for centuries. But in its way Augustus' solution was as Roman as what had gone before; it still left room for manœuvre and for the two component parts of the diarchy to arrive at a typically Roman compromise, and its solidity was well tested in the stormy 300 years of its existence. In fact the secret of Augustus' success lay not only in his natural political instinct, but in the fact that he was – unlike Caesar – innately and instinctively Roman, and this quality played a considerable part in the dexterity and tact which characterized his handling of his fellow Romans.

This is perhaps best illustrated in Augustus' choice of the means to indicate that a new era had begun in Rome. He did not date it from Actium or any of his victories, or even from the day he received the title of Augustus. He chose instead the year 23, the one in which he was given the tribunician power for life – the protecting power that was originally created to defend the interests of the plebs, the common people of Rome. The years of his tenure of this power were duly recorded in the inscriptions on his monuments, and posterity has endorsed the importance of this date, as for many historians it signalizes the end of the Republic and the beginning of Imperial Rome.

134 As the Republic faded and the Empire began, *Senatus Populusque Romanus* looked forward to a new age; part of a first-century A D marble relief.

Select bibliography

G.P. Baker *Twelve Centuries of Rome* London 1936

J.P.V.D. Balsden *Julius Caesar and Rome* London 1967

—— *Life and Leisure in Ancient Rome* London 1969

—— (ed.) *The Romans* London 1965

—— *Roman Women* London 1962

R.H. Barrow *The Romans* Harmondsworth 1960

A. Boëthius *The Golden House of Nero, Some Aspects of Roman Architecture* Ann Arbor 1960

G.W. Botsford *The Roman Assemblies* New York 1909

P.A. Brunt *Social Conflicts in the Roman Republic* London 1971

The Cambridge Ancient History vols. VII, VIII, IX, X Cambridge 1928

J. Carcopino *Daily Life in Ancient Rome* New Haven 1961

F. Castagnoli, C. Cecchelli, G. Giovanoni, M. Zocca *Topografia e Urbanistica di Roma* Rocca San Casciano 1958

A.M. Colini, M. Cozza *Ludus Magnus* Rome 1962

T. Frank *A History of Rome* London 1923

—— *Life and Literature in the Roman Republic* Berkeley, Los Angeles 1965

M. Gelzer *The Roman Nobility* Oxford 1969

M. Grant *Roman Literature* Harmondsworth 1964

—— *Julius Caesar* London 1969

—— *The World of Rome* London 1960

P. Grimal *La Civilisation Romaine* Paris 1960

M. Hammond *The Augustan Principate* Cambridge, Mass. 1933

G. Highet *Poets in a Landscape* Harmondsworth 1959

R. Lanciani *Pagan and Christian Rome* New York 1893

G. Lugli *The Roman Forum and the Palatine* Rome 1961

A.H. McDonald *Republican Rome* London 1966

—— *The Romans* London 1965

—— *The Roman Historians* London 1954

L. Macdonald *The Architecture of the Roman Empire* vol. 1 New Haven 1965

P. MacKendrick *The Mute Stones Speak* New York 1960

P. Murray *The Architecture of the Italian Renaissance* London 1963

U.E. Paoli *Vita Romana* Florence 1945

S.B. Plattner, T. Ashby *A Topographical Dictionary of Ancient Rome* Oxford 1929

P. Romanelli *The Palatine* Rome 1950

E. Strong *La Scultura Romana de Augusto a Costantino* Florence 1923

M. Rostovtzeff *Social and Economic History of the Roman Empire* Oxford 1957

E.T. Salmon *History of Rome from 30 B.C.–138 A.D.* London 1944

L.R. Taylor *Party Politics in the Age of Caesar* Berkeley, Los Angeles 1949

—— *Roman Voting Assemblies* Ann Arbor 1966

A. J. Toynbee *Hannibal's Legacy* London 1965
W. Warde Fowler *Social Life at Rome in the Age of Cicero* London 1965
M. Wheeler *Roman Art and Architecture* London 1964

Translation of Texts
R. Graves *Suetonius, The Twelve Caesars* Harmondsworth 1957
J. Michie *The Odes of Horace* Harmondsworth 1964
H. Morgan *Vitruvius, The Ten Books on Architecture* New York 1960
J. Roman *Sallust, Catalina* Paris 1924
I. Scott-Kilvert *Plutarch, The Makers of Rome, Nine Lives by Plutarch* Harmondsworth 1965
A. de Selincourt *Livy, The History of Rome from Its Foundation, Books I–V* Harmondsworth 1960
—— *Livy, The History of Rome from Its Foundation, Books XXI–XXX* Harmondsworth 1965
R. Warner *Plutarch, Fall of the Roman Republic, Six Lives by Plutarch* Harmondsworth 1958

List of illustrations

Aldobrandini wedding, 1st century AD. Vatican Museums. Photo Mansell-Anderson

103 Tullianum, Rome. Photo Anderson

104 Cicero. Marble bust, late 1st century BC. Vatican Museums. Photo Alinari

105 Boy on a horse. Limestone relief from Osuna, mid-1st century BC. Museo Arqueológico Nacional, Madrid

106 Roman bridge near Ascoli. Photo Professor S. Tiné

107 Gaul, from the frieze at Civita Alba, 2nd century BC. Museo Civico Archeologico, Bologna

108 Battle between Romans and Gauls. Relief from the Julius mausoleum, beginning 1st century AD. Plateau des Antiques, St-Rémy de Provence. Photo Lauros-Giraudon

109 Lictors. Marble relief, 1st century BC/AD. Museo Nazionale, Portogruaro. Photo Mansell-Alinari

110 Vercingetorix bound beneath a Roman trophy. Silver denarius of C. Julius Caesar, c. 50 BC. British Museum, London. Photo Peter Clayton

111 Caesar. Stone head from Tusculum, mid-1st century BC. Castello di Aglié. Photo Deutsches Archäologisches Institut, Rome

112 War-galley. Silver denarius of Q. Nasidius, 38–36 BC. British Museum, London. Photo Peter Clayton

113 Lepidus. Gold aureus of L. Livineius Regulus, c. 42 BC. British Museum, London. Photo Peter Clayton

114 Warship with legionaries. Marble relief from the Temple of Fortuna, Palestrina, 1st century BC. Vatican Museums

115 Caesar(?). Blue basalt head, 1st century BC. Museo Baracco, Rome. Photo Leonard von Matt

116 Cleopatra. Detail of a statue, late 1st century BC, nose restored. Vatican Museums. Photo Deutsches Archäologisches Institut, Rome

117 Curia Julia seen from the Comitium, Forum, Rome. Photo Fototeca Unione

118 Gaming-boards in the steps of the Basilica Julia, Forum, Rome, mid-1st century BC. Photo Fototeca Unione

119 Plaster fragments of the Fasti Antiates. Museo Nazionale Archeologico delle Terme, Rome. Photo Fototeca Unione

120 Bronze tablet of Caesar's Lex Cisalpina, c. 48 BC. Parma Museum

121 Personification of Parthia. Detail of a marble plinth, AD 145. Museo dei Conservatori, Rome. Photo Fototeca Unione

122 Brutus. Gold aureus of M. Junius Brutus, 43 BC. Staatliche Museen, Berlin

123 Octavian. Silver denarius, post-30 BC. Fitzwilliam Museum, Cambridge

124 Caesar deified. Silver denarius of T. Sempronius Gracchus, 40 BC. British Museum, London

125 Funeral procession. Relief from a sarcophagus from Amiternum, 3rd quarter 1st century BC. Museo Aquilano, Aquila. Photo Alinari

126 Roman soldiers. Detail of a marble relief from the 'Altar of Ahenobarbus', mid-1st century BC. Louvre, Paris. Photo Alinari

127 Garden scene. Wall-painting from the House of Livia, Primaporta, Rome, end 1st century BC. Photo Georgina Masson

128 Virgil and the Muses. Mosaic from Sousse, 2nd–3rd century AD. Bardo Museum, Tunis. Photo Roger Wood

129 Octavia. Gold aureus of Antony, 38–27 BC. British Museum, London

130, 131 Marc Antony and Cleopatra. Silver tetradrachm of Antony, c. 40 BC. Fitzwilliam Museum, Cambridge

132 Roman soldiers in Egypt. Detail of a mosaic of the Nile flooding, 1st century AD. Palazzo Baronale, Palestrina. Photo Alinari

133 Battle between four galleys. Silver denarius of Q. Nasidius, 38–36 BC. Nationalmuseet, Stockholm

134 Personification of the Senate and Roman people. Marble relief, 1st century AD. Vatican Museums. Photo Deutsches Archäologisches Institut, Rome

Index

189

Mithridates VI of Pontus 107, 112, *112*, 113, 114, 120, 125
Munda (battle) 156, 174

Naevius, Gnaeus 72, 73
Naulochus (battle) 175, 178
Nero, Gaius Claudius 60–1, 62
Numantia/Numantines 78, 84–5, 91, 99; *see* Spain
Numa Pompilius 12, 13, 39
Numidia/ns 52, 59, 60, 61, *61*, 63, 101, 153

Octavia, wife of 1. C. Claudius Marcellus 2. Mark Antony 174, 175–6, *177*
Octavian (Augustus C. Octavius) 9, 13, 133, 149, 159, 165–6, *165*, 167, 168–9, 170, 171, 172, 174–6, 178–81
Octavius, Marcus 88, 90, 92
Ogulnius, Gaius and Quintus 37
omens 7, 86, 87
Opimius, Lucius 96, 97, 98, 103
optimates 85, 92, 103, 112, 120, 128, 135, 136, 139, 140, 146, 148, 156
Orange (battle) 105
Ostia 13, 44, 74, 113, 114
Ovid (Publius Ovidius Naso) 154

Palatine 7, *8*, 9–11, *10*, 18, 24, 34, 41, 64, 82, 96, 108, 132; Casa dei Grifi 108, *109*; Temple of Victory 64, *65*
Palestrina, *see* Praeneste
Parthia/ns 144, 158, 159, *160*, 162, 174, 175
Paullus, Lucius Aemilius 55, 56, 74, 77, 78, 80, 81, 82–3
Pergamum 78, 90, 114, 152
Pharsalus 150, 151, 153
Philip II of Macedon 67, 68
Philip V of Macedon 57, 67, 76
Philippi (battle) 170, 172, 178
Phrygia 63, *160*
piracy 123, 124–5
Piso Caesoninus, Lucius Calpurnius 139, 149
Plautus, T. Maccius 73, 82
Pliny the Elder 118

Plutarch 46, 58, 87, 88, 91, 92, 94, 98, 103, 106, 107, 110, 112, 117, 120, 121, 122, 143, 147, 148, 149, 150, 152, 158, 161, 175, 178
Pollio, C. Asinius 147, 171
Pollux 24, *25*; *see* Castor
Polybius 23, 81, 82, *82*
Pompeia, wife of C. Julius Caesar . 124, 129, 133, 134, 136
Pompeii 110, *111*, *122*
Pompeius Sextus 156–7, 174, 175, 176
Pompey (Gnaeus Pompeius) 86, 112, 115, 117, 120–1, *120*, 122, 123, 125, 128, 129, 132, 135, 137–8, 139, 142, 143, 144, 145, 146, 148, 149, 150–2, 153, 156, 163, 174; against Spartacus 120; appearance *120*, *121*; assassination 152; in Asia 124, 132; in Spain 120, *121*, 149; marriages 121, 138; Mediterranean command 124–5
Pons Aemilius (Ponte Rotto) 73, 74
Pontifex Maximus 12–13, 100, 128, 134, 138; *pontifices* 12, 40
Pontus 107, 112, 125
populares 85, 96, 102, 107, 120, 140
Porcia, wife of 1. M. Calpurnius Bibulus 127 2. M. Junius Brutus 162, 170
Porcia, wife of L. Domitius Ahenobarbus 129
Porsenna, Lars 24, 30, 32
Porticus Aemilia 72, 74
Postumius, Aulus 24
Praecia 120, 131
Praeneste (Palestrina), 62, 115, 117, 118, *118*, 151
Praetor Urbanus 36, 150, 161
Propertius, Sextus 170, 173–4
Punic Wars 48–9, 50, 51–70, 78; *see* Carthage, Hannibal
Pydna (battle) 77, 81
Pyrrhus, King of Epirus 46, *46*, 47, 48, 69, 104

Quirinal hill 9, 18, 32, 34
Quirinus 9, 32

Ravenna 88, 146, 147
Regia 12, 44, 118, 128
Regillus, Lake (battle) 24, 25
Remus 6, 7, 38

Rhea Silvia 7
Roman army 16, 28, 48, 80, 83, 86, 93, 104, *104*, 117, 151, *177*, *178*; equipment 106; rank and file 25; recruitment 104; resettlement of veterans 106, 128, 136, 157, 170, *171*, 176; slaves in 69
Romulus 6, 7, 8, 9, 11, 12, 15, 16, 38, 72
Roscius Gallus, Q. 108, 110
rostra 36, *36*, 37, 45, 62, 92, 118, 154, 170
Rubicon, river 146, 148, 171
Rufus, P. Sulpicius 112, 114

Sabine hills 20, 69, 79
Sabines 9, 11, 13, 26; rape of Sabine women 9, *9*
sacrifice: animal 17, 71, *84*, 125, 133; human 57
Saguntum 50, 51, 101
Salinator, M. Livius 60–1, 62
Sallust (Gaius Sallustius Crispus) 130, 140
Samnites 35, 38, *39*, 40, 46, 47, 57, 69, 79, 112, 115, 116
Sardinia 14, 50, 92, 93, 174
Saturn, Temple of 24, 36, 44
Saturnalia 25
Saturninus, Lucius Appuleius 106, 107
Scaevola, Publius Mucius 88, 91
Scipio, Publius Corn. 51, 52, 54, 60
Scipio Aemilianus Africanus Numantinus, P. Corn. 78, 80, 81–2, 83, 85, 91–2, 96, 99, 102
Scipio Africanus Major, P. Corn. 52, 56, 60, 61, 63, 65–6, *66*, 68, 80, 81, 98, 103
Scipio Asiaticus, L. Corn. 69
Scipio Barbatus, L. Corn. 81
Scipio Calvus, Gnaeus Corn. 51, 60
Scipio Nasica Corculum, P. Corn. 80
Scipio Nasica Serapio, P. Corn. 80, 90, 91
Scipios 37, 69, 80, 81, 129
sea warfare 48–9, *48*, 149, *178*
Sempronia, wife of Scipio Aemilianus 81, 92
Sempronius Longus, Tiberius 51, 52, 53
Sena Gallica 61